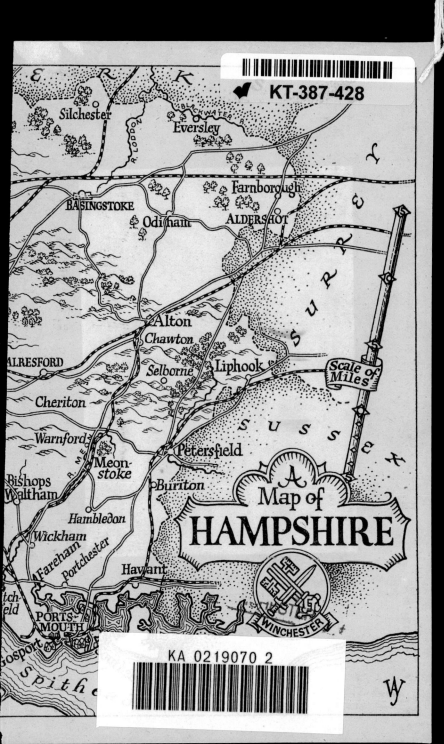

A
Map of
HAMPSHIRE

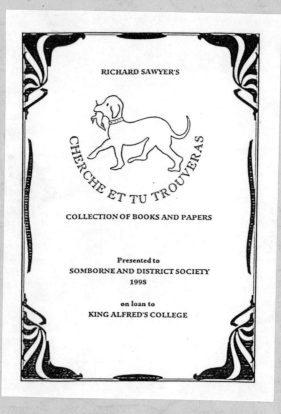

RICHARD SAWYER'S

CHERCHE ET TU TROUVERAS

COLLECTION OF BOOKS AND PAPERS

Presented to
SOMBORNE AND DISTRICT SOCIETY
1998

on loan to
KING ALFRED'S COLLEGE

R. Sawyer.

COMPANION INTO
HAMPSHIRE

Methuen's Companion Books

COMPANION INTO LAKELAND
by Maxwell Fraser

COMPANION INTO DORSET
by Dorothy Gardiner

COMPANION INTO KENT
by Dorothy Gardiner

COMPANION INTO OXFORDSHIRE
by Ethel Carleton Williams

COMPANION INTO SURREY
by L. Collison-Morley

COMPANION INTO ESSEX
by Herbert W. Tompkins

COMPANION TO TWEED
by George Burnett

COMPANION INTO WORCESTERSHIRE
by Maxwell Fraser

COMPANION INTO GLOUCESTERSHIRE
by R. P. Beckinsale

COMPANION INTO DERBYSHIRE
by E. Carleton Williams

COMPANION INTO CHESHIRE
by J. H. Ingram

COMPANION INTO SOMERSET
by Maxwell Fraser

AND THE PRESENT VOLUME

West Gate Winchester

COMPANION INTO HAMPSHIRE *BY*
L. COLLISON-MORLEY

WITH FIFTEEN PLATES
AND ENDPAPER MAP

THIRD EDITION

METHUEN & CO. LTD.
36 Essex Street, Strand, London

First Published . . March 28th 1940
Second Edition . . May 1947
Third Edition . . 1948

PRINTED IN GREAT BRITAIN

PREFACE

THIS book aims at providing an historical background to one of the most beautiful and interesting of our counties. Since Hampshire, even without the Isle of Wight, is also one of the largest of them, no attempt has, as a rule, been made to give detailed accounts of the churches. They are described with admirable fullness in the Little Guide to Hampshire. Nor have I devoted much space to describing the country-side. This kind of thing is so much the fashion at the moment that it is easy to come by in the many books that are appearing about its every aspect. And has not Hampshire Gilbert White and W. H. Hudson? I have, in fact, endeavoured to get together some of the kind of information which I want myself when paying something more than a fleeting visit to a county and which I find it difficult to procure, except scattered through a number of volumes; and I have tried to arrange it on clear topographical lines.

The list of those who have kindly helped me is a long one.

Portions of the book have already appeared in four articles in *The Times*.

Bomb damage along the coast has been heavy. Bournemouth has suffered severely and still more Southampton, where, however, the medieval buildings, owing to their wonderful powers of resistance, have escaped almost unscathed. Portsmouth and even more Southsea have been badly battered. Portsmouth High Street and the old streets round it have been almost wiped out, the Museum, the George and other well-known landmarks have gone, and, though the Cathedral has escaped, the Garrison Church and the Guildhall have been gutted.

L. C. M.

NOSTRA

v

CONTENTS

ILLUSTRATIONS

* *Photo: J. Dixon-Scott*   † *Photo: Will F. Taylor*

CHAPTER I: *Alton, Chawton and Selborne*

THE best way into Hampshire from Surrey is by Farnham along the wide, open valley of the Wey that leads to Alton. The contrast is immediate and striking. The moment you cross the border, bricks and mortar fall away and you are in genuine country. My acquaintance with rural England is less extensive than I could wish, but Hampshire seems to me to be the only one of the home counties that has managed to keep its country-side more or less as it ought to be, apart from the bad lapses along the coast. The towns and villages are not increasing excessively or losing their original character, while the woods and downs—even without the New Forest, is there a better wooded county?—preserve their beauty largely unspoilt.

Here you are in true Hampshire, for to my mind the great charm of the county lies in its valleys and its wealth of trees, of which you are soon conscious in the copses and timbered hedges that lead you on to Alice Holt, by Bentley. Bentley, once a part of Farnham, belonged to the see of Winchester from the eighth century. During the Commonwealth it was bought by George Wither, the Roundhead poet, a Hampshire man from Bentworth, who sold his estate to raise a troop of horse. But it was restored to Winchester. The church, long in the possession of Waverley Abbey, lies back from the road. As I came up the hill to it, I asked a little lady, by the gate of the hop field where she would be busy on the morrow, where it was. ' D'ye mean where all them grives are? ' came the answer in the full, rich, unalloyed cockney of the East End. ' I've not been there meself, but it's through them gites '; and the firm little arm pointed towards the avenue of yews, a good introduction to the magnificent yews in which the county

I

abounds, that leads up to it. In 1754 a parish meeting decreed 'that no relief be given to any of the poor people of this parish who drink tea or frequent the public house '.

If you happen to strike Bentley on the second Sunday of hopping—for it lies in the famous Farnham hop region—you may be met by an old dog-cart packed with gipsies, drawn by a spirited little nag trotting vigorously, with three others tied behind. It is the head of a small procession of weird old vehicles, horse- or pony-drawn, with a boy riding a great bay bareback and another leading a bunch of very mixed draft animals, all escorted by a cloud of bicycles. Even the cars prefer to creep gingerly along in their wake. For this is the Gipsy Fair, which begins about midday on this special Sunday and lasts most of the afternoon on the wide green. It is a humble little fair, with only a few coco-nut shies to detract from the horse-dealing, but the gipsies flock to it from all sides, crowding such teashops as are open, a rough lot of whom the owners are not sorry to be rid.

East of the station is Alice Holt, Alsiholt, Ailsholt, the ash forest, a royal forest under the same wardenship as Woolmer, but a forest in our sense, though here, too, pines are replacing deciduous trees. Once it supplied many oaks to the navy. An extensive Roman pottery site, long known locally, has recently been unearthed there.

Holybourne, now a suburb of Alton, where Mrs. Gaskell died, owes its name to a holy stream that rises here to join the Wey. This region was once infested with robbers. In the fourteenth century five mounted sergeants guarded the Pass of Alton during St. Giles' Fair at Winchester.

> ' Ye, through the pass of Aultone
> Poverte might pass
> Withouten peril of robbynge,'

says Langland. Here Adam de Gurdon plied his trade,

an outlawed follower of Simon de Montfort, winning such fame that the future Edward I wished to try his steel against him. After a long duel, in which he could not prevail, he offered to take him into his service and Adam became his devoted henchman. He subsequently became Warden of Woolmer and Alice Holt and settled at Selborne.

Alton straggles along the Winchester road for nearly two miles to the Butts, the pleasing green where the archers once trained. Most of it is new, but in the heart of the town are some charming Georgian houses and you get glimpses of old cottages, especially near the market and the centre of the High Street, though the fronts have often been stuccoed. Aubrey says Spenser lived here in his youth and a plaque marks the supposed cottage. Eggar's red-brick Grammar School, some of it sixteenth century, is the most attractive building. Alton, lying round the head waters of the Wey under the chalk downs, is an old town. Roman remains, among them a tessellated pavement from a villa found in the eighteenth century, are continually turning up. Some are in the Curtis museum. Alfred left it with Hurstbourne Tarrant and Bishop's Sutton to his son Edward. In Domesday it belonged to the Confessor's widow. The stripling Wey under the High Street divides the manor into Alton Westbrook and Alton Eastbrook, which ultimately came to the Knights of Chawton. The many early tradesmen's tokens prove the prosperity of Alton, which still grows and thrives with its breweries and ironworks. Thackeray mentions the famous beer in *Vanity Fair*.

We turned eagerly to the church off the market, where some geese were cackling in the churchyard, since it was the scene of Alton fight. There are some interesting carvings on the pillars of the Norman central tower, with the windows above now inside the modern church. The walls and the south door are freely pitted with the Cromwellian bullets. Lord Crawford, the Royalist commander at Alton, asked Waller to send him a runlet of sack and, when Waller sent him half a hogshead, he said he would bring him the ox he had promised himself. On the same day, December 12, 1643, Waller left Farnham in a hard frost, as if for Basing, then turned south to Alton. Crawford at once galloped for Winchester with most of his men, pursued by Haslerig's Lobsters, so called from their iron shells. Not only had he 'left his sack at Alton', but his hat and his cloak. He also left behind Colonel Boles and his men, who were driven into the churchyard and the works prepared there by a far greater number of Roundheads. Some 80, with Boles, retired into the church. 'Nay, at the entry of the church, dreadful to see the enemy opening the door ready to receive you with their pikes and muskets, the horses slaine in the allies (aisles), of which the enemy made breast-works,' wrote the Parliamentary Colonel Birch. They were quickly overwhelmed by numbers and threw down their arms. Boles with a few others refused to surrender and was killed, after accounting for some half a dozen of the enemy, but not in the pulpit, as has been said. There is a monument to him in Winchester Cathedral. Charles I is said to have exclaimed, ' Bring me a mourning scarf, for I have lost one of my best commanders.'

Medstead, to the south-west, is becoming a suburb of Alton, though the road thither is well wooded. From its 694 feet it commands a fine panorama of down, largely cultivated, to the north and west, round Nutley to the downs above Alresford. Wells are useless at this height and water is a problem. There is a large underground tank, but most of it is rain water. The old village is picturesque. The church tower, like that of Alresford, was a noted depository for smuggled goods, as were the vestries, since no one came near them in the week : a keg or two of this unusual spiritual comfort might even find its way to the vicarage, where it was not unwelcome at a time when public opinion was all on the side of the smugglers, or at least of the cheaper smuggled goods, to ensure secrecy.

Farther off lies Wield (Weald), about the most northerly point to which the greensand of the Weald, once covered by the great forest of Anderida, stretches to the chalk. This small unspoilt village, high up on the down, clusters round its pleasing little aisleless church, which has been rather gaudily painted. It has a finely beamed roof and an elaborately decorated, perfectly preserved alabaster monument to William Wallop in full plate armour (1617) and his third wife. He was a younger son, but had a distinguished career.

You may go round by Wield to the peaceful Candover valley. I tackled it from Alresford. On Saturday afternoon the bus was full of villagers bound for Basingstoke and the pictures, dark and bright-eyed, the type Kingsley and Hudson admired; among them a young man who might have been Italian with a feather in his hat. To the right of the road, at Chilton Candover, a fine avenue of yews, of unknown origin, runs up the hill for nearly a mile. The great fields stretch up the down, the little bits of hedge contrasting with the brilliant yellows and greens and browns, darkening to purple, of the autumn soil. Cows and sheep abound. This valley of the Candover has been a sad destroyer of churches. Chilton and Brown Candover, like Swarraton, deliberately pulled theirs down, while that of Preston Candover was burnt, only the chancel remaining as a mortuary chapel. A charmingly remote village, Preston Candover, with some good cottages. A little girl in a long dress was enjoying a dancing lesson from an elder sister in front of a row of cottages, just as I had seen one in Avignon, with the north downs looming up beyond a wooded stretch in the distance.

Duthy grumbled a century ago because the fairs were giving way to Maying ' on the Nythe, a swelling knoll of turf which juts out into Alresford pond, and certainly presents a pretty and lively scene, when it is adorned with green bowers filled with dancers, with sauntering parties of spectators in their holiday dresses, and with boats plying across the water '. He thought the British peasant clumsy and dull judged by those of the Loire. Miss Mitford, too, found the dancers too quiet and decorous in ' Bramley Maying ', and preferred the merry crowd outside, the children round the stall, the old men in their ragged coats and the young ones lounging with them because they were not allowed in in their smocks. The may-houses were covered alleys on the green with garlands and flowers hanging down among the dancers.

Chawton is a mile from Alton, whither Jane Austen and her sisters often walked in to shop—small and thatched and tiled. To-day it is visited for the two-storeyed, red-brick house by the fork of the Gosport and Winchester roads which was Jane's last home. The tranquillity, of which a niece speaks when the coaches had gone, is hopelessly shattered. The house, divided into cottages, has little more than the outside that Jane knew. But here she prepared all the novels published in her lifetime for the press, and here she wrote *Mansfield Park*, *Emma* and *Persuasion*. Into *Mansfield Park* alone does she introduce a Hampshire setting, at Portsmouth. This was the first novel she wrote at Chawton, and it seems to me to express her joy at escaping from the ' stinking fish ' of Southampton into the country and the surroundings she loved. Certainly Thornton Lacey is a Hampshire down village. ' I was suddenly, upon turning the corner of a steepish downy field, in the midst of a retired little village between gently rising hills, a small stream before me to be forded, a church standing on a sort of knoll to my right.'

' The front door,' says a niece, ' opened on the road; a very narrow enclosure on each side protected the house from possible shock of any runaway vehicle. . . . Collyer's daily coach with 6 horses was a sight to see . . . and most delightful was it for a child to have the awful stillness of night frequently broken by the noise of carriages.' 'I heard of the Chawton party looking very comfortable at breakfast,' wrote a friend, ' from a gentleman who was travelling by their door in a post-chaise.' Jane wrote in the drawing-room in the midst of the family, who must often not have known what she was doing. She objected to having a creaking door mended, because it gave her notice of approaching visitors, when she could slip her paper out of sight.   Part of it is to be a museum.

The house was given her mother by her brother Edward, who had changed his name to Knight on inheriting Chawton, which the Knights had owned since the sixteenth century.   The manor belonged to a Normanizing Saxon in Domesday, who exchanged it to swell the De Port estates. Chawton House stands on a hill in a beautiful park of elms and beeches, facing the cottage.   You catch a glimpse of it from the church.   It is Elizabethan.   The front has been spoilt, but the panelling and woodwork are handsome. The church is modern, its predecessor having been destroyed by fire the first time it was used after being restored.

Close by is an even more famous Hampshire shrine.   To Selborne you can go from Alton by the direct road through the open country with the hanger to guide you till the road dips and turns and suddenly shoots you right into the heart of the classic village.   But a better way is to follow the wooded valley with its parks beyond Chawton to Faringdon.   Gilbert White was curate here for a quarter of a century, and the yew can fairly look that of Selborne in the face.   At East Tisted, the home of the Nortons who owned Rotherfield Park, you go under the railway, then up the hill and across the fields to the left and through a corner of Newton Valence.   This village is associated with William de Valence, Earl of Pembroke, and Aymer de Valence, half-brother of Henry III and one of the gayest of his set, whom the king forced upon the monks as Bishop of Winchester.

The view back across the wooded valley to the downs on a fine summer afternoon is enough to sacre the walk. The road drops down between the hanger and the Noar—the Noar lies between wooded Selborne and Hawkley Hanger—and then round into the village past the field where the hoppers camp. Selborne has lost but little of what endeared it to Gilbert White. Tourists and societies may swarm here on high days and holidays to do honour to the Natural History on which its fame rests. To my father it was a sacred book. But when these irruptions have subsided, Selborne remains an unspoilt village, set in as beautiful and characteristic Hampshire country as it is possible to find. I was there at the height of the Munich crisis of 1938 and the contrasting peace that it breathed, the peace ' man did not make and cannot mar ', is something to be remembered. Not a little of its charm it surely owes to Gilbert White. Without him it would have been merely a beautiful Hampshire village and possibly names like the Plestor and the Lythe would have been forgotten. As it is, everything seems to have combined to enshrine it in a place of its own.

However, there is the hanger, the hanger of hangers, loved by White, towards which you make your way through an enclosure where a family of fine Hampshire pigs is taking the afternoon sun. The straight path up, though steep, is quite possible for a well-girded man, even though he be no longer young, and the sun hot. But at the other end is the more comfortable zigzag, at the top of which stands the wishing stone. This is the vast chalk hill, 300 feet, to the north-west of the village, commanding a very engaging view to the downs of Surrey and Sussex. Its covert is still altogether beech, and in season it is a mass of bracken and wild flowers. It is now safe in the hands of the National Trust. A path runs through the wood to Selborne Common, wild and almost forest-like, where the volunteers and felicities of all kinds once delighted Anna Austen, Jane's niece. Cobbett, talking, it is true, of Hawkley Hanger, found the spot beautiful beyond description in December, but 'I must leave to imagination to suppose what it is when the trees and hangers and hedges are in leaf, the corn waving, the meadows bright, and the hops upon the poles'. Except on holidays, when it is a pilgrimage place, you can enjoy the woods and the view almost as undisturbed as White himself.

Selborne lies between the chalk and the clay of the hop-gardens, while under it is a white freestone that endures heat; and beyond the clay is the lower greensand of Woolmer Forest. The village, 400 feet up, nestling under the hanger, is long—Longparish might almost be a generic name in Hampshire—with a charming street of varied houses and cottages, the village cart-rut, as White called it. One likes to remember that the manor belonged to the Confessor's widow in Domesday. Later, it was given to the Bishop of Winchester, Peter des Roches, for Selborne Priory. And it was to the priory that Adam de Gurdon, restored to respectability, granted the little square facing the church called La Pleystowe, or Play Place, now Plestor, in 1271, for a market. The 'vast oak' in the centre, referred to by White, was a victim of the Great Storm of 1703, and has been replaced by a sycamore, already venerable.

On the opposite side of the street is the Wakes, where White was born in 1720 and died in 1793. It belonged to his grandfather, vicar of Selborne, to his barrister father, to himself and to his brother, the publisher, who brought out the *Natural History of Selborne*. All the brothers were interested in natural history, a fact which must have com-

forted White when, like other men with a hobby, he used
to complain of the absence of neighbours with similar
tastes. Farther down are three of the four limes he planted
to shut out the butcher's shop. A fellow of Oriel, White
refused all offers of ecclesiastical preferment. In 1784 he
was curate here, and the burial entry before his own is
signed by himself. With a true instinct for his life-work,
'the upright little man who rode a pony and wore a wig',
as he was last remembered, and refused to have his portrait
taken, settled at Selborne. The district offers no specially
wide field to the naturalist, but he observed with the
utmost accuracy and he observed at leisure. He tells the
story of the village in his *Antiquities of Selborne* with the
same absorbed detachment with which he describes the
birds. How revealing is the memory of the last person to
recall him, an old woman. 'He was a still, quiet body,
there wasn't a bit of harm in him, I'll assure you, sir; there
wasn't indeed.' The Wakes has been much enlarged and
altered, but the room where White died, and the dressing-
room, scarcely 5 feet square, where he wrote, are there,
with the beamed hall and kitchen and the sundial in the
garden running up to the hanger.

You cross the Plestor to the yew, probably the largest in
Hampshire, now said to measure 25 feet. Some of the
branches are supported on posts. The striking church has
been severely restored. The altar-piece, given by Benjamin
White the publisher, is a good Flemish sixteenth-century
triptych of the Magi, flanked by St. George and St. Andrew.
There is a tablet to Gilbert on the south wall. His grave,
the fifth from the north of the chancel, has only G.W. and
the date on the stone.

Under the yew is buried the trumpeter, whose story is
told by W. H. Hudson. He was a leader in the riots a
century ago, when the villagers in a bad year broke into
the poor-house and marched to Headley, where they were

surrounded by troops from Winchester, many being transported. The trumpeter escaped to the woods, where he was fed by friends. When he returned to the village, he was not molested.

Down the village beyond the chapel gushes out the perennial stream which was harnessed to supply Selborne with water as a memorial to White. He notes that the Noar, ' a noble chalk promontory ', is remarkable for sending forth two streams into two different seas, this, the Oakhanger, a tributary of the Wey, the other of the Arun. Down the Lythe from the churchyard you go for the really beautiful walk along the Oakhanger valley, ' where skirting woods imbrown the dimpling brook ', as White sings in his *Invitation to Selborne*, to Priory Farm. Virtually nothing remains of the priory except some coffin lids and some tiles, much less interesting than those in Alton museum, in Selborne Church.

The fate which gave Selborne a place of its own among English villages decreed that we should know more about this small Austin priory than about almost any other of its size, for it was granted to Magdalen College in 1485 when in a hopeless state and all the documents are preserved there. It was founded by Peter des Roches in 1233 and possessed the churches of Basing and Basingstoke. Bishop Waynflete helped it twice when it could support only half its 8 canons, and at last there was no one left but the prior. Magdalen College continued the chantry priest for the souls of its benefactors and still holds the courts at the Grange.

Another delightful walk follows the macadam lane to Temple Farm, standing 500 feet up, with a goodly view across Woolmer Forest to Bordon and Hindhead. Adam de Gurdon certainly lived in Selborne, but there is apparently no proof that his heiress gave this land to the Templars, who had probably long owned land here, which they leased to the priory. The medieval farm White knew has gone, but as the long-horned cows go by two by two in a leisured orderliness impossible to their hustled Surrey sisters, conscious that nothing will disturb their progress towards the solemn rite of milking, you wonder whether they are not reincarnations of the Templars of old.

From here you continue down a quiet country road through the ample woods of the greensand to Woolmer Forest, where the pond had shrunk in a dry summer. In White's day it was nothing but bracken and heath, not a single tree upon it, nor a single deer. Queen Anne once rested upon a bank, the Queen's Bank, and saw the whole herd of 500 driven past her. The Butcher Duke of Cumberland sent them all to Windsor. There are firs upon it now, and large parts of it are thickly wooded. Formerly forest meant a tract of land subject to forest law, whatever there was upon it. It is still royal forest, but it is given up largely to the troops.

In 1861 a regiment going from Aldershot to Portsmouth marched, camping the first night on Woolmer Common and being billeted in various villages on the second. The baggage went by canal. The newly joined ensign who describes the march was modern enough to refer to the Exhibition as the Ex.

CHAPTER II: *Alresford and Cheriton*

BEYOND Chawton the road to Alresford is finely wooded, except for the bad patch at Four Marks; then open country, with wide downland views. Bishop's Sutton, with Sutton wood beyond on the right, belonged to Harold at the Conquest and then to Count Eustace of Boulogne, perhaps the most powerful of the Conqueror's knights. Later it passed to Stephen, who exchanged it with his brother Henry of Blois, Bishop of Winchester. The bishops had a palace north of the church, which was probably slighted by the Roundheads, for not a vestige remains, and a park. Here were their kennels, where on occasion the king's hounds were housed. Selborne had sometimes to provide wood for heating the royal horses and dogs.

A mile beyond is New Alresford, which has been Bishop's land since king Kinewald gave it to the see of Winchester on his conversion in the seventh century. Legend says that New Alresford arose when some Saxons beat some Danes at West Tisted and gave them their lives on condition that they were baptized in the Alre, the Itchen stream that gives the town its name. But it owes its prosperity to Bishop Lucy who, in the twelfth century, built the dam and made the pond, now much shrunken, into which he gathered the head streams of the Itchen, thus making it navigable to Alresford. He, too, is said to have rebuilt this pleasing, comfortable market town, noted in coaching days, with its wide streets and its market square, when King John rewarded him with a market and a fair. The sheep fair is one of the most important in the county, the average being still 8,000. Henry III built the first real road hither, probably the green lane from Alton that comes out by the pond. It was a wool town and sank when the staple was removed to Calais, but recovered somewhat under the Tudors. The only old houses are in the lane at the bottom of Broad Street, to the left, by the old bridge with its unspoilt, possibly fourteenth-century, arch, and they are worth a visit for their quaint variety. Alresford was continually being burnt, in 1689 when the church went, and again in 1736. The fires lit by the Cavaliers after Cheriton were easily put out. In the French wars a number of French and Spanish prisoners were here and some of their tombstones survive. They won popularity by the energy with which they fought a fire in a wood yard, thus saving the town from yet another conflagration. Old customs lingered. In 1780 a gratis dinner was offered to all who brought a good dog for baiting the bull and a silver collar for the owner of the one that pinned oftenest.

Miss Mitford prophesied truly when, in a fit of high spirits, she wrote that Alresford would be celebrated in history for two things, ' the first, to speak modestly, is my birth, the second is cricket '. The cricketing fame of Alresford has vanished, but you turn instinctively to the roomy grey house on the left of Broad Street where Mary Mitford was born in 1787, though Our Village lies just over the Berkshire border at Three Mile Cross. How often, in imagination, though she left it when she was six, she must have looked back longingly upon it, with its lofty, spacious breakfast-room literally lined with books, as ' a very nest of English comfort ', in the later years of struggle to keep her handsome, plausible, gambling humbug of a father, who had dissipated her mother's fortune, as well as the one that fell to her with a lottery ticket, out of a debtor's prison. In its present form it is symbolic of Alresford, for the charm of the town, as a whole, dates from her day. Ian Hay wrote *The First Hundred Thousand* in billets here.

For Old Alresford I turned to the right over the bridge

and along the causeway of the bishop's pond. It is now preserved and a great haunt of birds. In the eighteenth century 2½ tons of eels are said to have been taken from it in one night. The fishing rights were profitable. Farther on is a delightful view down the valley of the Alre on its way to join the Itchen. The church has a good eighteenth-century brick tower.

I breasted a stream of tanks and lorries, for the autumn manœuvres were in full swing, laden with cheerful, bronzed khaki. They were a fitting escort to the manor-house, the home of Colonel Norton, father of ' Idle Dick ', who seems to be permanently saddled with this casual reference in Cromwell's letters. It is said that his knowledge of the country, which enabled him to bring up some troops by by-ways, proved a decisive factor in Cheriton fight. Cromwell used to visit him at Alresford. Laud's biographer, Peter Heylin, was expelled from the living here, and Waller annexed his valuable library. Later Old Alresford House belonged to the Rodneys. There is a monument to the great admiral and his wife in the church.

Some 3 miles farther on, in lonely country, is Godsfield, long the chief Hampshire preceptory of the Hospitallers. The chapel is still standing, little altered externally, by a farm-house, and the living-room at the west end. Till recently it was a Youth Hostel. It dates from 1360. Henry of Blois founded it in 1170 and Adam De Port gave it all his lands near. The Order held it till the Dissolution.

A noble avenue of limes and beeches escorts you out of Alresford. I took the left fork, the main Winchester road, and a glorious road it is up to the downs which Gilpin thought ' heavy, uninteresting swells of ground ', above the ancient capital, even under a sky like grey flannel and in an atmosphere suggesting that it was being wrung by hands no less expert than those of St. Swithun himself. Then the sun came out, bringing the view over the Itchen valley and with it memories of over 30 years, for it has hardly changed, in spite of the cars and lorries and the worried young khaki driver who had lost his convoy. Foot passengers there were none. I carried on past the woods to the open down and an aged rustic steering a plough across the road. 'Next bus? There'll be one to-morrow.'

The road to Cheriton branches left a little outside Alresford. It takes you up on to the down and through the top of the Tichborne woods with good views over the valley. You enter the village after leaving the wood under the down well to your right: a beautiful village, clustering round the head streams of the Itchen.

The gardens are unusually good for these parts. In spite of the tile-hung and half-timbered cottages, Cheriton no longer looks, as Cobbett put it, as old as the hills that surround it, and why he called it a little hard, iron village, except that he saw it in mid-winter, I fail to see. You cross more than one brook that feeds the Itchen on your way to the green and the not unpleasing Early English church on its hill. The manor belonged to the Bishop of Winchester.

The village can have seen little of the important battle that goes by its name, though it is also called Alresford fight, on March 3rd, 1644. The Royalists were anxious to prevent Waller, who was at West Meon, from advancing west. Hopton was joined at Winchester by Lord Forth, who at once seized Alresford, important because it commanded the road to London, Waller's base. Some Royalist cavalry advanced as far as West Meon and engaged the Londoners stationed there; but they failed to catch them at church, as they hoped, for the 'godly body of Londoners' had prudently kept the fast ordained for that day a week earlier. Forth then occupied the hills beyond Alresford that look down upon Cheriton. Waller was not comfortable, but by the 29th he had made up his mind. The forces engaged were about 10,000 on each side. In a thick morning fog he seized Cheriton wood, thus outflanking the enemy's advanced posts, and spread his men along the down towards Cheriton. The Royalists, full of hope, cleared the wood, but did not press their success home. Waller also occupied the open ground below with his cavalry, a wise move, for the Cavaliers ruined their chances with their usual want of discipline. Contrary to orders, some of the horse charged down, and the Round-head horse dealt with them before they could form up from the lanes. Forth was compelled to support them, but though his horse scattered the cavalry, they could make no headway against the foot, well sheltered behind the hedges. Waller again showed himself ' the best shifter and chooser of ground when he was not master of the field '. Finally, seizing a chance, the Roundheads pushed in between the horse and the foot and forced the enemy to retreat. The Royalists lost no guns, retiring in good order along the Winchester road. Forth threw the enemy off the scent by making for Basing House, whence the road was open to Oxford. The battle, which they had had every chance of winning, ' altered the whole scheme of the king's counsels '. All idea of joining hands with the Royalists of Kent and Sussex was abandoned. Some mounds on the down to the north-east of Cheriton are said to be the graves of the slain. An old man had never heard of the battle, but the younger generation knew all about it.

For Tichborne you take a winding lane, possibly used by the Royalists, along the Itchen valley, with the down above. The church, standing with its seventeenth-century brick tower well above the village on its hill to the left, is most interesting, with its little Saxon chancel and its wealth of old woodwork. The north aisle, railed off, is the

B

property of the Tichborne family. On the Elizabethan altar-table a portable altar is said to have been placed for secret mass—the family is Romanist—in the days of persecution. There is a coloured alabaster monument to Sir Benjamin Tichborne, the first baronet, with Amphillis his wife and their kneeling children. He was in high favour with James I, whom he proclaimed at once at Winchester, and was not only made a baronet, but often visited by the king, who, when bored with the affected humility of his hosts, said that he would go back to old Ben and his honest hospitality. There is another to a child, said to be a son of Ben, drowned in a pond here. The manor was given the Bishops of Winchester by Edward the Elder in 909. From the twelfth century, if not earlier, it has been continuously held by the Tichbornes of the bishops.

The legend of the founding of the Tichborne dole is famous. In the days of Henry I the wife of Sir Roger Tichborne was a lady of great wealth and boundless charity. A brand had been given her by a saint, who told her that her life would be safe so long as it remained unburnt. When she was old and bed-ridden, she begged her husband to set by a sum of money to provide a dole for all who asked for it on Lady Day. When he promised her as much land as she could crawl round, the old lady was carried to the park and managed to crawl round the 20-odd acres still known as Crawls. Then she was carried back and her life ebbed, like that of Meleager, as the brand was consumed. The story is not unique in the county, but here is the most famous of the Crawls. The 1,900 loaves, which were regarded as talismans against various maladies, were regularly distributed till 1794, when the dole was converted into a charity because of the unruly crowds it attracted.

When the old house, parts of it Norman, was being

pulled down in the early nineteenth century, some of it fell, thus, it was said, fulfilling the prophecy that the house would fall if the dole were abandoned. A more real disaster was the famous Tichborne case, which lasted two years and cost the family £80,000. Arthur Orton, a London butcher, claimed to be the eleventh baronet, Sir Roger, who had disappeared at sea. He lost his case, admitted the fraud, and was sentenced to 14 years penal servitude. The road continues through the picturesque old village to rejoin the Winchester road.

A later Sir Benjamin Tichborne fought at Cheriton and is said to have hidden in the oak, the shell of which still stands in the field beyond the church at West Tisted, where he held land. There are plaques to himself and his wife in the church. There is a beautiful view, just before you drop down into the village, through a gap in the wood out towards the downs above Winchester. Firm believer though I am in walking as the only way of getting to know country, nothing is more delightful than a good run on a dull March day, when the almond is beginning to flower, among out-of-the-way Hampshire villages. Choose them far apart, say Wield, Silchester, the Tisteds, Hursley and East Wellow, with a romantic peep at the Awbridge Danes lake. Follow only the lanes, zigzagging across the main roads and avoiding the towns. In this way you will cover most of the best of the county, in praise of which it is impossible to say too much, that lies between the north downs, the Wiltshire border and the Meon valley, with its infinite variety of field and down, the wealth of wood in its spinneys and copses and avenues scattered everywhere, all wonderfully unspoilt, and its unmatched chalk streams. You may sprint back along an almost deserted road up the lovely Test valley. We had good friends to take us.

CHAPTER III: *Winchester*

THERE can be few towns in these islands more attractive than Winchester. It has, of course, grown, but it keeps its suburbs tucked away in quiet corners, where they are not allowed to obtrude. Its one serious indiscretion is the by-pass near St. Catherine's Hill, which, at least during construction, is a disturbing eyesore to old lovers of that region. Winchester is a country town still, with virtually no industries; a town worthy to be the capital of a county like Hampshire—the Hampshire of the downs and the New Forest—and a shrine of the history of England which long outstripped London in importance. At Hereford is an Anglo-Saxon map of the world where London and Winchester are the only English towns marked.

The importance of Winchester is obvious. It lies in the gap in the chalk through which the Itchen makes its way from the north, a gap which also cuts in two the downs that break the great forest that once covered the south; and at the mouth of the Itchen is the ideal harbour of Southampton Water. The earthwork on St. Catherine's Hill is there to show how early the position was appreciated, but there was also a prehistoric British settlement on the peat on the site of Winchester, Caer Gwent. In the museum at the entrance to the cathedral yard are finds from excavations on the site of Woolworth's in the High Street which stretch without a break from the Bronze and Iron Ages to Roman, Saxon, Norman and medieval times.

Naturally the Romans made Venta Belgarum one of their Romanized tribal capitals. The actual remains are buried too deep beneath the modern town to be numerous; but that Rome was early on the site is proved by the finding of coins of Claudius. The medieval walls probably followed pretty closely the line of the Roman, and the main gates were in the same places, the roads that joined them dividing the city unequally in true Roman fashion. The High Street was a Roman street, like the Jewry and Southgate Street. But there is no proof that the car-park by the museum was the site of the Forum. Nor do we know that the well in the cathedral crypt was Roman. A pavement, doubtless of a villa, was unearthed outside Eastgate on St. Giles' Hill, and there were other remains laid bare during the making of the railway outside Westgate, showing that the town had spread beyond the walls. Roman bricks are also built into the walls of Wolvesey Palace

Venta Belgarum was an important road centre. Roads to Silchester and Cirencester, Old Sarum and Bitterne and Portchester left its gates. This explains the inscription put up by a soldier on special duty to the Three Mothers, goddesses very popular in Gaul and among the legionaries, which was found in the Jewry. In Winchester, too, was an imperial weaving factory, for British cloth had won fame in Rome itself. Possibly the medieval fulling-mill at Coitebury had a Roman ancestor. Burial urns and tombs have also been found outside the gates. Haverfield is inclined to think that, like Silchester, Venta Belgarum was sparsely inhabited. But the importance of the position saved it from being abandoned. The Saxon pirates had no more use for towns than they had for villas, nor, in the early days, were they in a position to settle Winchester. But they seem to have used it as a fortress.

Winchester comes into history again when Kynegils, king of the West Saxons, who made it his capital, was converted to Christianity by Birinus. He was baptized at Dorchester, near Oxford, and it was not till 676 that the 'bishopstool' was transferred thence to Winchester. His son Kenwalh built the first cathedral, probably of wood, and confirmed his father's grant of land for seven miles round the city to the church. This was the beginning of the Soke (Anglo-Saxon Sòc, liberty). Egbert, whose bones are in one of the chests on the cathedral choir screen, was the first king of all England to make Winchester his capital. Under his son Ethelwulf the Danes appeared, as also did St. Swithun, and it was on the saint's advice that a wall, the foundation of the modern wall round the Close, was built, which kept this part of the city safe from attack.

The most imposing personality in Winchester to-day is undoubtedly King Alfred since, finely conceived by Hamo Thorneycroft, he took up his place in 1901, the year of his millennary—other good authorities place his death in 899 —outside the Guildhall. Nor can anyone waiting by him for a bus grudge this prominence to the greatest of our Saxon kings, since it is to the Saxons that Winchester owes her place in history. He made Winchester his capital after he had divided England with the Danes. His palace was at Wolvesey, which apparently the kings shared with the bishops. Here Alfred gathered his men of learning and set up his school for the sons of nobles, himself translating works for their use, and here he began the *Anglo-Saxon Chronicle*, writing it with his own hand down to the year 891. He placed a chained copy at Wolvesey so that all might read it.

Ethelwold, son of a rich citizen of Winchester, was summoned by Dunstan to restore church discipline in his native city. One day in St. Swithun's Priory he gave the easy-living canons, most of them married, the choice between putting on one of the Benedictine cowls he brought with him and becoming monks or leaving. Only three took them up. The others were replaced by monks from his own monastery of Abingdon. When the expelled canons asked that they might plead their cause, Dunstan presided over a meeting in the refectory, when the crucifix there is said to have uplifted no uncertain voice against their claims. Ethelwold built the first stone cathedral with its mighty tower, and its weathercock. It had a tremendous double organ with 26 bellows blown by 70 perspiring men cheering each other to the work. Two brothers were at the keyboards and the noise could be heard all over the city. King Edgar, with the aged Dunstan, came to the consecration. St. Swithun had, as he wished, been buried outside the church, where the rain of heaven might fall upon him, but he was now transferred to a shrine in front of the altar —had not the New Minster its miracle-working saint?— and, in protest against the change, he saw to it that it rained for forty days. But he did his duty as a worker of miracles.

Cnut the Dane also made Winchester his capital and proved a generous benefactor. After the scene with his courtiers by the sea he is said to have hung up his crown over the altar of the cathedral and never to have worn it again.

At the Norman Conquest, Winchester accepted William. Like the monks of St. Swithun, Edith, the Confessor's widow, the Old Lady, was pro-Norman and she advised the city to submit. The Conqueror was often here on his way to Normandy. Here he was solemnly crowned a second time in the cathedral by three papal legates, and here he wore his crown at Easter. William deposed Bishop Stigand, replacing him by Walkelin, a kinsman and a man after his own heart, who built the cathedral we know to-day. The work was finished in 1093. His brother was prior of St. Swithun's and most tactful in leading the monks along the straighter Norman path. In order to wean them from their fondness for flesh, he had the cook taught to dress fish so daintily that they wanted nothing else.

The Saxon cathedral lay a little north of the present building and was pulled down when it was finished. Some of it may survive in the crypt. The Norman cathedral was then the largest in existence and is still the longest, with the

exception of St. Peter's; indeed, its length detracts somewhat from its appearance externally. It will always remain
the chief glory of Winchester, and the impression made by
the magnificent nave the moment one enters is lasting.
Walkelin is best seen in the great Norman arches of the
transepts. The existing beams of the vaulting of the roof
are his. In 1107 his tower fell because, people said, Rufus
was buried under it, badly damaging the choir, which had
to be rebuilt and the present tower added.

Bishop Edyndon found the west front and the west end
of the nave in such a state that he set about rebuilding
them. Edyndon is said to have refused the Primacy with
the famous remark, ' If Canterbury is the higher rack,
Winchester is the deeper manger,' being the richer see.
His chantry, where the swastika appears on his robes, is
in the south aisle, by the choir. Some say that he entrusted
the work to the young William of Wykeham. However
that may be, it was William of Wykeham, when over
seventy, who undertook the transformation of the nave
from Norman to Perpendicular, ' one of the most curious
instances of the complete transformation of one style of
architecture to another that has been preserved to us '. It
would be hard to find a nobler Gothic nave. Wykeham
employed the same stone from Quarr in the Isle of Wight
to case the pillars. Portions of the Norman work are still
visible, as in the arches behind the triforium. Wykeham is
buried in the chantry he built for himself—a beautiful
specimen of a fourteenth-century chapel—on the spot where
he loved to come and pray when a boy.

The west window is a memorial of the attentions of the
Roundheads. It is filled with the fragments of the beautiful
glass, for which William of Wykeham left a handsome sum
in his will, that were collected after they had dealt with the
windows. Waller's men easily forced their way into the
town and the castle made but a feeble resistance. Troopers

rode up to the altar and did no little damage, though much that has been attributed to them was really the work of the Reformers. But they pillaged the houses of 'the sweet Cathedralists' and rode about the town in their vestments with prayer-books and broken organ-pipes in their hands. Many of the treasures of the cathedral library were hopelessly scattered or lost. Colonel Nathaniel Fiennes, father of touring Celia, a loyal Wykehamist, stood by Wykeham's chantry himself to protect it from damage and saw that the College was similarly defended.

The font, possibly the gift of Henry of Blois, is the best of the four marble fonts from Tournai in Hampshire. Round it is the story of St. Nicholas, patron of sailors and others, a saint dear to the Normans. The figures wear Saxon clothes, but the church is Norman. In it was baptized Henry III. In this north aisle are buried Jane Austen and Mrs. Montagu, the Queen of the Blues, whose home was at Sandleford Priory, just over the Berkshire border.

The solid north transept is the oldest and most characteristic bit of Norman work in the cathedral. Here is the modern Mariners' Chapel with a model of the *Mauretania*. In the charming Chapel of the Holy Spirit are a number of thirteenth-century wall-paintings of the life of Christ. In the south transept, the other great relic of Walkelin's work, is Prior Silkstede's chapel with his rebus of a skein of silk. Here is buried Izaak Walton, 'whose well-spent life did last full ninety years and past', and the modern east window is a memorial to him and the gentle art of the angler. He died at the house of his son-in-law in Dome alley, now No. 7 The Close.

The stalls of the choir have beautifully carved canopies and misericordias. Beyond them is the magnificent reredos, which was admirably restored and the niches filled with figures, the originals having been destroyed at the Reformation. On the screens at the sides Bishop Fox, who built them, placed six chests containing the bones of early bishops and kings, among them Kynegils and Egbert, Cnut and Emma. The glass in the east window, also given by Fox, is admirable, though it has suffered badly from restoration. Fox's chantry is by the reredos in the south arcade. Founder of Corpus Christi College, Oxford, he was Lord Privy Seal to Henry VII. He christened Henry VIII.

In the centre of the choir is the tomb of the Red King. His body was brought to Winchester on a cart—he had started on his expedition from the castle—and buried hastily, with little ceremony. His tragic end makes his tomb one of the most memorable, and the finds when it was opened, an arrow-head, some twigs and nutshells among them, tend to confirm the view that the tomb is really his. In front of the altar lies Hardicanute, the last of the Danish kings. In his day there were four banquets spread where all might feast, and he died while drinking. Somewhere here, too, is buried the great Earl Godwin, who collapsed with a seizure while eating with Edward the Confessor.

In the middle of the arcade behind the reredos, its position marked by a stone, was the shrine of St. Swithun. Bishop Lucy enlarged the east end of the church to make room for the crowds that visited it. The fine iron gates, probably the oldest wrought-iron work in the country, that lead from the south transept to the choir, and a stone screen across the south end of the nave, shut them off from this part of the church with the cloisters. The shrine of 'plated silver gilt and garnished with stones' was carried off with the rest of the cathedral treasures in 1538.

To the south of it is the splendid chantry of Cardinal Beaufort where, however, the crimson-robed figure dates only from Charles II. The legitimized son of John of Gaunt and half-brother to Henry IV, he is a striking contrast to his predecessor, William of Wykeham. He sided with the future Henry V against his father and was very powerful when he succeeded. A statesman and a man of character, he was guardian to Henry VI, whom he crowned in Paris. An able financier and very wealthy, he lent enormous sums to the Crown and his benefactions were endless. On the other side of the shrine is the chantry of his successor, Waynflete, a Wykehamist who was Head-master and first Provost of Eton and founder of Magdalen College, Oxford. Though a warm Lancastrian, he was treated with the utmost respect by Edward IV, whom he had christened. The three great statesman-bishops ruled the see for 120 years.

Aymer de Valence, half-brother of Henry III, was un-worthy of the monument recently raised over his heart at the end of the north aisle. A dissipated, grasping illiterate, he was forced upon the unwilling monks of St. Swithun by Henry, and his whole career was a scandal. He refused to be consecrated so that he could keep all his other bene-fices. He bore a grudge against St. Swithun's for the opposition to his election and continually persecuted the monks. Once in winter he shut them in the cathedral for three days and nights without food. At last the barons drove him, with other Poitevins, into banishment, where he died, his heart being sent to Winchester in a cup of gold.

In the north aisle is the last of the chantries, that of Bishop Gardiner, the last Catholic monument to be raised in the cathedral. He played a leading part under Henry VIII and Edward VI, but under Mary he came into his own. He crowned her and was made Chancellor. In his chantry is kept the chair used by Mary at her marriage with Philip II, which Gardiner celebrated. Philip had ridden from Southampton with 250 Spanish nobles, all in black velvet, at a leisurely Spanish pace in pouring rain, preceded by the official with the white wand whom Mary had sent a mile and a half out to meet him and who firmly refused to be covered. The Mayor and aldermen welcomed him at Westgate. Philip was lodged in the Deanery, the queen at Wolvesey, where the banquet was held, Gardiner alone dining at the royal table. The marriage ceremony, probably the most splendid ever celebrated in the cathedral, took place on July 25th, the day of St. James, the patron of Spain. Philip was attended by 60 Spanish grandees. The day after the pair rode to Basing House, where they were entertained by the Marquis of Winchester, returning to Winchester that evening. Winchester does not seem to have supported the Reformation with much enthusiasm. Naturally, under Elizabeth, the tomb of a Protestant-burning bishop like Gardiner was not well treated, but his bones are still there.

Of the eastern chapels that of the Guardian Angels is decorated with beautiful thirteenth-century angels. Here is buried Bishop Mews, ' Old Patch ', who had fought for Charles I, and, though seventy-one, was at Sedgemoor, where the loan of his carriage-horses was invaluable in getting the guns on to the field and routing Monmouth; but he was no fanatical supporter of James II. There is graceful wood-carving in Bishop Langton's chapel with his rebus, a long tun, and that of the see, a vine springing from a tun, and a hen and a tun for his prior, Henton. In the handsome and varied Lady Chapel, where the arms of Henry VII and his Queen, Elizabeth of York, and the Prince of Wales, are among the shields, the eastern extensions, with their well-proportioned, elaborate Perpendicular windows, were given by her as a thankoffering for the birth of Prince Arthur. He was christened in the cathedral in a special font.

The chief treasure of the Library is the illuminated Vulgate of the days of Henry of Blois. Winchester long enjoyed fame as the great home of illumination.

The Priory of St. Swithun was closely associated with

the cathedral. In early days there seems to have been no distinction between the property of the monks and the bishop. At the end of the twelfth century the huge fief owed the service of 60 knights to the king. But there were differences. Under Henry I, when Bishop Gifford leased some manors belonging to the priory without consulting the monks, they were much displeased. When the bishop would not acknowledge his error, ' they reversed their crucifixes and went in procession barefoot and contrary to the course of the sun and the custom of the church, to imply that, as the bishop had, contrary to the canonical decrees, deprived those who served God of their necessary food, so they would serve the church in a way opposed to law and to the ecclesiastical decrees '. The king was for the monks, most of the nobles, naturally, for the bishop. At last peace was made through the efforts of the king, the good bishop admitting his error and ever afterwards treating the monks with the utmost affection, being with them whenever he could, sitting by preference among the humblest novices : and in the Priory of St. Swithun he died. William of Wykeham, as usual, kept his end up, insisting upon all his rights. In his day it was agreed that the monks must repair the bridge over the Lock Burn in College Street and provide half the upkeep of the bridge over the Itchen : also, that they should cease to feed sheep and snare rabbits in his chase at Morestead. From that time, after the Black Death, there were never more than about 40 brethren, which hampered them in their duties. At the Reformation they were merged in the cathedral, the prior becoming dean and the monks the chapter.

The Deanery was formerly the prior's house, and the handsome arched gateway, like the hall, dates from Henry III. Here Charles II stayed while his house was being built, and Ken, then a prebend, refused to give up his dwelling to Nell Gwynne. ' Where is the good little man who refused his lodging to poor Nelly?' asked the king when the see of Bath and Wells fell vacant. Izaak Walton, by the way, married Ken's sister, Kenna, as he called her. Nelly was lodged in Colebrook Street. The chapter-house, where Langton gave King John absolution after the raising of the papal interdict, stood between the dean's garden and the south transept. The Norman arches opening on the close led to it. The cloisters of the priory stood in the close. The walls are the most solid remains of it.

There was never any good will lost between town and bishop, and in the Barons' Wars the town stood for the king. The monks of St. Swithun sided with Simon de Montfort. Their gate virtually commanded Kingsgate. The city, fearing that the monks might let Simon in, attacked the gate vigorously and killed several of the defenders, probably servants, who put up a good fight. Failing to storm it, the men of Winchester fired it. The fire spread and burnt Kingsgate with its chapel of St. Swithun. Later, the monks let in Simon de Montfort the younger with his men through their windows in the wall. He sacked the city and slew all the Jews, who were good friends to Henry. After the defeat of the barons the monks had to rebuild both Southgate and Kingsgate and provide watch and ward for them.

For Wolvesey Castle you cross the Lock Burn by the bridge in College Street, the successor of the one the monks had to keep in repair. This brook was the ditch along the walls. Wolvesey, wolf's island—legend says because the tribute of wolves' heads which was brought annually to King Edgar from the Welsh was delivered here—was a prehistoric settlement and the site of at least two Roman villas before the Saxon kings and bishops built their palace. Henry of Blois, the lordly brother of King Stephen, rather a great noble than a churchman, was long a powerful figure in England. During the troubled reign of Stephen,

Henry was as noted a builder of castles as the barons, and he turned Wolvesey into a strong fortress. It is now a ruin, but the walls of the hall and large sections of the outer wall remain. Like the barons, Henry fought for his own hand, and when Matilda swore to follow his advice he deserted his brother and took an oath of allegiance to her. At a synod at Winchester he even declared that it was for the prelates to choose the king. He also intrigued to get Winchester made an archbishopric. As Stephen was a prisoner, Matilda felt secure, but her haughtiness alienated the bishop, as it had the Londoners. However, she seized Winchester Castle with the help of her devoted half-brother, Count Robert of Gloucester, as well as Andover and Wherwell, to keep the way open to the west. These were both taken and burnt, the nuns of Wherwell fleeing 'with shrieks and lamentations'. From Wolvesey the bishop shot fire-balls into the northern and eastern parts of the city, which sided with Matilda, causing great destruction among the wooden houses. Hyde Abbey and Nunnaminster were burnt to the ground. Matilda made no reprisals, but she was so hard pressed that she was obliged to flee. Winchester was delighted at the accession of her son, Henry II, when the bishop lost all influence and Wolvesey was made harmless. He escaped privily to his old monastery of Cluny, but returned later and made an exemplary end. He was buried in the choir of the cathedral, and his massive ring, now in the library, was found in his coffin when it was opened. Henry II, who was often at Winchester, gave it a mayor and bailiff before London.

Under John the dauphin occupied Wolvesey, which was slighted by Cromwell. Bishop Morley, who is buried on the north side of the cathedral dais, rebuilt part of it from plans by Wren as the bishops' residence. Brownlow North pulled down a wing in 1820. The chapel is Tudor and there is Norman work in the walls. Morley, who, in a less splendid age, was almost as munificent as Henry of Blois, also built the college for widows of the clergy on the north side of the cathedral which bears his name and preserves his portrait.

In the great hall at Wolvesey Sir Walter Raleigh was tried in November 1603. James was at the palace, since there was plague in London. The trial was a mockery, like that of the Cobham Plot conspirators whom Raleigh watched from a window in the castle as they were led out to death and then pardoned. At first the citizens were all for the new king and pelted Raleigh with tobacco-pipes; but by the end of the trial he had become a popular hero. He was not executed till fifteen years later.

Across College Street, beyond the brook, was ' the greenery and promenade of St. Swithun ', the pleasant meadow dear to the monks, which they ceded to William of Wykeham in exchange for the manor of West Meon that he might build there his College of St. Mary. Wykeham had been educated at the grammar school in Symmond's Street, where I like to think King Alfred and more probably his son were educated, and he wanted other poor scholars to enjoy such advantages more easily than himself. Hence the foundation and that of New College, Oxford. It is the father of all public schools, and upon it Henry VI modelled his own foundation of Eton. Moreover, the old buildings are much the same as they were when the school was opened in 1394. At the Dissolution it acquired St. Elizabeth College, founded by Bishop Pontoise for promoting learning and piety among his clergy, from Wriothesley, and was given the Carmelite monastery, where Sickhouse was built in the seventeenth century. The rather forbidding front was intended for troubled times, when windows invited attack. In the tower over the gate-house is the Virgin. William of Wykeham is over Middlegate, where were the former lodgings of the Warden, so that he could keep an eye on every side. The grotesque figures over the buildings in the inner quadrangle, indicating the uses to which they were put, are distinctly amusing. Here, under a shed at the conduit, the scholars performed such ablutions as were deemed necessary in those simpler and hardier, if dirtier, days that ended barely a century ago.

It is pleasing to remember that the bell still tolls 70 times, once for each of the scholars on the foundation. Here is the fine lofty chapel, with its magnificent east window of the Tree of Jesse, though the priceless glass of Wykeham's day was virtually all restored away in the 1820s. The roof with its fan tracery in wood, the first of its kind, is beautifully delicate. Above the sacristy in the muniment room are the original fourteenth-century worm-eaten lockers for vestments and drawers for documents. In the cloisters, where school was long held in hot weather, with their oak roofs and handsome windows, is the really beautiful chantry in memory of John Fromond (1420), which is now the chapel of the junior scholars. The glass in the east window is old, and the bosses of arms on the roof, John of Gaunt and Henry VI among them, are interesting.

Then there is the finely panelled hall up a flight of stairs with its open roof. Over it presides the well-known portrait of William of Wykeham. The tapestries, showing the union of the white and red roses, date probably from Henry VII. In the passage outside the kitchen hangs the Trusty Servant, said to have been given Wykeham by a German monk. He has changed his clothes more than once, and he owes his present Brunswick uniform to the visit of George III in 1778. Royalty has often been at the College since Henry V. Edward IV sent the boys a lion to look at. Henry VIII brought the Emperor Charles V. The crop of Latin verses these visits produced touched high-

c

water mark under the precocious dying young Edward VI with 45. In 1410 a pair of porpoises were cooked in the great kitchen in honour of a visiting bishop. In 1415 the college engaged a French prisoner taken at Agincourt as cook.

School, with its handsome ceiling, dates from 1687. Among the arms of subscribers on the beautiful cornice are those of Morley and Ken, the latter a Wykehamist, whose morning and evening hymns first appeared in a collection of prayers he wrote for the scholars. His name is scratched in the cloisters (1665). Colley Cibber—founder's kin—was not accepted, but before his father sent up his second son he presented the statue of the founder over the entrance to school, whereupon, says Colley, ' the door of preferment was opened '. The South African War Memorial is the gate in Kingsgate Street, which leads to the cloisters built in memory of the Wykehamists who fell in the Great War.

From a window in No. 8 College Street Cassandra watched the funeral of Jane Austen making its way to the cathedral in 1817. All this region lies in the Liberty of the Soke, the West Soke, and was under bishop's control.

Now let us make a fresh start from the railway station on the east. The traveller arriving by train has a picturesque entry through Westgate. The station is in the new suburb of Weeke, or rather Weeke Within, on the Stockbridge road, with its tiny church dating from the twelfth century. Opposite the door is half of a brass of St. Christopher, the saint's feet in the water, above the Compton brass. The church stands high and beyond it stretch delightful open Teg Down and Compton Down, which are ecclesiastical property. On the golf-course on Teg Down Mr. O. G. S. Crawford discovered from the air a Romano-British village. Winchester is one of the healthiest of cities. Keats, who stayed in the neighbourhood of Minster Street, considered that the air on the downs was worth sixpence a pint. Perhaps it helped him to write the ' Ode to Autumn ' on his walk through the stubble field that Sunday evening. But this was not the case till quite recently, especially in the low-lying quarters by the river. As in all old cities many of its streets were ' very filthy and noyfull ' owing to the ' castynge of donge ' and other refuse, which stood in heaps. Winchester naturally suffered badly from the plague, and into the obelisk outside the gate is built the stone on which in 1666 the country folk put their provisions. People from the city then came out and took them, leaving money in their place. This was picked up with tweezers and dropped into vinegar before being touched. Outside the gate was also the Domus Hafoc, the house for the king's hawks, in a park, and a spital home for lepers.

Westgate, on the site of a Roman gate, is largely fourteenth century, the central arch being original. On the outer and least restored side are two heads through which ran the chains of the drawbridge. The ditch protecting the walls was some little way beyond. Originally the royal fish-stew, which the monks of St. Swithun had to keep stocked from their ample supplies at Botley, it survived till 1824. So did the picturesque ruins of the walls, running among shrubs and trees down Tower Street to the Hermit's Tower, then following the backs of the houses on the west side of City Road to Northgate. The rooms above Westgate were long a prison, especially for debtors. Till quite recently the cage or lock-up for disorderlies stood at the bottom of the steps leading to it. The rooms are now a museum. The fact that Athelstan established six mints in Winchester testifies to its importance, and Edgar ordained that there should be but one money and one weight and one measure, that of London and Winchester. To Winchester Henry I, disgusted at the state of the coinage, summoned the moneyers of the kingdom, and all except the three of Winchester were mutilated for making bad money. By the custom of Winchester mutilation and blinding were the punishments for capital offences. Hence a number of standard weights and measures, as well as the moot-horn for summoning the citizens, are kept here.

To the right of the gate was the castle, the wall of which was the city wall to Southgate, at the junction of Southgate Street and St. Swithun's Street. It then followed the backs of the houses in Swithun Street to Kingsgate. Kingsgate is largely fifteenth century. The chapel of St. Swithun upon it is still in use. The wall ran then through the gardens on the north side of College Street, as some fragments show, till it joined the wall of Wolvesey opposite the college.

Castle Hill, with its municipal buildings and the view out towards the downs from the parapet, suggests the piazza of a small Italian hill town. Here William the Conqueror built a fort: the stone castle dates from the twelfth century. It was a favourite residence of Norman and Angevin kings. Here Henry I married Matilda of Scotland, and here their eldest son was born. Henry III, Henry of Winchester, was born here and, with his love of beautiful things, rebuilt it. All that remains is his magnificent hall, the County Hall, more like a cathedral than a hall, and some underground passages. There are no finer windows of the time. Henry was fond of his birthplace, but it was in his day that it began to go down hill owing to the loss of Normandy and the transference of the mints and the flight of capital to London. When the hall is fitted up as a court of justice it is hard to appreciate its proportions and its arcades as they deserve. Most of the early parliaments met in it. At the end of it are the remains of the royal dais with a King's Ear over it, so that the king could hear all that was said in his own apartment.

In this hall Judge Jeffreys opened his Bloody Assizes

after Sedgemoor with the trial of Dame Alice Lisle. She pleaded that she believed Hickes was a fugitive for preaching illegally, and that she did not know that he and Nelthorpe had fought at Sedgemoor. The jury was unwilling to convict, though her guilt was palpable, but was cowardly enough to allow itself to be browbeaten into doing so by the brutal judge, who surpassed himself in his treatment of the prisoner. The old lady of seventy was condemned to be burnt alive that very day. She was so exhausted that she was dozing when sentence was pronounced. But public opinion was roused. The bishop and clergy protested. She came of a Royalist family and had shed tears for the execution of Charles I, and one of her sons had fought for James at Sedgemoor. But he had restored her property on petition after the Restoration when Duke of York, and he was not one to forgive. She behaved with becoming dignity when she was beheaded in the square outside the museum. She was the first and perhaps the most famous of Jeffreys' victims.

Here, too, hangs the famous Round Table with the names of the knights painted round it and a Tudor rose in the middle. It is, of course, the original, whatever the French book may say, and it led Malory to identify Winchester with Camelot. The earliest reference to anything of the kind is an order for the making of a Wheel of Fortune under Henry III. It appears to be a table of about that period and may have been made for some tournament. Henry VIII took Charles V to see it.

James I gave the castle to his friend Benjamin Tichborne, whose son restored it to the Crown during the Civil War. It made its final appearance in history in 1645. The Royalists had recovered it and strongly fortified it. Cromwell's artillery decided matters. His main battery of six guns was at Oram's Arbour, with ' parties ' by St. Lawrence's church and in old St. Thomas's churchyard.

He opened fire on Friday, and on Sunday, Ogle, who was further distressed by the death of his wife, beat a parley. The castle was very strong, well provisioned, and had a garrison of 680, and Cromwell was thankful to have got it so cheaply. Both sides felt that it should have put up a better fight. The castle was thoroughly slighted.

Charles II, who gave the city his portrait by Lely which is in the Guildhall, took a fancy to Winchester and decided to build a palace there. The town sold him the castle site for five shillings. Wren was architect. All the ground between it and the cathedral was to have been cleared and laid out with formal gardens sloping down the hill, while a park was planned to the south. Such ruins as the Round-heads had left were used for building material. Horace Walpole called the unfinished result a mixture of town hall and hospital, the worst thing of Wren's he ever saw. Queen Anne meant to complete it for her husband, but could not raise the money. Wren, by the way, found a Roman pavement on the site. During the eighteenth-century wars it was used for French and other prisoners, and some of their ingenious toys, made of odds and ends, are in the museum. A terrible epidemic broke out among them, and the number of dead buried in the ditch raised the level. During the French Revolution 660 French priests were quartered there. When they chanted the office the mighty wave of sound was heard all over the city. It was used as a barracks till it was burnt down and the present one built in its place.

Inside the Westgate begins High Street, the ancient Cyp Street (Cheap Side) or Market Street, first laid out by the Romans. There is a noble view down it and over to the hills beyond from the top of the gate. On the left was the house of beautiful Queen Emma, to whom Ethelred granted Winchester as part of the morning-gift after his marriage to her, and hers it remained when she married Cnut. Win-chester was her home in her widowhood and hither Edward the Confessor, whom she had treated harshly, sent the three earls to seize her great treasure. She and Earl Godwin led the English party in opposition to Edward and his Normans. As long as his mother lived, Edward avoided Winchester.

A little below was the Wool Staple Hall. The removal of the staple to Calais in 1363 dealt a fatal blow to the city. Then comes the Jewry, formerly Scowertene (Shoemaker) Street, the Roman road that led to Northgate; over which was the church of St. Mary. It was pulled down, like Eastgate and Southgate, in the eighteenth century, because they were unsafe and the entrances too narrow. Westgate was saved only because of the fears of the owners of the adjoining houses. It is Jewry because the Jews were settled here by William the Conqueror. They were well treated in Winchester, and the colony was important. Under Richard I Winchester alone spared them, ' being prudent and persevering and a city of unceasing civility '. At the corner was the George, dating at least from the fourteenth century, long the best inn, now, alas! doomed.

At the corner of Southgate opposite is the Black Swan, which had a fifteenth-century ancestor. Down it is a fine red-brick Georgian house. There is so much in Winchester that it is impossible to mention its many good eighteenth-century houses. At the corner of St. Thomas's Street are the clock and the statue of Queen Anne over the old Guildhall that dated from Edward IV and, when rebuilt in 1713, was used till 1873. The leaden statue of the queen was given for the Peace of Utrecht in 1713. There were shops under the Guildhall in Elizabeth's day. From it the curfew still rings at eight.

On the left again is St. Peter's Street, Fleshmonger Street, the butchers' quarter. The gateway of the Roman Catholic church here was once the west door of the Magdalen Hospital. Down the middle of this part of the High Street were stalls and shambles, with what effect upon the sanitation of the town can be imagined. On this side, too, was a row of shops or stalls belonging to the Confessor's widow, Edith. At the corner of St. Peter's Street was the manor and liberty of Godbeate, which Queen Emma granted to St. Swithun in complete freedom from all taxation or jurisdiction: and so it remained till the Dissolution, a sad thorn in the flesh to the city, since, with its church of St. Peter in Macellis, it gave sanctuary to criminals. The striking Godbegot House, half-timbered, with overhanging storeys, is Elizabethan.

The opposite side now becomes the more interesting. Here is the piazza or pentice, which still preserves some Tudor gables with carved bargeboards. The confectioner's shop, the front of which seems to be Elizabethan, is on the site of the old tenement of Helle; that of Hevyn runs along by the church of St. Lawrence. In the corner is the beautiful Henry VI City Cross or Butter Cross, which has been carefully restored. In 1770 it was actually sold to Thomas Dummer of Cranbury Park, but when his men came to take it away they were driven off by a mob of outraged citizens.

Here stood the Conqueror's palace, stretching back to the precincts of St. Swithun. He got the land from the New Minster in exchange for Alton and Kingsclere. Not only did he not rob them of it, as has been said, but they bested him, according to Domesday, since it was royal demesne. The palace stood in a court round which were the offices. The kitchen and the forges were along the High Street: the stables beyond Minster Street. Across the High Street was the prison, or Blockhouse, for robbers, with the cottages of the executioners. In this palace the Domesday survey, in which Winchester, like London, does not appear, was compiled. On its completion in 1086 the king rode out of Westgate along the Roman road through Buckholt Forest for Salisbury Plain to receive the homage of the landowners, sleeping, it is said, at Norman Court, just this side of the border. Stray remains of the palace can be seen under the museum and elsewhere. But the one real relic is St. Lawrence's Church, shut in by houses, which, though it dates only from the fifteenth century and has suffered much from the restorer, is almost certainly on the site of the palace chapel. To it the bishop comes before being installed in the cathedral to ring a bell, probably a memory of an act of homage to the Norman kings.

Across the High Street again were formerly the churches of St. Mary Kalendar and St. Mary in the Wold. In medieval days every street seems to have had at least one church. The city abounded in them, a veritable 'Isle Sonante'. In its decadent seventeenth century, Taylor, the water-poet, said it had almost as many parishes as souls. Down the three Brook Streets streams, now covered, ran open till about 1850.

Below the palace was New Minster, promised by King Alfred to St. Grimbald, a monk of great learning whom he had brought over from Normandy, and built by his son, Edward the Elder. Just then a number of refugees arrived from Ponthieu, driven out by the Danes, with the bones of their St. Josse which were enshrined here and soon achieved a great name for miracle working. Hither Alfred's bones were transferred from the Old Minster, as St. Swithun's was now called by contrast, where his ghost was troubling the monks. Naturally there was rivalry. In 1066 the Old Minster was for the Normans, but the abbot of the New was Harold's uncle. He and twelve of his monks and doubtless all of his available retainers fought for Harold at Hastings with armour over their cassocks, the abbot and the monks all being slain in the king's bodyguard. Hence William favoured St. Swithun's. When the Normans put mills on the Itchen—the best mill in the city belonged to the Abbess of Wherwell—and brought water to fill the town ditch from above, the lower town became very damp and the New Minster suffered severely. Moreover, it was cramped for room and the nearness of the two churches resulted in the chanting of one interfering with the other. If the new organ had any of the power of the old, the effect must have been awful. So New Minster moved out to the banks of Hyde Brook, on the east of the road to Silchester. Hyde Abbey was burnt down by the fireballs of Henry of Blois. He even annexed the molten metal of the great jewelled silver cross which had been presented by Cnut and Emma. Later he gave them an imitation substitute. Rebuilding did not begin for forty years. At the Dissolution the abbey fell to Wriothesley with a number of its manors. He pulled it down at once. All that remains is a fine gateway and some ruined masonry, with some fragments in the neighbouring church of St. Bartholomew. Towards the end of the eighteenth century a bridewell was built on the spot and a number of relics were found and scattered, among them a stone bearing the name of Alfred, now at Corby Castle. Three stone coffins, very probably those of Alfred, his wife and Edward the Elder, were broken up for road metal. Eighteenth-century Winchester has a black record for the destruction of historic relics.

On part of the site of the New Minster is the modern Guildhall. There is no proof of the existence of the Corporation before Henry I, though a Guild existed in Saxon days. It became a free corporate city under Queen Elizabeth. It sent two members to Parliament from 1295 to 1839.

Below are the Abbey Gardens, tastefully laid out, the site of the important Benedictine Nunnaminster, founded by Alfred, where his queen spent her widowhood and where their saintly daughter, St. Edburga, became not only abbess, but a patroness. Here the nuns of Romsey found refuge from the Danes. Beyond it is St. John's Hospital

for the needy poor, a still existing charity, built in 1289 by
Bishop Pontoise. Behind it was a hall of the Knights'
Guild, dating from Saxon times: they had another near
Westgate. It lasted into the Norman period and in early
days the knights played a part in the rule of the city.
Across the street is the old Town Mill, over the Itchen, now
a Youth Hostel. A little to the east of the bridge is old
Chesil Rectory, now a restaurant, an early sixteenth-century
half-timbered house. Eastgate faced the bridge. From it
the wall ran south to the wall of Wolvesey and north to the
postern at Durngate, then west along North Walls to
Northgate. St. Swithun built his Soke bridge of stone over
the Itchen. Doubtless the Romans had anticipated him.
In the peat near here was recently found a large assortment
of keys, Roman, Saxon and medieval. The Itchen formed
the town ditch. Chesil (popularly Cheesehill) Street gets
its name from the bank of gravel which troubled the boats
coming up with goods from Southampton.

Beyond is St. Giles' Hill, which affords the best view
over the city, and above all of the cathedral, across the roofs
of the Soke, with most of the buildings up to the City Hall.
In the valley to the left is St. Cross by the Itchen and
beyond it St. Catherine's Hill. To the east rise the great
downs. Truly a goodly view, English of the English. On
the top of the hill was the chapel of St. Giles, already ruinous under Henry VIII. In 1080 the hill was the scene of
a tragedy. Earl Waltheof, of the English Royal House,
husband of the Conqueror's niece, 'in stature and form
as fair as a second Absalom', joined the Danes and rose
against the Conqueror in 1069 when the rebels took York.
He was somewhat feeble-minded and William pardoned
him. But when he rebelled again, William imprisoned him
at Winchester. As he was the last male of his line and very
popular, he was dangerous: so one May morning he was
hurried out to the hill at dawn and executed.

St. Giles' Hill is the best known spot in the Soke, the bishop's liberty. The West Soke included Sparkford and St. Cross and all the quarter round the cathedral. The bishop ruled the Soke from Wolvesey through his bailiff of the Soke and the bailiff remained its mayor till 1835. This control of a large section of their city by the bishop was not popular with the townsfolk, who had also the authority of the king to clip their wings still further.

On the hill was held St. Giles' Fair, one of the great fairs of the Middle Ages. Rufus granted it to Walkelin and the fees were most helpful in financing the cathedral. Originally lasting 3 days, it later grew to 16 and even to 20 days. When it opened on St. Giles' Day (September 1st) nothing might be sold except at the fair for seven leagues round Winchester. The bishop's officers were given the keys of the city and the weighing beam, thus superseding the mayor and civic officials. Legal business was transferred to Cheyney Court, held in the fine half-timbered house in The Close. Even at Southampton, by special agreement, food only might be sold. The bishop had been known to excommunicate Southampton for infringing his privileges. There were whole streets of booths, each selling one type of merchandise, brought from all over England, as well as from France, the Low Countries and even Italy. Cloth was the chief article and London merchants, who abounded, dealt largely in it. Cloth-making, thanks to the sheep on the downs, was a considerable industry in Winchester. At Coitebury was a large fulling-mill, and the two mills the rent of which John gave the city for the repair of the walls. Wine was also important. The bishop received rent from the booths as well as dues on all goods brought to the fair. The monks of St. Swithun did a good business with their grocery stall, as can be judged from their wholesale purchases about 1333, only a small part of which can have been consumed by themselves. They bought 40 tuns of wine from Southampton; 136 sheep; 11,300 white herrings; 42,000 red; 220 salted salmon, with large quantities of salted cod, eel and other fish; large quantities of spices; 550 quarters of almonds; 20 of rice; ginger, cinnamon, pepper, mace, saffron, sugar, raisins, wax, dates, comfits, besides plenty of cloth and furs.

Winchester and the roads round were a sight during the fair. The people from the villages came pouring in to make purchases for the whole year and enjoy the fun. Besides the merchants of every kind with their long strings of pack mules, there would be the minstrels, jugglers and buffoons, the light-fingered pedlars, the brothers of Autolycus, and all the riff-raff that battened on such places, not a few of whom would find their way to the Court of Pie Powder (Pieds Poudrés, dusty-footed travellers) that dealt summarily with these cases. All Chaucer's pilgrims might be met here from the Knight to the Clerk of Oxenford, not a few rascally friars and priests among them. No wonder Winchester was a centre for the chapmen who carried their goods round the fairs all over England and who had a hall there.

The fair was at its greatest under the Angevins. It declined rapidly in the fourteenth century, when the wool staple went to Calais, and with it the trade of Winchester. In 1516 the city petitioned Fox, ' the most excellent kindest and loving Bishop that was ever Bishop of the See ', on account of the ' dekeying and desolacion of the city ', to be spared the expense of clothing the 16 or 20 persons who had to present the mayor in London and to be permitted to present him before the outgoing mayor instead. The city still pays 100 nobles (£33 6s. 8d.) to the Marquis of Winchester, the creation fee of his Tudor ancestors.

Beyond St. Giles' Hill is Magdalen Hill, where was the hospital of Mary Magdalen, founded by Toclive, for the sick and infirm. Spared at the Reformation, it suffered so badly in the Civil War that in 1788 it was sold for building material.

Some authorities, wrongly, of course, stage the fight between Guy of Warwick and the Danish giant in the Vale of Chilcomb, between Magdalen Hill and St. Catherine's Hill. But we know that it took place in Danemark Mead, near the Fire Station, and that, though armed with the spear of Constantine and the sword of Charlemagne, he only just managed to overcome the monster Colbrand in the days of Athelstan, who from the walls watched the contest that delivered Winchester from a two years' siege. The story was sung before a bishop visiting the Prior of St. Swithun by a famous minstrel in 1333.

A CHARMING way to get to the Worthies—or rather to Headbourne Worthy, the only one that matters much—is to go out by Hyde Abbey and follow the Nuns' Walk by the Hyde Brook. All but some half a dozen trees of the fine avenue have been cut down and when I was last there a number of them were still lying prone, their branches stretching up into the air in mute appeal. It is peaceful there, with an occasional trout rising in the brook, along by Abbot's Barton Farm, which belonged to the abbey. Farther on the railway embankment, now firmly established in the landscape, acts as a useful screen from the glaring novelty of the by-pass till you turn up on to the road for Headbourne Worthy. Egbert is said to have given St. Swithun's the Worthies, which later passed to the Mortimers. Henry VIII gave them to Jane Seymour.

It is, of course, for the church that one goes to Head-bourne Worthy. It preserves ' in its nave and the west part of the chancel the plan and a good deal of the walling of a pre-Conquest church ', probably of the date of Edward the Confessor. Tradition says that Wilfrid built the first church. Its chief interest is the great Saxon rood outside on the west wall, over which a large chapel was built in the fifteenth century and an altar erected up in front of the rood. It was very roughly handled at the Reformation. In the church is the fifteenth-century brass to John Kent, the Winchester scholar, in his gown.

Away to the west, on the Stockbridge road, at Lainston House, the notorious Elizabeth Chudleigh was secretly married to Augustus Hervey, grandson of the Earl of Bristol. She had met him at the Winchester races and captivated him, as she was to captivate many others, with her robust charms. Shortly afterwards they parted after a violent quarrel. She had married him only because she did not hear from her lover, the Duke of Hamilton, whose letters were intercepted by the aunt with whom she was staying at Lainston. In an evil hour for her, she compelled the vicar on his death-bed to enter the marriage in the registers. The evidence went against her in the famous bigamy trial when she was Duchess of Kingston.

The well-girded walker may, if so inclined, follow the road up the broad Itchen valley to Itchen Stoke, which belonged to Romsey Abbey. In the country behind lies the Grange, the house which Henry Drummond, the banker, built in place of a stately Inigo Jones mansion. The Regent occupied it for a time, after he gave up Kempshott. Then it was bought by Lord Ashburton, for we are here in the Baring country. It is as difficult to imagine Carlyle in this valley, where he often stayed with Lady Ashburton, as it is easy to imagine Kingsley, as the story goes, so intent on the trout that he forgot a service when he was at the inn there.

However, Itchen Abbas was my goal and I reached it by bus from Headbourne Worthy. It belonged to the Abbey of St. Mary of Winchester, and Henry VIII gave it to the Paulets. Here the wise man will turn down to Avington Park, crossing the Itchen by the bridge, where it comes bustling out of Avington mill, and get on terms with the river in its very home. And it would be difficult not to love it as it flows through these rich meadows. This, not the Alresford road among the Worthies, is the real Itchen valley. Through the park you go—and a beautiful walk it is—to the good thatched village of Avington. The red-brick eighteenth-century church is an interesting period church : high pews, a two-decker pulpit, elaborate carving over the altar, all in mahogany, and a good tower. To

The Gatehouse, St. Cross

The Itchen at Itchen Abbas

the north is Hampage wood, from which, it is said, the
Conqueror allowed Bishop Walkelin to take as much wood
as he could cut in four days for his cathedral. Walkelin
mustered every available man and cleared it completely
within the time, leaving only the Gospel Oak, the shell of
which is still pointed out, where the gospel was read at the
beating of the boundary and where tradition has it that
St. Augustine preached. When next he passed that way
the king was amazed. ' Am I bewitched? Had I not a
beautiful wood here? ' On hearing what had happened
he was in high rage. Walkelin fell on his knees before
him, offering to resign his see, if he could but be his
chaplain, and was forgiven.

On through the park the road goes and past the lake.
This was formed from the Itchen by the first Duke of
Buckingham and Chandos, who bought Avington with
Itchen Abbas in 1820: ' one of the prettiest spots in the
whole world", Cobbett called it. Below Avington the
Itchen gathers in the Alre and the Candover and swells
to its full size before entering Winchester. Across the
pond is the red-brick house with its white portico. It has
its history. One of its mistresses was the widow of Lord
Shrewsbury, who was killed in a duel by the Duke of
Buckingham, when she held Buckingham's horse disguised
as a page. Charles II stayed here with Nell Gwynne.

The road brings you out into the quiet valley, where
comfortable, well-thatched Easton spreads itself lazily. It
has a good Norman church. On the south wall is a monument to the widow of William Barlow, an interesting
Reformation prelate, who, from being an Austin Canon
and Prior of Bisham, ultimately held three bishoprics, going
into exile under Mary and dying Bishop of Chichester
under Elizabeth. All her five daughters married bishops,
one of them being the wife of Toby Matthew. A son was
vicar of Easton. A path leads across the water-meadows

D

and the river back to Headbourne Worthy.

Was Easton the village half-way between Alresford and Winchester where W. H. Hudson stayed? He loved the Itchen and the Test, but above all the Itchen. ' Through this infinite variety of refreshing greens and graceful forms flow the rapid rivers, crystal-clear and cold from the white chalk, a most beautiful water.'

For St. Cross there is the path up by the Meads, the College playing-fields. This hospital is a splendid memorial to the munificence of Henry of Blois, almost too splendid a foundation for the support of the ' thirteen poor men, feeble and so reduced in strength that they can hardly or with difficulty support themselves without another's aid ', and for giving a daily dinner to 100 other poor men. The Knights of St. John were his trustees, but they abused their trust, and under Henry II they were forced to give up the Hospital to the Bishop of Winchester. But the bishops were no better. The mastership was ' a scandal and a byword for full six centuries '. William of Wykeham found the great hall had fallen in, the 100 poor men were no longer fed, and the 13 brethren had been turned out. During the twilight of piety which generally ushered in the end of these worldly bishops, Cardinal Beaufort added to it the ' Almshouse of Noble Poverty ' for men of gentle birth, planned on a splendid scale. But it never materialized. The ground, having been purchased from Henry VI, was claimed by Edward IV.

St. Cross weathered the Reformation, but the abuses continued. John Lisle and Cook, the regicides, were Masters under the Commonwealth. It maintains 9 decayed footmen, wrote Gray in 1764, and a Master who draws £800 a year out of it. There is nothing more elusive than a man's conscience, which is as a rule conditioned by his times; but the sight of Bishop Brownlow North at his prayers, by Chantry, in a position of such prominence in the cathedral, fills one with even more disgust than the elaborate tomb erected over the heart of the worthless Aymer de Valence. He gave the Mastership to his son, the Earl of Guildford, vicar of New Alresford, who drew a salary of £1,400 a year and levied fines amounting to £33,000 in 20 years. He also granted relatives leases of Church property on nominal terms for long periods.

The charity has been thoroughly reformed. The foundationers, Henry de Blois's men, wear black gowns with silver crosses and tell you proudly that they are 300 years older than the Cardinal's men with their crimson gowns and tasselled hats. At the porter's lodge you may knock and receive the wayfarer's dole, a horn of beer and a slice of bread, which is given to all who ask for it until the 32 slices and the 2 gallons of beer have been exhausted. This is almost the only remaining case of the carrying on of the duty of charity once imposed on all such institutions. The lodge is in the gate-house, over which rises Beaufort's solid tower. He himself kneels in the central niche.

The hall, with its high, handsome open roof, its gallery and its dais, suggesting a college hall, lies to the west of the gateway. On the dais are Henry of Blois's table, Beaufort's chair and William of Wykeham's rickety-looking one. Like the kitchen, the hall was built by the Cardinal, whose arms appear in the graceful windows. But it is in the garden, with the cottages of the brothers round it, that you come under the influence of the place. A few minutes on one of the seats there on a fine May morning, looking across to St. Catherine's Hill, bring a feeling of utter peace, of complete escape from the world of to-day, though you know that the traffic is roaring along the by-pass, such as no other such place in England that I remember can give. Doubtless the charm does not always work on the inmates, since they are human. Each of them has his three rooms and a garden, and they can now marry.

The Lock Burn, which flows behind their dwellings, was formerly the drain.

No better contrast between the shoddiness of to-day, which goes hand in hand with the vast sums spent on creature comforts, and the Middle Ages, ' as lavish of architectural beauty on what modern habits would deem a receptacle for beggars as on the noblest of royal palaces ', than the magnificent cruciform church, with its massive central tower, which can look the cathedral itself squarely in the face. It is as glorious a specimen of thirteenth and fourteenth-century Transition Norman as is to be found in the country. The arches and pillars are wonderfully varied and the execution approaches perfection. The clerestory and the fine west window are fourteenth century. In front of the altar is a good brass to John de Campenden, a Master appointed by Wykeham, who carried out a quantity of work in the church. The remains of a thirteenth-century painting of the murder of Becket—there are other remains of painting in the church—in the south transept show where his altar stood. The fifteenth-century screen, like the font with its Norman bowl, comes from the church of St. Faith, destroyed in 1509 : for St. Cross is also a parish church. There are some highly interesting fourteenth-century tiles with animals and the motto, ' Have Mynde ' on them. Above the altar of the south chapel is a Flemish triptych.

From St. Cross you go over the Itchen to St. Catherine's Hill. It lies on the other side of the by-pass, which has sliced into it, though it has not damaged it in essentials. It is a spur of the main chalk range, cut off from it by a deep valley, in which are the Death Pits, where the victims of the plague were buried. A narrow ridge, where is the sewage farm, connects it with the downs, along which runs the track right into Sussex. St. Catherine's Hill is the first good defensive position along the Itchen valley from the

sea. Here was the original settlement from which Winchester sprang and which was abandoned for the site by
the river about 200 B.C. This latter was a Belgic settlement. The Belgae never occupied the hill.

The site has recently been thoroughly excavated. The
chapel was the special object, so far as the beeches on the
top, which were almost certainly first planted by the troops
here in 1762, would permit, but their 'roots are no less
deeply embodied in the fabric of the chapel than they are
in the sentiments of the Wykehamical body'. It was a
chapel of some importance, dedicated to St. Catherine, like
other chapels on heights, which was demolished by
Wriothesley.

This is the Hills of the Winchester boys, and by the
chapel is the maze, their Labyrinth. These mazes played
their part in folk-dancing, especially on May Day. There
were numbers of them before the Commonwealth, when
they were destroyed as ungodly. This one is a square of
40 yards and was, as all Wykehamists know, cut by the
boy who was forced to spend his holidays at school, a
punishment sometimes really inflicted. When he had
finished it, he pined away and died under the elm called
Domum tree by the Itchen, on the last day of the holidays.
But before dying he had cut the verses of Dulce Domum
on the elm. The Winchester boys long claimed a right to
the hill for their games, and in 1811, when there was a
beacon there, the Watch was told to prevent them doing
mischief, 'but to be civil to the boys while at their exercise
on the hill'.

The old road takes you between the by-pass and the
Itchen to Twyford. The 'queen of Hampshire villages'
is now afflicted with an outcrop of bungalows and villas,
though there is good country round. Like Owlesbury, it
belonged to the see of Winchester from Saxon times. Pope
was at school here and is said to have been expelled for

writing a satire on one of the masters.

The Welles family, who lived at Brambridge, which is in Twyford, facing Otterbourne across the river, were recusants, one of whom was hung in London under Elizabeth for saying mass there. They were succeeded by the Smythes, also Romanists, whose daughter Mary Anne became Mrs. Fitzherbert. She endowed a small Catholic chapel at Twyford, which was abandoned and the endowment transferred to Eastleigh. There were many recusants in Hampshire, and Gasquet has thrown a good deal of light on their fate. In 1583 some poor Catholics, who were unable to pay their heavy fine for not going to church, were whipped through the streets of Winchester. Nicholas Tichborne of Hartley Maudit, who belonged to a junior branch of the family, died after nine years in prison, a loyal subject of the queen. All his property was gone and the family lived on charity. Yet their lot was easy compared with that of Protestants in a Romanist country.

At Twyford House, a large red-brick mansion, dwelt that princely absentee Bishop of St. Asaph, Dr. Shipley. Benjamin Franklin is said to have written much of his autobiography while his guest there.

You will be rewarded if you take the road to Morestead. The beautiful down is spotted with much that is unlovely, but if you turn off by the waterworks, you find yourself in a good lane, which brings you up by a great field and then runs on through woods. There is a glorious backglance across to the downs above Winchester. Follow the path over the other side, among fields and woods, till it joins the road. This passes the Shearer's inn, beyond which is a path up the down to the right leading to Owlesbury. The church stands high, looking straight across to Southampton. At Marwell Park was a college of priests, which Henry VIII gave to Sir Henry Seymour, his brother-in-law. When one of them persisted in saying mass, Sir Henry is said to have torn him from the chapel and bade his servants shoot him. Legend wrongly places this scene at Owlesbury church. The Bishops of Winchester owned Marwell, and Henry VIII is said to have married Jane Seymour at Marwell Hall. This has been largely rebuilt, but the Seymour arms are on a stone slab in the hall. Marwell Hall is one of the claimants for the Mistletoe Bough story. Fuller records that the rector of Upham near by used to show the chest to the curious. At Upham, Edward Young, author of the *Night Thoughts*, was born.

From St. Cross the modern road follows the Roman road by the Itchen and the railway, past Compton Down and over the hill to the village, pretty and unspoilt, nestling in its valley, with a well-restored church lying up the lane to Pitt Down. The original tiny Norman church is now the north aisle. Goldfinch was a name here, and the sons were either Richard or Joseph. In 1645 a party of Roundheads demanded quarters at the house, where a birth was imminent and a cask of ale already prepared for the christening. This the Captain promised to spare on condition that, if the child was a boy, it should be called after himself. A Barnard Goldfinch thus appears for the first time in the family.

The lane by the church leads round past the farm and up to Compton Down, much the best way back to Winchester. Here is Oliver's Battery, said to have been used by Cromwell during the siege of Winchester. It is nearly two miles from the town, but guns were then regularly removed to a place of safety at night. The vallum and ditch are Roman, but were occupied only for a short time. There is a prehistoric site below. Here, in his grave, on the breast of a Saxon chief was found a beautiful gilded bronze bowl with enamel bosses. There is a replica of it in the Winchester Museum, the original being in the British. It

is sixth century, and it is suggested that he was killed
during the siege of Winchester in 550.

Beyond Shawford Down is Otterbourne, the next of these
Itchen villages. William of Wykeham bought it for his
family. Then it was sold to Waynflete, who gave it to
Magdalen College, which still owns it. Dr. Routh, the
last man to remember Dr. Johnson, was the last President
to hold a court at the Moat House. Owing to its position
by the railway the old church was pulled down in Keble's
day, with his unwilling consent—Otterbourne was then
part of Hursley—the chancel alone being spared. Its ugly
successor was built by Mr. Yonge, a retired Peninsular
officer. He was the father of Charlotte Yonge, the novelist
and prolific writer, who was a devoted disciple of Keble.
Her *John Keble's Parishes* gives an interesting account of
this district, where she lived and died. Keble and his
wife censored her work as long as he lived, allowing no
reference to drunkenness or madness to appear, and at a
family council it was decided that a woman must not earn
money by her pen, so all her profits went to charities. Yet
one remembers the influence *The Heir of Redclyffe* had
upon the young Pre-Raphaelites. At least one little girl
dreaded the awful historical guessing games at her children's parties—did she not write the Cameos from English
History?—and ever afterwards maintained that history was
not a fitting subject of study for a lady.

On the right, as you go up Otterbourne Hill, are the
beautiful grounds of Cranbury Park. After the Restoration it was owned by Sir Charles Wyndham, whose wife,
by the way, was Jacoba, and one of his many daughters
Beata, names not to be neglected by parents in search of
a name out of the common. From the Wyndhams it went
to Jonathan Conduitt, who married the beautiful, brilliant
niece who kept house for Newton. Conduitt was Newton's
successor at the Mint. Newton spent his last years at

Cranbury, where the sundial is said to have been designed by him. Later it was sold to the Dummers.

Off to the right, on the Romsey road, lies Hursley, a singularly pleasing Victorian village, which belonged to that model landlord, Sir William Heathcote. The old cottages look as comfortable as the new, which blend admirably with them. The village stands at the foot of the chalk downs, ' uneven ground with gravelly hills rising above valleys filled with clay, and both alike favourable to the growth of wood ', in the beautiful valley that runs from Winchester to the Test. Hursley belonged to the Bishops of Winchester, and Edyngdon is said to have built the church, of which the tower alone survives. At Merdon the Danes defeated Alfred and Ethelred in 781. For Merdon Castle you escape from the main road along the path by the allotments. It winds delightfully through the fringe of the well-kept woods of the park and then you follow the road to the left. The ruins lie just inside the park gate at the top of the hill. The castle was built by Henry of Blois. It was in good repair till about 1165, but in the next century only the residential part was habitable. It stands on a spur of the chalk, sloping gently, in the middle of a prehistoric camp, where the bank encloses some 11 acres. Some ruins remain. The well is very deep and is saddled with the not uncommon legend that ducks put into it come out at Hursley without their feathers.

Hursley came to the king at the Reformation, and was granted to Sir Philip Hobby, who built the first lodge in the park. On his death it passed to his brother, who married the widow of Thomas Sternhold, part author of the famous Sternhold and Hopkins version of the psalms. Sternhold was Groom of the Robes to Henry VIII, who left him 100 marks in his will, and he acquired Slackstead, which lies to the north of Ampfield, at the Reformation. Like Marot in France, he tried to make the psalms as popular as profane songs at court. By 1639 Hursley belonged to Richard Major, a devout Protestant, who raised a troop for the Parliament. Oliver Cromwell arranged a marriage between his daughter and his son Richard. Quiet and retiring, Richard was the type of son whom a man like Cromwell sometimes has and loves from contrast. The last man to wish to have greatness thrust upon him, he was quite happy at Hursley. In his day was planted the double avenue of walnut trees leading to the old house, as well as the noble limes, which were then fashionable as they were thought to purify the air, round the church. These Dick is said to have planted himself.

At the Restoration he retired to France and changed his name. On the death of his wife, Merdon went to his son, Oliver, who predeceased him. Then his daughters claimed Hursley, but the Court gave it to Richard. He died in 1712 and was buried at Hursley. There is a large mural monument under the tower, transferred to the new church, to the Cromwell family, where poor Dick's one distinction would appear to be that he was father to his daughter Elizabeth. The only relic of him is the set of bowls said to have belonged to him, some of which are shown at the inn.

The new, not unpleasing church was built by Keble in place of an ugly eighteenth-century one, for which the original Norman building had been destroyed. Portions of the tower alone survive. Keble, who was first curate and then rector, is buried in the churchyard, near the vicarage. He gave the profits of his *Christian Year* to the new church.

The first Sir William Heathcote bought the estate from Cromwell's daughters. He is said to have pulled down the lodge, which was in bad repair, because he could not live where an 'arch rebel' had dwelt. The seal of the Commonwealth before Cromwell abolished Parliament was then found hidden behind a wall. The new house stands higher up the hill. In it is the beautiful Charles II panelling shamefully removed from the chapel of Winchester College.

Beyond Hursley you get the first taste of the New Forest in the woods round Ampfield, with its picturesque well under the church. This, too, was once part of Hursley. The church, looking down on the turnpike and out over the country from the woods, was built by Sir William Heathcote. In fact, the combination of Keble and Heathcote shows the Victorian squire and vicar at their best. A liberal and wealthy landowner, a generous and earnest rector, who knew how to stir the enthusiasm of his parish and his friends, provided this great parish with necessary, if not remarkable churches, and with incomes for the incumbents.

Another way to Southampton is along the railway route by Eastleigh (Bishopstoke), where are the carriage works of the line, a modern red-brick town. You have but to turn off from the main road to find yourself amid fields. Where a lane crosses the Itchen by a water-splash stands the church of North Stoneham, virtually in the park which is still owned by the Flemings who acquired the land from the Wriothesleys. A church existed here in 885. Parts of the present church are thirteenth century. In the south aisle is the large monument to Sir Thomas Flemyng and his wife (1613). He was made Solicitor General over Bacon's head and was a judge after the heart of James I, whose claims he supported. He helped to try Guy Fawkes. At the west end of the aisle is the monument to Lord Hawke, victor of Quiberon Bay, which battle is ' elegantly displayed there on in white marble '. He lived at Swaythling.

Here, too, is a tangible relic of the Venetians. The church is dedicated to St. Nicholas, the saint of those voyaging by sea, and under the matting in the chancel is the beautifully preserved slab bearing the inscription ' sepultura de la Schola de Sclavoni ', dated 1491. The 180 oarsmen of a Venetian galley — never slaves — were mostly from Dalmatia, Slavonians. This was the burying-place of the fraternity, such as they had at Venice. Why does it bear the Imperial eagle? Venice was a refuge for people in trouble in the Empire, but Dalmatia belonged to her or to Hungary.

Across the Itchen are South Stoneham and Swaythling. The Roman road to Clausentum, which left the modern Southampton road at Otterbourne, followed that bank of the river.

CHAPTER V: *Southampton*

THE road enters Southampton by a fine avenue fringing its suburbs on the east. To the west lies the magnificent Common, 400 acres, with every variety of woodland scenery and sports ground. Part of the original common land of the town, it still has much the appearance of a stray bit of the New Forest. On the right, where the avenue becomes the London Road, is a large building now badly damaged to which every one interested in the perambulation of his own country or in geography should mentally doff his hat, for it has been the Headquarters of the Ordnance Survey since 1841. University College, by the way, is out in Hampton Park. It is the lineal descendant of the Hartley Institute, formerly in the High Street.

The importance of the well-protected harbour was grasped by the Romans, who had their post of Clausentum at Bitterne. Southampton stands on the rising tongue of gravel that lies between the mouths of the Test and the Itchen. Together they form the noble estuary of Southampton Water running down to Calshot, the mouth of which is protected by the Isle of Wight. Certain remains give reason to think that the original settlement was in the neighbourhood of St. Mary's Church, on the Itchen, to the north-east of the medieval walls; but early in the eleventh century the nucleus of the town was already forming along the Test. The Saxons were here by the eighth century, when it gave its name to Hamtunscire, and in 925 it had two mints. To-day, with its suburbs of Shirley, Freemantle, Portswood and some of Bitterne, it has a population of about 177,000. In Domesday it is Hantune. Henry VI gave it an Incorporation Charter and two years later, in return for a heavy fee-farm, payable to the king, it was made a county, Portsmouth being within its liberty, for it stretched from Hurst, including Lymington, to Langstone.

As the road proceeds it becomes apparent that the life of the place is centring more and more above Bar, where are the most up-to-date shops: it is drifting out towards the imposing and dignified Civic Centre, which lies off the main road on the right. Here are now the courts and the Guildhall and all the labours and splendours of municipal activity, and here, too, will soon be the School of Art. This is by no means a disadvantage to the sentimental tourist, bent on investigating old Southampton with as little allaying modernity as possible; and he will soon find that the district deserves a longer stay than is usually accorded to it. Indeed, it would, to my mind, make a far more interesting centre for a regular holiday than most of the mushroom watering-places that lie like a blight along the coast.

Above Bar, on the left, was the Congregational Chapel, now destroyed. It was a memorial to Isaac Watts, who was born in French Street, where his father kept a school. Small, delicate and extraordinarily precocious, he wrote hymns for a chapel in his boyhood. 'How doth the little busy bee . . .'—'Dog's delight . . .'—we love them and laugh at them; but he also wrote 'O God our help in ages past' and others that have a permanent place in our hymn-books.

You reach the walls at Bargate—gate is the Anglo-Saxon for street—the north gate, formerly entered by a draw-bridge over a double moat that reached the sea by what is now Orchard Street. If Bar has not been offered up on the altar of progress, it has undergone changes that shock its old friends. It has been detached from the houses and the traffic now flows round it instead of under it. The Guildhall above, where a court existed under Elizabeth, has followed the fashion and gone north to the Civic Centre. Bar, if a little jagged about the edges, looks larger and more impressive than of old. Its active days are over. It has become an ancient monument, playing no further part in the life of the town. But it is still Bargate, 'large and welle embatelid'. The towers and the arch facing us are four-teenth century; the gates in the towers, which now serve no purpose, eighteenth. The other side, with its quaint statue of George III in a toga, and the Jacobean shields, which are bad heraldry, is much inferior. The pictures of Bevis of Southampton and his esquire-giant Ascapard, noticed by Pepys, have long retired inside the Guildhall. In his day you entered Bargate 'between the jaws of 2 rampant lions and 2 thundering warriors' with Queen Elizabeth above. Pepys, one remembers, dined with the Mayor and had sturgeon of their own catching, 'which do not happen in twenty years'.

The north wall can still be traced among the houses down to Arundel Tower, named doubtless after the horse of Bevis of Southampton. Where it reaches the water is Catchcold Tower. These walls, about 25 feet high, were strengthened by 29 towers : in some places, as in Bargate, Norman work survives. They stretch, an almost unique relic of medieval fortification, right away to the Pier. Till the road was made in front of them in 1850 they were lapped by the waves, as they appear in the old prints. They were built on the shore without foundations, but with a row of piles in front. Lighters were bound to bring a load of stones to shoot among these piles to strengthen them, and their owners were given a barrel of beer for each 20-ton load. From King John's day there are numerous references to the expenses of the repairs, which were a severe strain on the town. The continued grants from the fee-farm prove the importance the Crown attached to these defences.

Next comes the mound of the castle, first mentioned in the agreement between Stephen and Henry II. As coins of King Offa have been found here, it may have been

fortified in Saxon times. Speed describes the castle as
' most beautiful, in forme, circular, and wall within wall,
the foundation upon a hill, so topped that it cannot be
ascended but by stairs '. It had its quay, the barbican.
In 1386 the king's chaplain, an expert gunner, was put in
charge at a salary of £10 a year paid from the wool duty.
It was from his ' Chastel de Hantonne au rivage de la mer '
that Henry V indited a letter to the King of France. Under
James I the castle was ruinous and he sold it. Lord Lans-
downe built himself a castellated mansion here about 1800,
and his heir drove a phaeton drawn by ponies little bigger
than Newfoundland dogs. Jane Austen spent four years
in a corner house in Castle Square, then fashionable, with
a garden, said to be the best in the town, running up to
the walls, by which she used to walk with the sea below.

Beyond the castle lies the best known and most interesting section of the walls—the arcades. Obviously this was
a weak point, since the walls of the houses here offered
no adequate defence, so 19 arches were built, providing
the defenders with a platform, while the machicolations
enabled them to deal effectively with an enemy below. The
windows of the houses were blocked up, as they still are.
The arcades are said to have been erected after the disaster
of 1338. On Sunday, October 4th, while Edward III was
in France, a combined French, Spanish and Genoese fleet
appeared off the Gravels, where, at the east end, the
fortifications were weakest, ' and full fast they slogh and
brend ', as Minot sings. The inhabitants fled, but next day
they plucked up courage, returned with the peasants round
and drove the enemy back to their ships with great
slaughter. Among them, says Stowe, was the son of the
King of the Sicilies, to whom the French king had given
whatever he could get in England. ' But he being beaten
down by a certain man of the country, cried out, " Rancon,
rancon " : notwithstanding which the husbandman laid

The City Walls and West Gate, Southampton

Titchfield Abbey

Buriton

him on with his clubbe till he had slain him, speaking these
words, "Yea . . . I know thee well enough; thou art a
Frencon, and therefore thou shalt die," for he understood
not his speech, neither had he any skill to take gentlemen
prisoners and to keep them for their ransome.' The town
was so badly damaged that it was long before many of the
rents could be paid. God's House was lucky, as only 29
of its 108 houses were destroyed.

West Gate, so unpretentious now, leading to West Quay,
was long the chief gate of the town. It was defended
by no less than 3 portcullises, as the grooves show, and
the quay was also protected by a stone barbican. From
here the men-at-arms for part of Richard I's fleet embarked
for Palestine and through it may have gone the 800 Hampshire hogs the sheriff gave them. Here the English archers,
with Edward III and the Black Prince, marched out to
prove the worth of their long bows against the noblest
chivalry of France at Crécy. Froissart refers to the expedi-
tions that left the port: and it was from this gate that the
army of Henry V embarked to win Agincourt, when the
town supplied 21 ships and over 500 sailors. Two of
Henry's great ships, the *Holy Ghost* and the *Grace Dieu*,
were built at Southampton. It is good to remember these
things as one's eye follows the line of the old grey walls,
though their feet are no longer in the sea; and it was
consoling to see a little girl taking a friend at full speed
along them, proud to pour out her knowledge of their
story: at least children are now taught to appreciate local
history.

In the eighteenth century this was the quay for the
Channel Islands, with which there was a busy trade, among
other things in runaway matches. You could hire a cutter
for five guineas and be married in the islands as easily as
at Gretna Green.

This was an important district, too, while Southampton

E

had its brief summer of fashion. Horace Walpole found it crowded in September in 1755 owing to the baths, and Keats enjoyed the quiet of Winchester in August when the fashion had gone to Southampton. The chalybeate spring was near by, at the bottom of Orchard Street, and behind West Gate were the Long Rooms, where the assemblies were held in summer; in winter they were at the Dolphin. Close to these were the baths. Mr. Martin, the owner of the Rooms, was allowed to remove for his own convenience not merely portions of 3 round towers, but even the top of the West Gate, which was not too safe.

The walls now turn east. Bugle Street gets its name from Bugle or Bull House, the town house of the Earls of Southampton, built round a courtyard, which was burnt down in 1791. At the corner is the Wool House or Weigh House, now destroyed, also called the Spanish Prison because Queen Anne kept a number of Spanish prisoners there. The Earl of Warwick under Edward I held a messuage in the town by sergeantry of weighing, being in charge of the beam or tron for weighing the wool. There were also many wool warehouses in the neighbourhood. Wool was the chief item in the trade of Southampton.

Among the great trading fleets dispatched yearly from Venice were the Flanders Galleys. Most of them sailed to Antwerp or Sluys, but 3 or 4 came on to Southampton. So strictly were they controlled by the Grand Council that a special decree was passed to permit the captain to go ashore at Rye or Hampton to hear mass. Their arrival, which was very irregular, was as eagerly awaited by the Venetian ambassador as by the merchants. The first visit was in 1317. Their path was not always peaceful. In 1488 they were ordered to strike sail by 3 English pirate vessels. They refused, and in the fight 18 English were killed. They brought eastern goods of all kinds, Venetian luxury goods and wine, notably malmsey.

In spite of the Hampshire yew, we looked to them for the best bow staves. Edward IV allowed them to trade only on condition that they brought 10 staves with every butt of malmsey and Tyrian. They took away leather, coal, cheese, lead, but above all cloth and wool.

The Tudors valued these visits. Henry VII arrested the highwaymen who had killed some Venetian merchants and hung them in sight of the fleet. Henry VIII was entertained on the Venetian flagship and greatly impressed by a performance on the slack rope hung between the masts. The glasses used on the occasion were distributed among the guests. The king had the guns fired off more than once, being much interested in their range. The galleys were sometimes confiscated, as by Henry V and Henry VIII when at war with France; and when Henry VIII returned them, he kept six bronze guns. Henry VIII put an end to these visits. He complained that the galleys brought no spices, only glass and such like rubbish. Venice pleaded that the spices went to Portugal and that they brought wine and their purchases were important. But the king put an embargo on the wool and in 1532 the galleys came for the last time. Thus Venice lost her English market owing to the rounding of the Cape. But individual galleys long called at Hampton on private ventures.

So badly did the Londoners treat the Italian merchants under Henry VI that they migrated to Winchester and Southampton in a body. This fact, with St. Giles' Fair, increased the importance of Hampton as a port of call. All these coasts were infested by pirates, especially in war-time, when hostilities invaded our very harbours. In 1536 the French cut out Flemish ships both from Southampton and Portsmouth. Just before the Armada the ambassador of Henri III had to wait for an escort to take him home from Southampton.

Beyond the end of French Street is the twelfth-century

house known as Canute's Palace. It is only right that the
name should stand and that Canute should have his street
here, because all good citizens know that this was the scene
of his famous rebuke to his flatterers by the sea. Moreover,
Southampton played an important part in pre-Norman
history. It was attacked by the Danes, who were driven
off in 837. Ethelwulf and other kings dated charters from
' the celebrated place called Heantun '. When the unpleasant attentions of the Danes rapidly became more pressing,
Southampton, like all this coast, suffered badly. Olaf and
Sweyn wintered here in 994, and so powerful was Danish
influence that the town, not unwisely, supported Canute,
who was here elected king.

The Sun Hotel occupies the site of the old watch-tower
by South Gate, which protected the sluices of the east ditch,
filled by the sea. It was long called Bridewell Gate,
because, with the tower, it was the town gaol. Water-gate
Quay was built early in the fifteenth century and provided
with a crane and a custom-house, a very unpopular
innovation with those who had hitherto evaded the customs.
Winchester entered a protest. Here, too, was the platform,
protected by artillery. There was a town gunner, whose
guns were seemingly kept in store till required. In 1475,
when the French were beaten off, his ' organs ' were not
ready : nor did they escape damage in the fight, for
' Thomas with the beard ' needed two new ' forlokkes '.
Here is now the Town Quay. The Mayor was given
Admiralty rights by Henry VI and the Admiralty gallows
was here. He could thus regulate fisheries and claim
wrecks. He was, in fact, Admiral of the port. Hence a
silver oar, which still exists, was carried before him. Here,
too, is the Royal Pier opened by the Duchess of Kent and
Princess Victoria. The invitation was carried to their
yacht on a state barge with the silver oar in front.

This town quay, on the Test, is the centre of local and

coastal traffic, and beyond it lie the docks, opened in 1842, two years after the railway. Their great expansion commenced with the acquisition by the railway company in 1892. The newest section, to the north-west, along the Test, has been built on reclaimed land. Southampton has long been the most important passenger port in the kingdom and it is now the fourth commercial port. Its double tide always gave it a great advantage. Over 18,000,000 tons of shipping use it yearly and its trade is not far short of £55,000,000.

The fortunes of Southampton have ebbed and flowed. In early days, when Winchester was not much less than the capital, it prospered greatly, for it was the chief port to Normandy, and it continued to prosper so long as we held Aquitaine and Guienne. It was the great port for the wine trade, and a number of Norman cellars have only recently been improved away. Some held the king's prisage, when he claimed two tuns of wine at his own price out of every ship carrying more than 20 tuns. Warwick the Kingmaker had a pension on the fee-farm, which was often paid in wine, doubtless from the prisage. So wealthy was Southampton that the queens were often dowered from the fee-farm or the customs.

The ebb began in the sixteenth century. After the Fire of London it took occasion to advertise its advantages, with its good harbour and its many empty houses and warehouses, but with small success. By 1683 ' the late Rebellion had robbed the Chamber of all public moneys: the plague had consumed the inhabitants, the Dutchmen had spoiled them of nearly all their ships, their looms were useless owing to the late Act of Prohibition, their revenues had sunk, their burdens increased '. It was difficult to find men to undertake the municipal offices. Under William and Mary, Celia Fiennes found Southampton very neat and clean, ' the streets well pitched and kept so by their carrying all their carriages on sleds as they do in Holland, and permit no cart to go about in ye town and keep it clean and swept '. But it was almost forsaken and neglected owing to the failure of its trade. The revival began when it became a fashionable bathing resort. Hence the privileges allowed Mr. Martin.

The walls now turned north by the Town Ditch, which was double and later formed part of an abortive canal. Their line was long marked by an unpleasant alley called Back of the Walls, which has been cleared away.

It is best to enter the old town by Bargate, at the top of the High Street, formerly English Street. This was long enthusiastically admired. 'The town is one most gallant street,' said Pepys. 'One of the fairest streets that is in England,' echoes Leland. The compliment can hardly stand to-day, though it is a fine, broad, straight street lined with shops which have been more modernized than the houses into which they are built. But it is no longer the lounge of the neighbourhood for miles around, as it was till the middle of last century, in the days when the fashionable world drove out along the half mile of causeway under the elms to Itchen Ferry. In its smartest days Southampton was well served with coaches. In 1803 stage-coaches left for London at 5 a.m., returning the same evening : inside fare 21s., outside 14s. Night coaches ran three times a week, starting at 7 p.m.: fares, 18s. inside, 12s. outside. There were also plenty of local coaches and coaches to other parts of England, as well as vans and wagons. Hackney coaches, it is true, there were none, but the gentry were 'accommodated with sedan-chairs on reasonable terms'. As early as 1655 the Southampton coachman set up another coach with 6 horses, and 'there is another sett up lately in Winchester '.

In Leland's day the High Street was 'well bylded for timbre bylding ', but the upper part is now externally almost completely modern. On the left is East Street, leading to the now vanished East Gate. On the other side is Simnel Street—Simnel means manchet bread—the bakers' quarter, one of the picturesque but dirty alleys that once formed a notable feature of this old port town, especially under the walls. They were swept away in the nineties of last century. Close by was Butchers' Row. Bridge Street on the left takes its name from the bridge over the Town Ditch. At the corner is Holy Rood Church, now known as the holy ruin, of which the tower alone is ancient. Here Philip of Spain heard mass after landing when he came to marry Mary in 1554. In front of it, in the middle of the road, as usual, stood the Audit House or Market House, which was cleared away before the end of the eighteenth century. Opposite is St. Michael's Street, leading to St. Michael's church, the one church that has not been completely modernized.

The mother church of Southampton was St. Mary's, probably of Saxon origin. But in 1550 ' the great church of Our Lady ' was largely destroyed, as it has been again, seemingly because its tower was too good a mark for the French, and the rubbish was used to repair the streets. It long remained in ruins. The present St. Mary's, a memorial to Bishop Wilberforce, was designed by Street.

St. Michael's has also been badly gammoned, but the arches of the tower are Norman. Also it possesses one of the fine twelfth-century fonts of Tournai marble like that in Winchester Cathedral. This one bears the symbols of the Four Evangelists. Near it, on a stand, are the chained books, Foxe's *Book of Martyrs* and a *Commentary on the Gospels*. In the square outside was the Fish Market, the buildings of which nearly filled it.

Opposite the church is the striking Tudor House, with its gables and overhanging storeys, now, one is glad to say, the museum. In the sixteenth century there were many 'fair merchauntes houses'. Edward VI was impressed by his visit. The citizens had been at great expense in repairing the walls. 'The town is handsome and for the bigness of it as fair houses as be in London. The citizens made great cheer and many of them kept costly tables.' But, says Leland, 'the chiefest is the house that Huttoft, late Customer of Hampton, builded in the west side of the town', the Tudor House of to-day. Henry Huttoft, who finished it about 1435, was a wealthy merchant, during whose mayoralty Catherine of Aragon visited Southampton. He was a religious man, a benefactor of Mottisfont Abbey, for the preservation of which he pleaded. But when he saw its case was hopeless, he begged that he might have it towards his poor living. The north door, the museum entrance, led into the great hall of his dwelling, the south into his office. Later alterations have largely obliterated the interior plan of the house. The foundations and cellars are Norman, and the old house may have been destroyed in 1338.

Huttoft was a follower of Cromwell, by whose influence he was made Customer, as the excellent guide to the house relates. Another house named by Leland is that of his son-in-law, Guidotti, a Florentine wine-merchant of note, who bought for the king. He lived at 59 High Street, whence came the beautiful fire-places in the Guildhall offices. Guidotti absconded, leaving debts to the Crown of over £6,000, for £3,000 of which Huttoft was surety, so naturally he was in difficulties. Also three of his ships were taken by pirates. But he remained prominent in Southampton till his death. Guidotti made his peace with the Government and was knighted by Edward VI.

Tradition says that Henry VIII stayed at the Tudor House when he visited Southampton with Anne Boleyn, and that Philip of Spain spent his three days here before his marriage.

Behind the Tudor House is a garden laid out in Elizabethan style, with a vista of cranes and funnels that would
have appealed to Henry VIII. Here is the culverin he
presented to the town, said to be the third finest in the
kingdom. From the garden you look down into the
Norman house which runs along Blue Anchor Lane, where
is the arched doorway. This lane, leading to Blue Anchor
postern in the walls, was another noted rookery, which
was cleared out, and a large lodging-house for men built
in it by the Corporation. The house is early twelfth
century and is described as ' nearly perfect except the roof '.
It is probably one of the oldest houses remaining in
England. The basement suggests that it was used to store
wine. Many old cellars have gone, but the finely groined
one in Simnel Street has fortunately been spared. The
house was certainly destroyed in 1338, for it looked out on
the sea under the arcades. It has been little altered
externally since then.

Bugle Street and French Street run up to St. Michael's
—St. Michael was the patron saint of Normandy—parallel
to High or English Street. In Domesday there were 76
burghers in Southampton and William settled 65 French
and 31 English in French Street, whence doubtless its name.
At that time many nobles and officials had houses in
Southampton wherein to lodge on their frequent crossings
to Normandy.

Charles I is said to have lodged at No. 17 High Street,
where there is some good carving, in 1625, when the Treaty
of Southampton was made with the Dutch. Towards the
sea end the ordinary world is left more and more behind.
The shops are less modern. Nautical instruments and
charts and clothes begin to appear in the windows, and you
become aware of the peculiar smell of the great warehouses
and of things stored wholesale. You are in the midst of
the concerns of those who go down in ships to trade, an

atmosphere which will always have a romantic flavour for any one to whom the London docks were a chief delight in boyhood. From the end of the pier you can gaze out on that great highway of ships, Southampton Water, with its background of the peace and beauty of the New Forest. For a good view of the town and a glimpse at its shipping, take the ferry over to Hythe. On your way you will pass the docks, where you may get a sight of the huge bulk of the *Queen Mary*. Nor must we forget that it was from here that the *Mayflower* sailed in 1620, though Plymouth was the last port at which she touched, to found the New England colonies.

At the bottom of High Street, to the left, is Winkle Street, once running under the walls. It leads to another interesting building, God's House, or rather what was God's House, for rarely has an ancient building been so badly mauled by an Oxford College. It is comforting to turn to the good row of red tiles of the cottages on the left. God's House, or Domus Dei, was founded by a wealthy citizen for aged and poor sisters and brothers. In 1343 it was granted to Queen's College, in which Edward III's queen was interested. At that time, when the wardens were generally non-resident, the poor brothers and sisters were allowed, in addition to their food, a farthing every other day. All the old buildings, which went back to the foundation, were replaced by the present commonplace structures for four brothers and four sisters in 1861, when also the gateway and the chapel were spoiled by restoration. In the chapel were buried the three conspirators against the life of Henry V before Agincourt. The Earl of Cambridge and Lord Scrope of Masham were paraded through the town to the north gate and executed just as the fleet set sail. The fact is recorded on a plaque.

This was the chapel granted by Elizabeth to the Walloon

Protestant refugees; 'she appointed us unto this youre towne, where we should freely and peaceably make our abode and quietly exercise marchandizing'. The registers contain interesting information. There are many cases of expression of penitence at having heard mass to escape persecution. The minister was the only one in the town not to desert his post during the plague of 1665. After the Revocation of the Edict of Nantes there was a considerable increase in the community and some of the refugees started the manufacture of silk in Winkle Street. The Walloons conformed to the Church of England in 1712, with the disapproval of their fellows in England, and the service is still read in French.

Among distinguished citizens of Southampton are Millais and Charles Dibdin, a Wykehamist, and the writer of 'Tom Bowling', 'The Lass that loves a Sailor' and many other songs.

There is ample information about the history of the borough. The number of officers it employed was varied and peculiar. There were, to make a selection, the wardens of the gates; the keepers of the various keys; the town crier; sand-walkers to look out for wrecks, who, as they might not be pressed, later rose to 20 or 30; auditors; beadles; a scavenger; two constables; a town carpenter, sweep and brickmaker; the pavier who had a house and a yearly gown and had to 'searche the pavement' and repair it when necessary; a cow-herd with 14 overseers and 12 drovers to look after the common land. This was extensive and included not only the common, but most of the parks with which Southampton is not ill provided. There were even the town musicians, whose number varied, there being 3 in 1433. In 1615 the town cook was given the monopoly of the oyster-beds in the harbour on condition that he retailed them at 2d. a hundred and supplied 500 for the Mayor's fish dinner. In 1637 the foot-post to

London, wearing his silver badge with the town arms, started on Monday or Tuesday.

The defence of the different towers was, in 1544 at least, entrusted to certain bodies of citizens. Bargate was assigned to the town, but God's House tower was in charge of the Mercers and Grocers and the tower against Mr. Huttoft's—the postern at Blue Anchor Lane—of the Weavers. Under Elizabeth all burgesses from the Sheriff upwards must wear a scarlet gown on high days and holidays, as also their wives. An alderman whose wife had not got one might be fined £10 and 10s. for every day she failed to wear it.

The Court-leet, still held on Hock Tuesday, existed before the Conquest, and its records contain, as always, much varied human information. In 1550 'Mr. Maire kepith a sowe in his Backsyde which is brought in and out contrary to the ordenaunce of the towne', where no hog was allowed. In 1557 Walter Ear was presented for wearing velvet guards on his hose and John Delisle's wife for wearing a petticoat guarded with velvet.

To the right of the Avenue as you leave Southampton towards the north is Bevois Town, which occupies the site of Bevis Mount. Whether it was thrown up by Bevis as a defence against the Danes or whether he is buried there with the fair converted pagan Josyan is still uncertain. But at least we know that it belonged in the eighteenth century to the brilliant, eccentric Lord Peterborough and that he spent his last years in ' my Blenheim ' that ' could not afford lodging for two maids of honour and their equipage '. Latterly he added to it considerably for his late-acknowledged countess, the actress Anastasia Robinson, to whom he had long been married. He would let strangers see it only at high tide, when it looked its best. Peterborough liked the company of men of letters. Swift, who liked him, calls him ' the ramblingest lying rogue on

earth '. With Pope he was intimate and he was often
at the Mount, which he calls ' beautiful beyond imagination '.

In the winter of 1683-4, the registers of Holy Rood tell
us, the river was ' covered with ice from Calshott Castle to
Redbridge. . . . And ye river at Ichen Ferry was soe
frossen over that severall persons went from Beauvois Hill
to Bittern farme forwards and backwards '.

Where is now the suburb of St. Denys, on a piece of
land between Portswood and the Itchen, was the Austin
Priory of St. Denys, founded by Henry I. All that remains
is a piece of wall by the Itchen. Henry II granted to it
most of the churches of Southampton.

At Bitterne, now a modern suburb, is the curve on the
east bank of the Itchen on which was the site of the Roman
settlement of Clausentum. Two parallel lines of defence,
30 yards apart, cut it off from the land side. ' If Clausentum was a fort,' says Haverfield, ' it was a fort only in
the fourth century, before that it was something else.' It
is situated on the estate of Bitterne Manor, which is being
developed, and numerous Roman remains have been found
there. The road runs right through it. The well is said
to be Roman. A road has recently been found through the
settlement ' leading towards the turn of the estuary just
above Northam bridge. . . . It would lead to the spot
where in 1918 two pigs of lead with the name of Vespasian
were found and makes it probable that there were quays
hereabouts.' There was a Roman road from Clausentum
to Chichester, the course of which has now virtually been
established.

The railway follows the coast. Netley long ago sacrificed
its rural simplicity to the hospital which roused the formidable wrath of Florence Nightingale and the rest of it is now
disappearing under suburban streets, though you get a
glimpse of the Solent from a stray corner. The private

owner has shut off the view from the sea on the road to the abbey, but once there, you escape into another world. It still stands, as in Gray's day, 'in a little quiet valley, which gradually rises behind the ruins into a half-circle crowned with thick wood'. Walpole was enchanted : 'they are not the ruins of Netley, but of Paradise'. The ivy and the trees which he admired among the ruins have gone, and the abbey is now in the appreciative charge of the Office of Works. It has doubtless suffered somewhat from time and tourists, for Netley was long a vulgar resort of trippers of all kinds, with swings and merry-go-rounds. But the ruins can still awaken much the same enthusiasm they did in Walpole, and it is possible to understand how this lonely site appealed to the Cistercians who came here from Beaulieu in 1239. Henry III was their patron and he endowed them well, giving them a fair at Wellow and a market at Hound, to say nothing of a tun of red wine for communion from the royal prisage. The position had its disadvantages. Sailors made heavy claims on the hospitality of the monks, while those stationed in the neighbourhood, as they complained in 1338, were continually raiding their sheep-folds and, after the sack of Southampton, they dared not till their fields. Henry VIII's commissioners spoke highly of the generosity with which they dispensed hospitality.

Much of the church remains, including the noble east window and the stairs in the south-east corner of the transept that led to the tower, a well-known landmark for shipping, where was probably the light kept burning for a beacon. The plan follows the usual Cistercian model. The church is to the north of the beautiful cloisters, and on the east is the chapter-house, of which, as at Beaulieu, there are three arches remaining.

At the Dissolution the Marquis of Winchester secured Netley. Later, the Earl of Huntingdon divided the church into a tennis-court and a small chapel, using the nave as his kitchen. In 1700 the church was sold to a Southampton builder, who was warned of the danger of destroying sacred buildings. Much impressed, he dreamt that the key-stone of an arch fell on him and killed him. He consulted the father of Isaac Watts, who advised him to have no personal concern in pulling down the church. But he persisted, and his skull was in due course fractured by a stone falling from a window. To this circumstance we owe the preservation of the ruin in its present state.

In front of the abbey in Gray's day was a thicket of oaks, on each side of which you could catch sight of the sea covered with sails. Behind this screen was the gate-house which Henry VIII converted into one of his castles along the coast. The tower was added when it was made into a private house.

After the abbey it is pleasant to escape from the purlieus of Netley over the railway past the woods to Hound in the open country. The farm and the interesting little Pointed church with its wooden belfry and the great yew in the churchyard take you back into the real Hampshire. Hound was yet another De Port manor.

CHAPTER VI: *The Portsmouth Road*

THE Portsmouth road was bound to grow into one of the great roads of the south with the development of Portsmouth into a naval station and a favourite route to the Isle of Wight. The Elephant and Castle was its starting-point, and it duly made its way to the gap in the downs by Guildford before plunging south-west to cross Hindhead, where Pepys once lost his way. The first five miles over the border to Liphook are downhill, a gentle slope where a many-caped, white-hatted whip of the great coaching days could enjoy himself and spring his cattle, unless the snow were heavy. Towards the end of the seventeenth century the Portsmouth machine ' sets out from ye Elephant & Castle and arrives presently by ye grace of God ', and the length of the journey, owing largely to the state of the roads, was not brought under human control for another hundred years. In 1784, when the mail coaches started, the journey took 14 hours. Just before the coming of the railway upwards of 24 coaches crossed the border in a day. The Rocket, the best coach on the road, left Piccadilly Circus at 9 and reached Portsmouth at 5.30.

The liveliest and most characteristic sight on the way from Portsmouth was a coachload of sailors just paid off, often with prize-money in addition to their pay—one remembers Hogarth—during the French wars, throwing their guineas recklessly about and being robbed wholesale. At the inns they were generally given shake-downs in the barns. As they swayed with the coach instead of against it, it not unfrequently capsized; and, assisted by the liquor they generally had on board, they were liable to come to a violent end by falling off when asleep. The return journey,

80

when all their money was spent, was a much more sober affair, performed as often as not on foot.

The road enters Hampshire over Bramshott Common, which can be nearly as purple with willow-herb in July as it is with heather in August—Bramshott, Grayshott, Heyshott, you are in the Shott country. In 1900 Canon Capes could describe his parish, about which he has much of more than local interest to tell, as obscure, for it is on the inhospital greensand. But the car and the camps have changed all that. It is a large parish. Woolmer Forest runs into it and there is also Wheatsheaf Common. Close to the church is Old Place, now a farm, modernized, but with fifteenth-century windows.

By it is the lane down to Waggoners or Wakeners Wells, the beauty of which is in no way impaired now that it has been taken over by the National Trust. Tennyson loved the spot and there he wrote that curious little poem, ' Flower in the Crannied Wall ', which was often on the lips of my philosophy tutor in the early days of Greats. George Eliot saw it differently. ' What a good place for a murder in a novel! ' Ironworks were common in this corner of Surrey, thanks to the woods and the iron-stone, and Henry Hooke made these three ponds to supply water for his. They are the most beautiful I know. They drain into the southern arm of the Wey. A century ago there was a heap of ashes by the bridge, which were used for mending the road, and Henry atte Cinderheap was a local name.

Such ponds also supplied fish, which was long a necessity, because, after the Reformation, Saturday was a compulsory fish day and Wednesday was also recommended, with the object of keeping up the fisheries and the supply of sailors. Any one who said that fish-eating or fasting was necessary for salvation was punished, and any one not eating fish on Saturdays might be imprisoned for three months or fined £3. Exemptions on medical grounds had to be paid for.

F

Liphook has far outstripped Bramshott. It stands where five roads meet. It grew up as a hamlet of post-boys, stable-hands and the like, round the Anchor, an important posting inn in the eighteenth century. Perhaps its greatest day was when it entertained the Allied Sovereigns with Blücher and the Duchess of Oldenburg. George III stayed there with Charlotte. Jack Wilkes, who was often on this road on his way to the Isle of Wight, once complained of the ' dull, sour hostess ' and of the noise and dust of the recruits speeding to their ships and the sailors on leave carousing. William IV, when Duke of Clarence, always stopped to chat with the host, Dowling, who had been in his employ. He was a great patron of the Anchor. The Duchess of Kent came several times with Victoria and liked to walk in the garden, so that they might be seen. The opening of the railway left the Anchor sadly derelict. A traveller, coming suddenly upon the Portsmouth road at Hindhead in the 1870s, thought that, ' if I had stayed there till now, I should not have seen anybody or anything coming along it in either direction '. There are sash windows of five periods in the Anchor and a good panelled room up-stairs. The George coffee-room, like the Nelson, keeps its name. The gangs of chained convicts were shut up in the cellars.

Liphook marks the boundary between the army and the navy, between Aldershot and Portsmouth. To the north, beyond Grayshott, is Headley, high and healthy. Bordon Camp has robbed it of its old rurality, but not of the gorgeous views across the downs and to Woolmer Forest and the hangers by Selborne. The fine open roof was replaced when the church was rebuilt, and there is a panel of brilliant thirteenth-century glass depicting a martyrdom.

The Portsmouth road runs through great expanses of heath and woodland as you draw out into the country. When it gets on to the high ridge beyond Rake above

Harting Coombe, it opens up delightful wooded views across the Sussex Weald by Rogate to the downs. One of my most vivid memories of their rounded tops bathed in sunlight is from an old farm-house at Harting, looking out on to a lane that led straight up to them.

Then the road drops down to Petersfield, the first—and I am not sure it is not the best—of those bright, pleasing Hampshire market-towns that recall the days when towns were ' small and white ' oases of civilization amid the barbarous country. The streets are broad, the houses, rarely more than two storeys, belong to all periods from the sixteenth century, with plenty of Georgian red brick. It is a relief after escaping from Portsmouth to lean on the rails of the market-place and rest one's eyes on its peaceful charm, as the cars and buses make their way round it on their devious paths, just as did the coaches and pack-horses when the roads were very different; for here is the reason of its origin, the branching of the Winchester and Portsmouth roads. Petersfield was an important stage in coaching days, the railway added to its prosperity and the car has preserved it without spoiling it. It grew considerably under the Tudors, thanks to the cloth trade, which was at its greatest under James I, when the town put 40 men into the field for the service of the realm. Under Henry II the Earl of Gloucester gave Petersfield the same privileges as Winchester and they were confirmed by his widow, Hawise, whose charter still exists. It once sent two members to Parliament.

Castle House has gone, where Charles II stayed and Pepys records that he occupied the same room. I like to remember that Pepys was very merry here at bowls. But there is the much restored church, which still has some noble Norman features, and William III, once gilt, posing as Marcus Aurelius on the horse with the carefully plaited tail. He was presented to the town by William Joliffe, to whom

Gibbon's father sold the manor, and was moved here when Petersfield House was pulled down in 1793. There are good houses in Sheep Street, which leads to the Spain, so called because the Spanish merchants gathered there to buy the wool from the down sheep. Outside the town to the south-east lies the heath with its large pond.

The road continues through an unattractive suburb to the cleft in the downs by Butser. It is good to escape into the lane to the left for Buriton. On either side are great hazel hedges, and you actually pass a restive pony being long-reined, a notable tribute to the peace of the road. There is no better place to while away an hour than a village with an old church in good country, supposing you know something about its history, none more restful, at least for a stranger. Hampshire, to my mind, has some ideal ones and a few others which the cottages are enough to consecrate for me. Buriton is nearly perfect of its kind, a well-to-do eighteenth-century village, almost unspoilt, where the very car seems an anachronism, within a mile of the great high road. First come the cottages, then the fine group of limes in glorious leaf. Beyond, on the hill, is the stately tower of the church, with its Norman nave and the painting of the Virgin on the window of the thirteenth-century chancel. Above rises the great wooded hanger of the down. Parts of the roomy, green-clad rectory, behind its high wall, where Bishop Louth was born, go back to the fourteenth century.

On the other side, across a large courtyard with out-buildings round it, is the manor-house, with a distinct and not inappropriate suggestion of France about it. The scent of hot wall-flowers pervaded its Georgian peace. One almost expected to see young Gibbon step out of the door in the uniform of the South Hampshire militia, torn un-willingly from his books. His father had converted an old mansion in a state of decay into the fashion and convenience of a modern house, building on the three-storeyed wing. 'The spot was not happily chosen, at the end of the village and the bottom of the hill, but the aspect of the adjacent ground was various and cheerful; the downs commanded the prospect of the sea, and the long hanging woods in sight of the house could not perhaps have been improved by art or expense. . . . I never handled a gun, I never mounted a horse; and my philosophic walks were soon terminated by a shady bench, where I was long detained by the sedentary amusement of reading or meditation. At home I occupied a pleasant and spacious apartment; the library on the same floor was soon considered as my peculiar domain.' The large, low room on the third floor deserves his praise. Downstairs the house is finely panelled. Gibbon would hardly have made an ideal companion into Hampshire, but the village remains an admirable setting for him.

If you want to enjoy yourself, take the beautiful, steep wooded lane that winds up over Head Down, then through the remains of Bere Forest, along the Sussex border, by Chalton, clinging round its green under its down, and the little disused chapel of Idsworth in the park to the left. This contains some notable thirteenth-century wall-paintings. Chalton belonged to Simon de Montfort and also to Cromwell, who held it till his death, for it was part of the estate which Parliament compelled Charles I to give his 'beloved Oliver Cromwell' in 1645. You strike the busy world again at Rowlands Castle, an ugly village swamped by modern building Rowland, they say, was a giant who plundered this district, doubtless a memory of some Norman baron who built the castle and ruled it with no gentle hand. The mound stands in the park of Deerleap House on the left, but the house and the railway have played havoc with the plan of the castle.

All this region was infested with smugglers of the most

desperate kind, and Rowlands Castle was the scene of the
first act of one of the most brutal outrages ever committed
by them. A cargo of tea was seized at sea and placed in
the custom-house at Poole Harbour. The loss was a severe
one to the smuggling fraternity and a gang of 60 men
was organized, who broke open the custom-house, there
being no resistance, and carried off the tea. The raid made
a sensation and a crowd gathered to see the booty pass
through Fordingbridge, where a man called Chater recognized one of the smugglers and gave information. When,
in company with a customs officer named Galley, he
reached the White Hart at Rowlands Castle, the landlady,
who was hand and glove with the smugglers, became
suspicious and warned some of them. They came and
drank with their victims. Galley wanted to leave, as he
felt anxious, but the landlady prevented him. When they
retired, they were searched and a letter was found which
they were taking to a Justice of the Peace at Chichester.
Various ways of getting rid of them were proposed, the
women being more brutal than the men. Finally, they
were placed on a horse with their hands and feet tied and
flogged all the way to Rake. Galley was carried to Harting
Coombe and buried alive in a fox's hole, as was proved by
his body being found with his hands held over his face to
keep off the earth. Chater was chained up in a shed and
left more dead than alive for three days. Then they set
him once more on a horse and flogged him all the way to
Lady Holt Park, where they threw him down a well and
flung in stones to finish him. Information was given; one
of the gang was arrested and turned king's evidence. Ultimately six of them were hung at various places in Hampshire and along the coast.

From Rowlands Castle carry right on to Warblington,
avoiding Havant. Warblington church and the handsome
Tudor tower and gateway of the castle—all that remains

—stand away to the south in fields that have a touch of
Sussex, a welcome surprise after the noise of the Brighton
road. The manor belonged to Godwin's sons before the
Conquest; later it came by marriage to the father of
Warwick the Kingmaker and the boy Earl of Warwick
who was executed in 1499. It was restored to his heir, the
Countess of Salisbury, who was executed by Henry VIII
and buried in Christchurch Minster. Henry VIII granted
Warblington to Sir Richard Cotton, Comptroller of the
Household, who probably built the castle. He entertained
Edward VI there. The Cottons were for the king and
'this strong house' was taken by the Roundheads and
probably slighted. In the eighteenth century the manor
was bought by the famous nabob, Richard Barwell, of
Stansted.

The castle was protected by a deep moat and a high
ditch. The church, dedicated to Becket, is within the outer
ring. It has a beautiful fourteenth-century timber porch,
a particularly graceful arcade to the south aisle and a tower,
the lower storey of which is Saxon—the only bit of Saxon
work left, for the church was rebuilt in the thirteenth
century. In the churchyard is a yew, fine even for Hampshire, measuring 26 feet. Emsworth, right on the border,
at the mouth of the Ems and the head of Chichester
Harbour, has now been separated from Warblington. It
is a busy little place, a yachting centre with a considerable
oyster fishery.

However, we set out to explore the Portsmouth road
and to it we must return from Buriton, whence you can
make a variation by taking the more westerly lane that
follows the railway. Nor are you to be pitied on the
section of the road which runs between mighty Butser, the
highest point in the county, towering above you on the
right, and War Down, where they are eternally quarrying,
on the left. The great bluff of Butser, 889 feet, is far the

most impressive of the Hampshire Downs. A path leads
up from the road. It is the only one of the downs where
you are rarely alone; on the top is a crumbling windmill,
which has lost its sails. Once there you are lifted far
above the things of to-day. The ant-like traffic scurry-
ing through the gap below seems as remote as the French
prisoners who are said to have made the road. The view
is vast in every direction, across sun-touched Spithead to
the hills of the island and along the chain of the Harting
Downs into Sussex. To the north are the downs about
Medstead and the chain by the Cleres. To the south,
towards Portsmouth, ' hills, swelling above each other, and
undulations shapely and uncouth, smooth and rugged,
graceful and grotesque, thrown negligently side by side,
bounded the view in every direction '. Thus Dickens, who
brought Nicholas Nickleby and Smike this way from
Hindhead.

A narrow neck joins Butser to the main line of the
downs from Old Winchester Hill. Across it are traces of
a camp. It is pretty certain that the top was British, though
the details are confused and later diggings have helped to
increase the confusion. Butser is a spot where one lingers
willingly, loathe to take the plunge into the everyday
world. The wild flowers of the chalk, with the blue
butterflies hovering over them, are a delight to the botanist.

The downs continue bare and open for a space, stretching away east and west as they did when they formed part
of Bere Forest, a fine and restful prospect. This was a bad
patch for peaceful citizens in older days, where gentlemen
of the pad and the road often plied their trade. On the
left is the wayside inn, the Coach and Horses to-day, where
Nicholas and Smike put up when they heard that it was
twelve long miles to Portsmouth, a momentous stop, seeing
that it was here that they fell in with Mr. Vincent
Crummles and his talented family. The road has changed

indeed since then. After the turning to Clanfield it is in the grip of the tentacles of Portsmouth. Though at first there are considerable open patches of country or wood—scant relics of Bere Forest—on one side or the other, the fence of villas soon becomes continuous. Fortunately, there are broad expanses of unspoilt Hampshire behind it.

At the fork of the Havant road is Horndean and to the west, on its hill, the church of Catherington, early Norman, but much restored. Here are some Napier monuments, with the tomb of Admiral Sir Charles in the churchyard. He spent his later years on his farm at Horndean, which he called Merchistoun Hall after his birthplace. There is also a monument to Admiral Cradock, who went down at the battle of Coronel. Here, too, is buried the widow of Edmund Kean as well as her son, Charles. In the church is the monument of Chief Justice Sir Nicholas Hyde, uncle of the great Lord Clarendon. It is generally held that it was under his roof, in the predecessor of the present Hinton House, with its fine view, that the Duke of York, later James II, married Anne Hyde. This region was all in the Forest of Bere. Houses close in thicker and thicker as the road approaches Portsdown Hill.

CHAPTER VII: *Portsmouth*

FROM the top of the Portsdown Hills you look down on a wide panorama of low, flat shore with its great expanse of harbours, channels and bays, and the hills of the Isle of Wight in the distance. You are, as a matter of fact, already in the Portsmouth of to-day, which extends up here beyond the old George Inn. The obelisk opposite the Green Posts at Hilsea, which you pass on the way down, marks the limit of 1799, so rapidly has the town grown. As I gazed down on these acres of small houses and mean streets, I was still half obsessed with the idea of my childhood when I entered the station by train, that in every one of the cottages there must be a couple of jolly tars hitching up their trousers in unison, as they did in *Pinafore*—or was it some comic opera?—preparatory to embarking on a frigate or a three-decker, singing chanties and winning great naval victories for the Old Country. This is, after all, only the childish facet of the true significance of Portsmouth, now called Pompey by the navy. If it has ceased to be the chief harbour of the fleet, it is still the greatest dockyard in the world; and its heart is the *Victory*, no longer anchored in the harbour towards Gosport, which gave you the thrill of being rowed out to her, but resting peacefully in the oldest dry dock in existence, having been constructed in 1656. For Trafalgar was the crowning triumph of our sea-power, which was consecrated by the death of the greatest and most romantic of our admirals.

It is impossible not to realize the value of the harbour, unlovely though the slime and the ooze may appear at low tide. Much of it is being eaten up only too rapidly by streets hardly less unlovely. Below is Cosham, now a ward of Portsmouth, where William de Cosham once held land for the service of supplying one man for the defence of Portchester Castle. Beyond narrow Portsbridge Creek, spanned by the bridge that carries the only road into the town, is Portsea Island, with Portsmouth and Southsea and their suburbs, now all included in the borough. Portsmouth does not appear in Domesday, but Great Saltings already existed then at Conor, which belonged to Harold before the Conquest. There was early a village at Fratton, which belonged to Edward the Confessor. William I gave it to the powerful Earl De Warenne.

On the other side of the narrow entrance to the harbour, where the water is deep enough to float the largest ships, is Gosport, and beyond, separating it from the Island, Spithead, the great anchorage and review-ground of the fleet. It gets its name from the Spit, the sandbank three miles long running down from Gillicker Point at the south of Gosport. Portsmouth harbour, 4 miles by 2, has ample water to float the whole fleet at low tide. Portchester, where the Romans set their seal on the harbour in the castle, and even Fareham can be reached by a channel to the west. Portsbridge Creek, spanned by the road and the railway, connects with Langston Harbour, a favourite haunt of the Danish pirates, beyond which is Hayling Island.

Immediately after crossing the bridge you are engulfed in the great sea of bricks and mortar through which the London road threads its way. The railway runs over Victoria Park from the station to the pier. This, like many of Portsmouth's open spaces, was part of the old fortifications, the Esplanade. With their magnificent elms, they were the town promenade till they were pulled down in the seventies. Here, too, was the tidal mill-dam, crossed by a causeway, now filled up. All this will be familiar to readers of Besant's *By Celia's Arbour*. The arbour was the Queen's Bastion, the last of the series towards the harbour, from which you could get a clear view across to Portchester

Castle. Portsea used to be known as the Common and the town did not reach it till Queen Anne's day, as the names of the streets indicate. The military strongly objected to building near the walls. There are still 'garrison houses' left in Penny Street, and St. Thomas Street, gabled and low enough not to be seen above them. Near the station is the handsome Guildhall, one of the finest in England, facing an open square. Close here, in St. George's Square, where Sir Walter Besant was born, is the Georgian church, 'a great barn of red brick', of which he gives an amusing account in *By Celia's Arbour*.

Before making for old Portsmouth lovers of Dickens must follow the Commercial Road to the north into Landport, for he was born at No. 387 in 1812. The house is now a Dickens museum. This was then a new suburb, on the edge of the town, and the little row of houses, which had been a long rope-walk in the eighteenth century, was Landport Terrace. Dickens chanced upon the terrace when in Portsmouth to lecture. He walked up and down with his friends, wondering which house it was, suggesting one because it was so like his father.

In the other direction the Commercial Road passes the United Services Recreation Ground. Cambridge Road leads to the top of the High Street, the heart of old Portsmouth. Round here most of the history of the town is concentrated. The rush of the life of to-day passes it by and it remains an oasis to which one willingly returns. The quaint shops are interesting. At the corner is the Grammar School and opposite it the barracks that has replaced the Theatre Royal, where Crummles ruled, and Nicholas Nickleby appeared as Romeo with Smike as the Apothecary. It is of them we think returning to their lodgings, to the neglect of all the great men to whom High Street was as familiar as their quarter-decks.

No. 10, on the right, is the oldest house in the street,

though only a small part of it goes back to the seventeenth century. In 1628 it was the home of a Captain Mason, who was Governor of Southsea Castle and later founded Portsmouth in New Hampshire. Handsome, attractive ineffectual Buckingham, the Steenie of James I, was often in Portsmouth, and from there his disastrous expedition to relieve La Rochelle had sailed in the previous year. Hither he came for the sailing of another expedition and here, early in the morning, as he was going through the hall to his coach, he was stabbed, while some one whispered in his ear, by John Felton, a soldier with a grievance. Exclaiming 'villain' and pulling out the knife, he staggered back into the arms of his attendants. The Duchess rushed from her bedroom to the gallery, as did his sister, Lady Anglesea, and saw him weltering in his blood. 'Ah, poor ladies,' writes Dudley Carleton, ' such was their screechings, teares, and distractions, that I never in my life heard the like before, and hope never to heare the like againe.' Felton suffered at Tyburn, but his body was gibbeted near the Clarence Pier of to-day. The last piece of the gibbet is enclosed in the obelisk there.

A little farther down is the George, the best of the Portsmouth hotels, which has housed almost every man of note who has been here. Nelson reached the George at six on his last morning in England. His bedroom has been preserved intact, even to the old shaving-glass. It was the room he always had and opposite, also unchanged, is the one used by Lady Hamilton, who was not with him then. Somehow this room appeals to me more than the *Victory* of to-day, spick and span in every corner and restored exactly as it was when he sailed for Trafalgar—' Nelson's chequerwork ', as the Navy tells you. For me its patina has gone, possibly because I remember it black with white port-holes, like the three-deckers one sees in prints. They also show you the stairs down which Nelson slipped into the yard to escape the waiting crowd. He embarked from Southsea beach.

Next comes the classic portal of the Town Hall, now a local museum of much interest. The market-place was below, the Council Room above. Its predecessor, of similar plan, stood in the middle of the High Street. In 1814 the soldiers offered to clear it away in 24 hours for the visit of the allied sovereigns, but the offer was not accepted. Below it, in the eighteenth century, stretched a row of wood-roofed shambles infested at night by the worst that even Portsmouth could produce.

Opposite is the cathedral, dedicated to Thomas à Becket, built in 1180, only ten years after his death. It belonged to the Austin canons of Southwick. At the Dissolution it became a store-house. Charles I rescued it. It is a curious medley. The chancel and transepts are Early English. The nave suffered badly in the Civil War and in 1691 it was rebuilt with a tower at the west end. Though ' the inside beauty of the house was much admired ', the town fortunately objected to dipping into its pocket to the tune of six times the usual poor-rate in order to make the chancel a work of beauty equal to the nave. In the chancel is Buckingham's monument, put up by his sister the Countess of Denbigh. The fatal dagger is still owned by the Denbigh family. The marriage certificate of Charles II and Catherine of Braganza is here. Much of the church plate formed part of her dowry. A man used to be posted in the cupola under the great vane, formed like a ship, presented by Queen Anne's husband, Prince George of Denmark, in 1710, to signal ships entering the harbour.

Behind the cathedral is St. Thomas Street, where lodged Vincent Crummles at the house of one Bulph, a pilot; but I failed to locate the boat-green door. This is another oasis of Georgian houses, a welcome relief from the acres of shoddiness from which I had escaped, humble though many of them are. A few only have been reconditioned. One warehouse screens a walled garden with lawns. It is a thousand pities that more of those whose lot it is to dwell in Portsmouth do not think them worth the pains freely lavished on a derelict country cottage. Highbury Street branches right, St. Mary's Street in Tudor days, since there was a chapel to St. Mary hereabouts. Here, at Curzon House, lived Lord Howe, the victor of the Glorious First of June. The street leads to the old Gun Wharf, which separates Portsmouth from Portsea. Towards the end, on the right, is the simple cottage of John Pounds, now a show place. Crippled while working in the dockyard, he turned shoemaker : then, beginning with a crippled nephew, he became interested in teaching and taught many of the poorest children to read and write, thus founding the Ragged Schools.

Breezy Lieutenant Price of the Marines and his slatternly family lived off the High Street, and I am inclined to put them in Highbury Street. Fanny Price was Jane Austen's only Hampshire heroine. She shocked the geography of the Miss Bertrams of Mansfield Park by talking of the Isle of Wight as the Island. Jane, with her sailor brothers, knew Portsmouth well, and the navy comes in for its due in her last novel, *Persuasion*. Mrs. Price took her regular Sunday walk on the fortifications.

At the bottom of the High Street stood the cage, the town gaol, from the window of which a glove or a gloved hand was shown for the opening of the Free Mart Fair, dating from Richard I, which lasted a fortnight. The road curves round to the left past some very old houses, one of them Princess Christian's home, to the other interesting Portsmouth church, the Garrison Chapel. This was the old Domus Dei founded by Peter des Roches in 1214 for Christ's poor and dedicated to St. Nicholas. At the Dissolution there were complaints not only of the bad

bread and beer served to the ' powr pepull ', but also that
the Master, with his income of 800 or 900 marks, kept no
hospitality, ' wiche is a gret dekay to the towne '. It was
at first used for naval stores and gunpowder, but became
a church once more under Elizabeth. Originally the
chancel was the chapel and much of it is thirteenth
century. The nave was the Domus Dei proper, where the
sick were ranged in the aisles. It was restored in 1866.
It is filled with memorials to distinguished soldiers and
sailors : the brasses are as bright as the buttons of the
troops who keep it in exemplary order. The other buildings, on what is now Governor's Green, where the mound
is the last remnant of the older fortifications, were converted into a residence for the Governor under Elizabeth.
They were pulled down in 1826. Here, in the great hall
of what was then called the King's House, Charles II
married Catherine of Braganza and here they remained
a week. But this did not prevent him some years later from
making Louise de Querouaille Duchess of Portsmouth.
The Corporation still possesses the pair of silver flagons she
presented to it.

The Domus Dei, which was lavishly fitted up for the
occasion, enjoyed its greatest day during the entertainment
of the allied sovereigns in 1814. The road from the Portsdown Hills was lined with 11,000 troops. In the town,
according to custom, the Royal Dock Ropewalkers, habited
in white jackets and nankeen trousers, with purple sashes
across their shoulders, five conductors with short staves, the
others bearing white wands, followed the cavalry, preced-
ing the Prince Regent's carriage. The guests came after
their host. When rough old Blücher drove to the
Governor's house from his quarters, a number of Blue
Jackets stormed the quarter-deck of his coach. Most of
them capsized, but two hung on and danced all the way.
When Wellington arrived at the George in a chariot and

eight, the crowd took out the horses and dragged him to Government House.

The fine modern church at Kingston is the best of the other Portsmouth churches.

Opposite the end of the High Street is the Victoria Pier, looking out to the harbour entrance and the Island beyond. Close by is the old Sally Port, where Catherine of Braganza landed and where, as the tablet puts it, ' heroes innumerable have embarked to fight their country's battles '. Here, too, is the small section of the fortifications that survives, extending to the King's Bastion. They have given Portsmouth a line of precious open spaces, as they gave Paris her boulevards. Of the gates the Landport Gate, the entrance to the Men's Recreation Ground, is in its original position. The Unicorn Gate, from North Street, is now an entrance to the dockyard. King James II's Gate has been moved from near the Square Tower to the Officers' Recreation Ground. He deserves to be remembered here. He did much for the navy, both as Duke of York and as king, and it owes him not a little.

Here, too, is the Round Tower, dating, in its present form, more or less, from Henry VII. On its front is the curious gilt statue of Charles I, erected after his return from his expedition to Spain when Prince of Wales with Buckingham, without a bride. The Governor wanted the inn signs in the High Street to be set in the houses, as they obscured and outfaced the bust, and ordered that all officers and soldiers should doff their hats before it.

Near it, at Tower House, a boat-loft which contains some interesting ship relics, Wyllie painted his panorama of Trafalgar. At No. 74, with the wooden pilasters, where the High Street curves round to the right, lived Lord Anson, the circumnavigator. George Meredith was born next door at No. 73. Behind its fat, round windows dwelt the ' glorious Mel ' of *Evan Harrington*, with his

G

beautiful daughters, the tailor who never sent in a bill and who was Meredith's father. Peter Simple patronized Meredith the tailor.

High Street debouches into Broad Street with the modern successor of the old Blue Posts, dear to the middies of other days. Not for them the splendours of the George. The Soldiers' Institute has replaced another famous inn, the Fountain, in the High Street. Opposite the Blue Posts in the eighteenth century was a small Fisherman's Row, at the end of which was the post where the bull was tied for baiting on Shrove Tuesday.

The Point was outside the gates and here is another well-known hotel, the Star and Garter, where all the great seamen of the days of the three-deckers have forgathered. The table where Nelson and Howe have sat is still shown. Here have stayed William IV in his sailor days and Louis Philippe in exile. Franklin slept here the night before starting on his fatal Arctic Expedition. Thackeray knew it and liked the view over the harbour.

But the Point was generally frequented by rougher company. It was the resort of the seamen in their wildest days. In 1746 there were 41 public-houses there and from them Jack would reel out to the boat that was to take him to his hammock in the close quarters of his crowded ship. It was the right place for the gibbeting of the tarred corpse of Jack the Painter, as he was called, and his ghost long haunted it. James Aitken had been highwayman and then rebel in America. In 1776 he tried to burn down the dockyard and did some damage to the Rope Walk. He was caught at Hook and hung off the yard on a very high gibbet.

Behind Point is the Camber, the commercial dock. This has never been of much importance, for Portsmouth is essentially a naval harbour. Here yachts are built and tramp steamers unload. On a quiet evening it is as peaceful as a village harbour, though the biggest warships are secured alongside Middle Ship Jetty opposite.

Facing the main entrance to the dockyard is the Hard, once a favourite haunt of old salts. Here, in the fifties, Besant used to talk with an old man who said he had been a cabin boy with Captain Cook at the time of his murder. On the Hard, with its pubs and dance-halls, used to be the offices of the rascally pay-agents. I am not going to say anything about the dockyard. In days like these the visitor is, quite rightly, shown very little. But it is well worth a visit.

Gosport, to which you cross by the ferry from Point, getting a good view up the harbour on the way, was christened God's Port by Bishop Henry of Blois, when he took shelter there in a storm. From the Round Tower at the mouth of the harbour, built originally by Edward IV, to a smaller tower on the Gosport side, a mighty iron chain was stretched under Henry VIII. It is said that some of the links can still be seen at the bottom of the sea. You land on the Hard, at the end of the High Street. There is little of interest in the town, which has grown considerably. Its importance lies in the great Royal Clarence Victualling Yard, facing the dockyard, and the Naval Hospital at Haslar to the south, beyond the bridge over the creek.

Portsmouth suffered much from the Press Gangs, and Haslar was the scene of one of the hottest presses known. A body of marines arrived and it was rumoured that they were sent to put down a serious mutiny in Haslar. They marched off at night with a large and rapidly growing crowd following, eager to see the fun. When they had all crossed the bridge into Haslar, it was closed and the record number of 500 good recruits was secured. Only the few who plunged into the water escaped by swimming.

Southsea, with the curious curving streets that seem

planned to prevent a direct approach to the sea, is a recent growth. The Common was long marshy, and wild fowl abounded there. About 1800 it was infested by footpads. In the 1860s it was still ' an open heath behind a bank of shingle and sand, with a marsh and a tiny rivulet on one side and a broader marsh on the other; and, standing by itself, the grey old castle by the shore '. It now belongs to the War Office. It has been the scene of many famous camps and reviews. The great Chancellor Hubert de Burgh had a splendid army camped there in 1220, and there Edward III mustered the army with which he won Crécy. Along the Esplanade are a number of naval memorials, from an anchor of the *Victory* to the Naval Memorial of the Great War.

Henry VIII built Southsea Castle. He is seen entering it in 1544, in one of the well-known Cowdray pictures, when the French made their attack on Lord de Lisle's fleet, which had captured Boulogne and was preparing for another raid on the French coast. The French dared not pursue the English ships into the harbour. After some abortive attempts to land on the Isle of Wight, they withdrew, pursued by the English. During this engagement there occurred the first of the many naval disasters with which Portsmouth is associated. The *Mary Rose*, the finest ship in the navy except the *Great Harry*, turned over and sank between the two fleets with all its 600 hands. Some say it was over-weighted with its 60 guns. Relics of it, preserved in the museum, have been fished up from time to time. Henry VIII witnessed the disaster from the castle. This was burnt down in 1627, being entirely of wood, we are told, and quite deserted. It was rebuilt seven years later.

Southsea Castle was the deciding factor in the siege of Portsmouth, the most important event at the opening of the Civil War. Lord Goring, after obtaining large sums from

the Parliament for fortifying the town, announced that he
would hold it for the king. His decision was not popular,
and more than half his men deserted. He still further
alienated the inhabitants by the ruthlessness with which
he carried off everything from the farms on Portsea. The
Parliament pressed the siege by sea, as well as by land.
Goring could not do much with his disaffected garrison of
300 men. The few men he left to guard the bridge over
Portsbridge Creek were easily overpowered. Food soon
began to run short. The batteries on Gosport were proving
troublesome, one of them sending a shot through the tower
of St. Thomas's, where Goring had a look-out, and damaging the bell. He offered to surrender, if not relieved by
a certain date, but the offer was rejected, though the enemy
sent him the 2 fat bucks for which he asked. The capture
of Southsea Castle by Colonel Dick Norton, whose home
was at Southwick, brought matters to a crisis. It was considered the strongest fort in England for its size. The wall
was 3 or 4 yards thick and 30 feet high; the moat 3 or 4 yards
deep and 5 across; there were 14 guns mounted. 'It hath
dainty chambers for to entertain a Prince.' The garrison
consisted of some 25 men, of whom only about half were
on the spot. Norton had 400 infantry and 2 troops of
horse. He feinted with an attack on Portsmouth. The
castle guns were all on the north side, but he got into the
moat on the south side. The surprise was complete. The
commander had been in Portsmouth carousing with
Goring, 'and had more drink in his head than was befit-
ting such a time and service'. On being awakened he said
that he would discuss terms, if they would kindly wait till
morning.

Immediately the news became known there was a mutiny
in the garrison, most of the men deserting, while the mayor
and many prominent citizens fled. Goring had no choice
but to yield. He got good terms by threatening to blow up

the Square Tower, where he kept his powder. The loss, says Clarendon, ' struck the king to the very heart ', as well it might.

Southsea, like Portsmouth, has its literary associations. Conan Doyle was a doctor in the house next the chapel in Elm Grove, whence the elms have now gone. H. G. Wells lived in Southsea and it is to his experiences as assistant in a drapery shop in King's Road that we owe the immortal Mr. Polly. Kipling used to stay with relatives in Campbell Road when a child, where his treatment gave rise to that tragic story *Baa Baa, Black Sheep*.

The history of Portsmouth is the history of its development as a naval port, and its advantages were so obvious that they could not long be neglected. A fishing village must soon have grown up round the harbour, though there is no mention of it in Domesday. The luckless Robert landed at Portsmouth when he came to claim the crown which his brother Henry I had usurped : so did Matilda with her brother Count Robert of Gloucester when she was fighting Stephen. Henry II, in whose reign St. Thomas's was built, often crossed from Portsmouth to France, though Southampton was the principal Norman harbour.

To Richard Cœur de Lion Portsmouth owes its first charter and its emergence into something approaching a town. He was delayed here in 1194 before setting out to punish the treacherous King of France for his share in his imprisonment in Austria. He it was who ordered the construction of the King's Hall, of wood, probably on the site of the old King's Hall Green, where is now Clarence Barracks, and he granted land for others to build. Further, he gave Portsmouth a fair, later held in June, which was not unimportant and was attended by Norman and Dutch merchants.

And it was Richard's unpleasant brother John who began

to make Portsmouth a naval port. After he had lost his French possessions, instead of being a place of departure for another part of his kingdom, it became liable to attack from the French coast. John was often at Portchester Castle for the hunting, and it was at Portsmouth that he assembled the ships, with which he sought to recover his lost provinces, when the barons refused to support him. In 1212 he ordered the first dock to be constructed here under the direction of the Archdeacon of Taunton, William de Wrotham, the Keeper of his Ships. As the clergy then had a monopoly of brains, they also had a monopoly of organizing jobs, strangely inappropriate though some of them may seem to us for men of their cloth. The dock was to have penthouses against the walls to keep the needful stores. The basin seems to have belonged to the Abbey of Fontrevault, and as John had granted the abbey some mills, it was probably in the neighbourhood of the Gun Wharf, up the old mill-dam.

The town continued to grow, but it was quite unprotected. The barons of the Cinque Ports dabbled in piracy: indeed, for several centuries to come piracy and smuggling continued to loom large in the story of Portsmouth, as of other ports: and when the Cinque Ports were captured by Henry III, they took to the sea. Portsmouth was a rival, and now a prosperous rival, so they attacked it and destroyed not a little of it.

From the days of Edward I the borough has sent two members to Parliament almost continuously. The gaps were mostly in the fourteenth century, when the bailiffs sometimes omitted to return the burgesses owing to the cost, since they had to allow them 2s. a day. It now returns three members. During the Hundred Years' War Portsmouth suffered badly. In 1338 it was burnt by the French. As it was built of wood, St. Thomas's and the Domus Dei were almost the only buildings that escaped. There were

other attacks in 1369 and 1377. Some of the dues were
remitted and the town was even given the right to levy
customs for walling and paving. But as traders had also
to pay dues to Southampton, they began to abandon a port
where their expenses were doubled. The town had not the
stone walls of Southampton, only some poor earthworks.
But the men of Portsmouth struck back in 1374; ordered
by none, but ' spurred on by their own inborn courage ',
they attacked the French fleet with the men of Dartmouth
and burnt five ships.

However, under Richard II the defences were strengthened, and in 1403 the French, finding them too formidable, turned to an easier prey in the Isle of Wight till they
were driven off by the men of Southampton and Portsmouth.

The Tudors first made Portsmouth a real naval harbour.
Henry VII not only built the Square Tower, but rebuilt
the round wooden tower at the harbour mouth in stone.
He also constructed an important dock of a new kind where
ships could be repaired. It was situated near the King's
Stairs in the yard of to-day. Now, too, the first man-of-
war, a small one, the *Sweepstake*, was built at Portsmouth.
Henry VIII did much more, having the savings of his
father and, later, the money and often the building material
of the plundered monasteries to draw upon. Victualling
was a problem, so he built five brew-houses, one, the
Anchor, in St. Thomas Street, where biscuits were also
made, and four on what was known as Four House Green,
where Clarence Barracks now stands. The dockyard was
enlarged by nine acres. All this naturally gave a great
fillip to the town. Leland described the fortifications and
the great dock for ships. Here he saw the rotting ribs of
Henry V's *Grace Dieu*, the *Victory* of his day. ' There is
one fair street (High Street) from west to north ', and in
the middle of it a town house (the Town Hall) built by a

rich man, Carpenter by name. 'The town of Portsmouth is bare and but little occupied in time of peace.'

But it was ill protected still and Bishop Fox wrote to Wolsey in 1518, 'If war be intended against England, the Isle of Wight and Portsmouth are too feeble for defence.' In 1526 the town was 'in sore ruin and decay', and in 1538 the guns were not functioning. Some French ships were able to cut out a merchantman that had run aground from right under them. Soon afterwards the ramparts which had been hastily run up collapsed, to the wrath of Henry, who himself went to see that they were properly built. In 1544 the Governor asked for more men, pointing out the difficulty of reinforcing the place in a hurry, as there was only one bridge. The question of adequate defences continues to crop up.

Portsmouth fell on evil days under Elizabeth. Deptford was made the dockyard, being near London, though the fleet was generally at Portsmouth. Then there was a fire which destroyed most of Henry VIII's storehouses and much of the town. However, the fortifications were put in a better state. For the Armada Sir John Norris was stationed here with 1,000 men, and the English ships put into the harbour to refit with such food and powder as could be found. Nor were things better in the new century. It was Buckingham, of all people, who once more made Portsmouth our chief naval port. After his murder the defences, which had suffered severely from a great storm, were repaired with timber from the New Forest. Portsmouth paid £60 in ship-money for the £195 of Southampton and the £190 of Winchester, a fact which enables us to gauge its relative wealth and importance.

There was a great revival under the Commonwealth, when ships were once more built there, large additions were made to the dockyard and a new dry dock was built. Point had already got its bad name, in spite of Puritan discipline. Under the Duke of York, after the Restoration, the yard was further enlarged, the Dutch prisoners from Portchester Castle providing the labour; and more and more ships were built. The town, like others at the time, was filthy and unhealthy and the plague hit it badly, though it escaped more lightly than other places in Hampshire. A house was built in the yard for Middleton, the Chief Commissioner. Before that he had lodged with the mayor, he tells Pepys, where there were nine people in a room 16 feet by 12 feet and the household consisted of 26. No wonder that during the plague he preferred the yard, with a good sawdust fire ' and the sweet perfume of tarred ropes ' to the town, the air whereof, a physician told him, ' was naturally so harmful to man that any one who could put up with it would never be killed by plague '.

The lot of the seamen, ill-fed and irregularly paid owing to the lack of money, was hard. The wounded were generally placed in public-houses, though some of them went to Portchester Castle. But the town, the dockyard and the port continued to grow in importance.

Portsmouth firmly established its position during the wars of the eighteenth century and its activity was never greater. But its prosperity ebbed and flowed. As in Leland's day, in war-time it was much frequented, at other times scarcely at all. In 1784 Pennant found its pavements grass-grown; sales of furniture everywhere; the coffee-houses with scarcely a marine officer. After 1814 and the end of the Napoleonic wars the distress was acute. But in its yards a long series of famous ships was built and from it all the great fleets of the day sailed under the most noted of our admirals from Shovel under William III through Howe and Rodney and many others to Nelson in the *Victory*. Our kings were proud of it, none more proud than George III. In 1773, when he made his first visit, he had been welcomed by all the men of the dockyard with green boughs in their hats, so that at a distance they looked like a walking wood. These were the days of Garrick. Was the idea suggested by Birnam Wood coming to Dunsinane? 'My attachment to Portsmouth is too well known for you to doubt my desire of having every branch filled with able hands,' wrote the king.

Sir Marc Brunel, a Frenchman by birth, was one of the able hands employed in the yard, and it was at Portsmouth that his more distinguished son, Sir Isambard, was born. After working under his father on the Thames Tunnel, he became engineer to the Great Western Railway. He designed those famous ships the *Great Western* and the *Great Eastern* and was the first to succeed in introducing screw propellers into warships, a great boon to the navy which had never taken kindly to the paddle-wheel owing to its vulnerability.

Naturally Portsmouth was the scene of some important events, of the trial of Byng, for instance, after the loss of Minorca, which was a great blow to English prestige. The Government weakly sacrificed him to public feeling. Though found guilty, quite justly, only of not having done his best and recommended to mercy, he was shot on the quarter-deck of his own flagship, the *Monarque*.

Such a town, reflecting the life of its principal inhabitants, was rough in the extreme. Discipline was almost non-existent among the troops and the seamen on shore, especially when their pockets were full. Drunkenness was universal. Their life was hard enough, in all conscience, and their food a disgrace. There was ample justification for the Spithead Mutiny—'the breeze at Spithead'—of 1797, as was proved by the Government at once granting the men's demands. The Military Governor and the mayor frequently failed to see eye to eye. On this occasion it was only the tact and courage of the mayor that prevented more serious trouble. The men, doubting the promises of the

Admiralty, sent a deputation to the *London*, and when it was not received, a struggle occurred in which five of them were killed. The men insisted on burying their comrades on shore in the church of St. Mary Kingston, but the Governor objected and it was the mayor who induced him to give way.

Many, too, were the disasters, most of which have been long forgotten. Point would indeed be a fearsome place if it were haunted by the ghosts of all the seamen who have lost their lives here. The best-known tragedy was the loss of the *Royal George*, in August 1782, while the fleet was being prepared to go to the relief of Gibraltar. She was the flagship of Admiral Kempenfelt. In order to stop a slight leak, the guns were moved to one side to heel her over and the port-holes left open. Consequently, when a gust of wind struck her, she filled and sank. There were a number of women and children on board and upwards of 1,000 lives were lost, including the admiral, caught in his cabin. Only those on deck had a chance to escape. The wreck lay in the harbour, a serious obstacle to shipping, till it was destroyed by the Engineers in the 1840s. The *Edgar* blew up in 1711 with loss of 400 men, the officers being on shore, and a like fate overtook the *Marlborough* in 1776. The *Eurydice* sank much like the *Royal George*. But these had no admiral on board and no Cowper to sing their fate. Nor must the wives be forgotten who have endured the endless waiting, hoping against hope for husbands who never returned.

In the nineteenth century the importance of Portsmouth, both as a naval and a military station, rapidly increased. Not only did the dockyard cover 300 acres, treble its former area, but new barracks were built. Southsea grew no less rapidly, at first owing to the craze for sea-bathing, then as a residential suburb. The change over from sail to steam resulted in many novelties. The last naval sailing-ship was built at Portsmouth in 1848, the *Dreadnought* in 1905. For a charming picture of the place at this transition period, during the Crimea, you cannot do better than turn to *By Celia's Arbour*. Besant as a boy had cheered old Charley Napier as he walked down the pier to embark, seen the great fleet start for the Baltic, and the queen's yacht, the *Fairy*, threading its way among the ships. He knew the drinking-shops and the dancing-halls where the men's money vanished before the founding of institutes. And he gives you a sympathetic picture of the simple middle-class life of the town, not distorted by a twentieth-century mind. In those days, he assures us, the harbour was a forest of masts; they seem never to have broken up the old ships. There were hundreds of wooden ones lying idle up the harbour, some coal-hulks, some receiving-hulks, some convict-hulks, floating at high tide, and at low tide lying on the soft cushion of the mud. And the captain knew them all and could tell their story, from ' the French frigate, the most beautiful ship that floats '. He remembered the breaking up of the *Royal William* in 1813, which was launched in October 1679: built for Charles II, it sailed for James II. Well, there is still the frigate, the *Foudroyant*, and an old 74, the *Implacable*, once the *Duguay-Trouin*, which fought against us at Trafalgar and was afterwards captured and re-named, now a holiday-boat for sea scouts; and there is the *Victory*.

CHAPTER VIII: *Portchester, Fareham and Titchfield*

THE Fareham road runs under the fortified Portsdown Hills, which, in the early eighteenth century, were 'very pleasant for sports, hawking and hunting', with the mud flats and the harbour to the left. On a peninsula jutting into it at the head of a creek is Portchester Castle, for so they like to spell it now. The street that leads from the main road to it has the appearance and the quiet of a village. The Romans knew the value of this harbour and in it they set one of the chain of forts they built towards the end of the third century, when their grip was beginning to weaken, as a defence against the marauding Saxons, who may well have grasped its value too. They were under the Count of the Saxon Shore. Most of the great walls, 200 yards long, and the majority of the 20 bastions that strengthened it, survive. They are said to be the finest Roman walls in the country. The area enclosed is about 9 acres, and there were 2 entrances: a sea gate, where there is Roman work, and the land gate, facing it. The great bank on the land side, with the ditch, is almost certainly ancient British. The moat on the north is Roman.

The royal visits to Portsmouth in early days were really visits to Portchester. The keep that was built into the Roman fort is twelfth century, and it is here that the kings stayed, with the exception of Edward III, who preferred Southwick. Henry II, in whose reign it was built, was here several times and also used it as a prison. John was a frequent visitor, hunting in the forests. At Portchester he received the news of the Papal interdict. He ordered the castle to be destroyed in 1217, but the order was rescinded next year. Stores were kept in it for sending to France during the wars. At one time oaks were cut in the forests round for making 80 bridges and 600 good hurdles. From Portchester Edward II set out to oppose his queen's landing, when he was defeated and imprisoned. The most interesting of the royal visits was that of Henry V before Agincourt, when the conspiracy formed against him was discovered. The leaders were arrested at Portchester, but they were executed at Southampton. Henry VIII and Anne Boleyn hawked in the country round during a merry visit, and Elizabeth was here with her court.

The solid keep, a noble landmark, is the most interesting part of the castle. It juts out, beyond the line of the Roman walls. The entrance was, as usual, on the first floor, approached by a ladder : here, too, was the chapel on the south. Round the south and east walls was the moat. The early domestic buildings have gone, but the ruins of the fourteenth-century ones, completed by Richard II, on the south side, remain, all on the first floor with cellars beneath. So anxious was he to finish them that in 1399 the men worked at night by candlelight. Armorial glass—a great luxury—was prepared for many of the windows. From this time also dates the large main entrance on the west. The castle was already ruinous under James I. Since Charles I, who granted it to Sir William Uvedale, it has been privately owned, but the Government has often made use of it.

Since the Civil War it has generally been used as a prison during continental wars. Under Charles II the prisoners were Dutch. The French prisoners of the Napoleonic wars lingered long in local memory. There were actually 8,000 of them, with 2 militia regiments to guard them. They slept in two-storeyed wooden buildings erected in the garth or in the keep. In the hulks in the harbour were 9,000 more. They earned a little by making ingenious toys and knick-knacks out of meat bones and other odds and ends.

They were cheery and lively, on the whole, and did not fare too badly, though a regiment of West Indian negroes was almost entirely wiped out in a single winter. The benevolent and eccentric ' man with the black beard ', who made large sums as a hawker, a well-known character in Portsmouth, once gave them 1,000 lb. of bread.

The prisoners were employed to clean and paint the Norman church that stands in the south-west corner of the Roman fort. It was built for the Austin canons to whom Henry I granted land here in 1133. But within twenty years they removed to Southwick and the monastery buildings were probably used as a quarry for the castle. On the fine west front is the badge of Stephen, the centaur-archer, if we may so call it. The south transept has gone, but otherwise the church is an almost perfect specimen of a Norman church of the day. The Norman font is interesting.

To the north, beyond the great unattractive Nelson column on the down, is Boarhunt, with a wide view. The church, close to the old manor-house, now a farm, stands embowered in trees. The little chancel arch and the narrow light beyond prove it to be another of the Hampshire Saxon village churches, and the font is probably Saxon too. Near by, to the west, is Southwick, with some delightful old houses, in woody country, part of the Forest of Bere. The Austin priory from Portchester, of which there are scanty remains, was in the modern park. It possessed a famous image of the Virgin, our Lady of Southwick. William of Wykeham founded five chantries here, for the prosperity and for the soul of Edward III, for his own soul and for the souls of his father and mother, John and Sybil, whom he buried here. At Southwick, Henry VI awaited his lovely bride, Margaret of Anjou, who lay sick of the smallpox at Godshouse in Southampton. She had landed at Portchester, but was so ill from the voyage that the Earl of Suffolk carried her ashore. In spite of a heavy

The Sallyport, Portsmouth

storm, the men of Portchester had strewn the streets with rushes. She slept at Godshouse in Portsmouth. So scanty was the wardrobe of the daughter of the attractive but poverty-stricken King René, that an express was sent from Southampton to fetch an English dressmaker to wait on her from London.

At the Dissolution Southwick went to Wriothesley. He gave it to John White, a hanger-on of his, who pulled down the church and turned the monastery into a house. From him it passed by marriage to the Nortons. The news of the murder of Buckingham was whispered into the ear of Charles I while he was praying in the chapel, a guest of Sir Daniel Norton. In Dick Norton's day Dryden's *Spanish Friar* is said to have been acted in the Frater. Then Southwick passed to the Thistelthwaytes, who still own the fine park, as well as Portchester Castle. The monastic buildings, quite ruinous, were pulled down about a century ago and the modern house built.

Back on the main road there is still a stretch of country outside Fareham, and the core of the place bears the hall-mark of a Hampshire market-town. There are some pleasing Georgian houses in High Street, which branches north. The small, bow-windowed house where Thackeray stayed as a boy has been swallowed by the bus-centre. Fareham stands at the head of the creek which forms the most north-westerly portion of Portsmouth Harbour, a long, wide inlet known as the Cams, into which flows the Wallington from Southwick and Purbrook. Here is the old tide-mill, picturesque enough, and on the other side the wooded park of Cams Hall. Till well into the seventeenth century Fareham was a busy port, especially for wood from the forests round, but there is little traffic to-day. Though it contained 30 hides, it was only assessed at 20 in the old days, because it was an easy prey to Danish pirates.

H

On the Wickham road with its half-timbered gables is Roche Court; parts of the walls are medieval. Here was the manor of the same name, earlier West Fareham. Peter des Roches, the Poitevin Bishop of Winchester, was guardian of the heiress, whom he married to his nephew, Geoffrey des Roches. By marriage it went to Sir Bernard Brocas of Beaurepaire about 1380 and from the Brocases to the Gardiners.

Beyond Fareham is Titchfield, one of those quaint, attractive large villages, as they seem to us, though it had a market in Domesday, which linger in Hampshire and give the idea that they are lingering in the restful two-storeyed houses, mainly Georgian or Stuart, not specially notable, that look out on the twisting streets : in the fine beamed gateway at the end of East Street, for instance, with the really old houses near it. The parish once stretched from Wickham to Warsash, where the Crab and Lobster Inn testifies to its one industry. After shedding several new parishes it still reaches the mouth of the Meon and includes Titchfield Haven. The Meon flows east of Titchfield, which was a port till, as the registers put it, ' the shutting out of Titchfield Haven by one Richard Talbottes industry under God's permission '. The Earl of Southampton built the wall to drain the marsh. Titchfield was crown property and was granted to John de Gisors, who lost it through opposing John. Henry III gave it to Peter des Roches for his Premonstratensian abbey. The abbey was given many privileges, including a five days' fair, by Henry VI, who there married Margaret of Anjou. She received the embarrassing present of a lion, certainly prophetic of the qualities she was to display on behalf of her husband : it was sent to the Tower. At the Dissolution Titchfield Abbey fell to Thomas Wriothesley, Earl of Southampton, one of the worst of the Tudor men, who abetted Henry VIII in his cruellest tyrannies. In

1542 the French ambassador said he almost governed England. Two years later he was made Chancellor. Titchfield became his home and he converted the abbey, says Leland, into ' a right stately house embattled '. The south wall of the church was the front, and across the nave he built the handsome gate-house, Place House, with the four towers, that stands out strikingly to the north of the village, with the Meon below. It is now a national monument and the plan of the abbey is bricked out.

The second Earl entertained Edward VI, to whom his father was guardian, and Elizabeth at Titchfield. It may well be that Shakespeare has entered the gate-house and wandered by the Meon, when the guest of the third Earl, the patron to whom he dedicated *Venus and Adonis*, his first published work, and *Lucrece*. Southampton married the gay maid-of-honour Elizabeth Vernon, a cousin of Essex, and was imprisoned for taking part in his rising. He was released and restored to favour by James I. Quarrelsome and hot-tempered, he was a bitter enemy of Buckingham and was even under arrest for a time at Titchfield. He and his son died of fever in the Low Countries in 1624. The fourth and last Earl ' brought very much reputation to the Royal cause '. Charles I was at Titchfield with his fifteen-year-old bride and she remained at the mansion while he went hunting in the New Forest. Nor was her stay without trouble. At dinner there was a shouting match between her chaplain and an Anglican divine, each determined to say the grace, and once, while an Anglican service was being held in the hall, Henrietta Maria and her ladies twice walked through talking and laughing. To Titchfield Charles fled when he escaped from Hampton Court, only to go a prisoner to Carisbrooke. He chose it, well knowing the old Countess, Elizabeth Vernon, ' to be a lady of that honour and spirit that she was superior to all kinds of temptation '. In the eighteenth century Place House became a quarry for Cams Hall at Fareham.

The lower part of the tower of the church is Saxon, and there is much Norman work. The quaint shingled spire and the north aisle are fifteenth century. The large south chapel, the abbot's chapel, was reserved for the White Canons. Here is the handsome, elaborately carved alabaster and marble Wriothesley tomb. The second Earl left the then enormous sum of £1,000 for the erection of two fair monuments—there is but one—in the parish church of 'Tichel'. On the top, in the centre, is his mother, and on either side, a little below her, her husband and her son, the second Earl. The third Earl, a boy, kneels at the west end of the monument. A funeral helmet and two crowns also hang here.

CHAPTER IX: *The Meon Valley*

HAMPSHIRE has not anything to show more fair than the secluded Meon valley. The approach to it is worthy of it. The left fork by the Austens' cottage at Chawton is flanked by noble trees waiting to usher you down to it. You plunge right into it at West Meon. The Meon, which has come round to meet you from East Meon, where it rises 400 feet up, is captious still, vanishing into swallow-holes, but it soon becomes a clear, swift, bustling little stream, and round Droxford you used to be able to play about on it in a small boat.

The Romans, or rather Roman-Britons, had found out this lovely valley and built a villa in Lippen wood, but it is with the Jutish allies of the Saxons that it is associated. They were given the Meon valley with the north shore of Southampton Water and the Isle of Wight as a reward for their help to the conquering Saxons. Here the Meonwara, the men of the Meon, lived an isolated life on their farms, having little contact with outside influences. Even Christianity did not touch them till Wilfrid, who had a stormy career as Archbishop of York, came as a missionary among them at the end of the seventh century. Tall, dark and intelligent, the men of the Meon still stand rather apart and are often said to preserve the Jutish type, the long skull and face and nose and the big chin.

West Meon is a pretty village, thatched and tiled cottages everywhere. At the cross by the green branches the road to Winchester, which Waller took before Cheriton. The morning mist had not cleared when we started down the valley, where the cattle were grazing peacefully in the lush green water-meadows under the wealth of trees. The woods round Warnford Park make perhaps the best bit of this beautiful road. The Meon runs through the park past Warnford House, into which the Elizabethan original has been modernized. Warnford, which had formerly belonged to Hyde Abbey, was a De Port manor.

Beyond the house is the church. In the early nineties, when I spent some happy holidays in this valley, there was much indignation at the refusal of the lord of the manor to allow it to be repaired. But when I see it as it is now, tactfully restored, and remember what a Victorian vandal might have done to it, I can almost look upon him as a public benefactor.

'Wilfrit fundavit, bonus Adam, me renovavit',

runs the inscription under the porch. Adam De Port pulled down the Saxon church, but he recorded the fact that it was built by St. Wilfrid, who converted the Meonwara, and there is enough to interest in his own largely twelfth-century substitute with its broad aisleless nave, its Saxon dial under the inscription on the fine, solid Norman tower and the great variety of old woodwork.

Close by the church are the ruins of the Norman house known as King John's house, really St. John's, because it dates from the time when Adam De Port married the St. John heiress Mabelle and changed his name to St. John. Adam was a turbulent Norman noble. He joined the barons against the king after the murder of Becket. When they were beaten he was banished. Finally, in 1180, Henry II pardoned him after inflicting the heavy fine of 1,000 marks and confiscating some of his estates. He spent the rest of his life in peace.

As we left the park, the sun slowly fought its way out of the clouds and flooded the whole rich, peaceful valley, seemingly nothing but trees and meadows with their great herds of cattle. It stretches away to Beacon Hill, the highest point of the downs here, lying off on the right, and to the lower hills on the left, topped by Old Winchester. The Meon among its willows is a tiny stream still, only just beginning to busy itself with watercress beds and the sedges dear to the waterfowl that haunt its more secluded reaches. The rare cars and bicycles had no disturbing effect. I do not remember meeting any one on foot outside the villages. Along the road up to the down you find yourself in the street of the Breeding Sows, as a Roman might have called it, where, in a long row of wooden huts, a true son of his county is said to keep 600 of them. Exton we passed and then came Corhampton with its grand old yew, said to measure 22½ feet, arching over the path of the churchyard. The chancel of the simple little aisle-less church is Saxon, the pilaster strips standing out two inches. So are the chancel arch and the stone chair, the sundial, a twin to Warnford's, and the fine arcading round the north door : a little church that impresses, where Norman font or Jacobean pulpit and even traces of old painting pass unnoticed. Had Wilfrid a hand in it?

Over the Meon, now a respectable stream with the old mill beyond, is Meonstoke, a royal manor till it was acquired by William of Wykeham for his college at Winchester. It is the only Meon village that is breaking out into bungalows and, thanks to an eighteenth-century fire, there are not many old cottages to counteract them. But it clusters pleasantly round the Meon bridge, not without thatch in the older parts; and thatch can make all but the most hopeless of cottages presentable. The Perpendicular church is interesting and the presence of the rose, his emblem, has induced some to give the east end of the chancel to William of Wykeham.

From here you may tackle Old Winchester Hill, with its yews and beeches, standing out alone beyond Harvestgate Farm. There are the usual barbed wire and other impediments for the enthusiastic tripper to negotiate or circumvent, if he wishes to investigate these downs. It looks as if they were not often disturbed. When we used to come up here for picnics, years ago, the path was more open. It is a gentle hill, the top crowned by a fine, 14-acre oval camp, with a number of barrows round, and 3 good bowl barrows in the centre. Perhaps the camp, if it is not due to the name of the hill, gave rise to the tradition that Winchester was first founded here. Roman remains have been found in it. The views are glorious. To the south on a good day you can see right away by Petersfield and Butser to the sea and the Isle of Wight, but as it was misty, I had to be content with what looked like Butser. To the north are the downs and the plateau above Alton; to the west Salisbury Plain and the New Forest. You can still follow the track over the downs to Butser.

Wild and unspoilt it is up here and across the valley, with its farms and fields spread out before you. Above Corhampton, beyond Corhampton Down, is another delightful stretch of wild, high, healthy Hampshire, running out towards Cheriton and Alresford. The deserted roads and lanes are often separated from the fields by a broad strip of woodland; the rare cottages nestle among the trees. I remember starting out from Winchester, over the shoulder of St. Catherine's Hill, in the rain, on a July morning in 1916. At Hazely Down, the malign influence of St. Swithun happily ceased. The sun shone brightly as I entered Morestead and turned left. Then came more wood, followed by the climb up to Stephen Castle Down and then Corhampton Down. 'We did not half appreciate the women before the war,' remarked an old farmer, pointing proudly to a 9-acre wood which was to be cleared by 6 of them. In Soberton I passed a squad of German prisoners going cheerfully home from their work in the fading evening light.

Along the ridge from Wheely Down, behind Beacon

Hill, you look out over a wonderful panorama past Old Winchester towards the sea, grey and misty in late February, green and brilliant in the sun of early spring. Beacon Hill—660 feet, a shade lower than Old Winchester —has much the same view. These two ridges help to shut off the valley to-day as they did for the Meonwara.

Up here on Millbarrow Down is Preshaw House, with the group of tall lindens round the lodge. It stands back in its ample park, where the rabbits seem almost to be expecting to be fed, so little are they perturbed by a car. It is an attractive house, but nothing is earlier than the seventeenth century and most is later. Here lived Cary Verney, Lady Gardiner, of the Verney letters, with her second husband, genial John Stewkeley. A hospitable house it was. 'Preshaw House puts me in mind of the loaves and fishes. It increases and multiplies with its company,' wrote lively Dr. Denton, when Lady Smith appeared with 2 daughters, a chaplain, 2 maids, 3 men in livery and 6 horses, and there was only one spare room.

And then there was that bright young thing, Cary's step-daughter, Ursula, who found home intolerable after 8 months of gadding 'and now hath bin at all the Salsbury rasis, dancing like wild with Mr. Clarks whom Jack can give you a carictor of, and came home of a Saturday night just before our Winton rasis, at near 12 aclock, when my famyly was a bed, with Mr. Charls Torner, a man I know not, John Turner's son, who was tried for his life last November for killing a man. . . . She could not be pleased without dancing 12 hours in the 24, taking it ill I denied in my husband's absence to have 7 ranting fellows come to Preshaw and bring music.'

In Hinton Ampner church, with its Saxon pilaster strips, are the monuments of the Stewkeleys, who recovered the manor, which they had rented in 1637, at the Restoration. It belonged to St. Swithun. Ampner is a corruption of almoner, because it was assigned to the almoner for his expenses, and here he held his courts. The church, like the house, stands high and they command fine views. Below rises the spring that becomes the Itchen. The old house was haunted by a man in a drab coat, said to be the evil Lord Stawell, who died there, and a woman. Admiral Sir John Jervis (Lord St. Vincent) came to investigate on the complaints of his sister, the tenant, and is said to have advised her to leave. A number of secret passages were found in the walls when it was pulled down.

Near by is Bramdean, and in Brookwood Park, for a time the home of the once popular novelist, Charlotte Smith (*The Old Manor House*), were discovered two fine Roman pavements, belonging to a large villa approaching in size that at Bignor. They were left on the spot and are now completely ruined.

Beyond the hill is Droxford, where a Jutish cemetery was unearthed during the making of the railway. The finds are in the Winchester Museum. Izaak Walton's son-in-law, Dr. Hawkins, was rector there—part of the rectory dates from the seventeenth century—and here Walton spent his last years, leaving all his books at Winchester and Droxford to his daughter. And what better home could there be for the author of *The Compleat Angler* than this lovely valley in Hampshire, ' which I think exceeds all England for swift, shallow, clear, pleasant brooks and store of trout '? Among his intimates were John Derbyshire, the curate, and Francis Morley, a nephew of Bishop Morley, at the manor-house. The White Hart, too, dates from Walton's day. Doubtless it was then ' an honest alehouse, where we shall find a cleanly room, lavendar in the windows and twenty ballards stuck about the wall '.

Egbert granted the manor as a thank-offering for his coronation to the monks of St. Swithun. Later, like others round here, it came to the Bishop of Winchester. The church has good Norman and later features and the graceful figure of a lady, said to be the mother of John de Drokenford, Chancellor to Edward I, who was born here. It was found in a field, where it is thought to have been buried to escape the Roundheads, who destroyed her handsome tomb.

You pass out beyond the village to Middlington Park, and then across the valley—as usual, there was a camp down by the Meon—to Soberton, with its striking Perpendicular church up on the hill. It has a wide prospect over towards Droxford and the downs. As there is a man's head by a key and a woman's head by a pail with a skull between them, on the tower, it is reputed to have been built by a butler and a dairymaid. Hence, during the sensible restoration of 1882, the money for the Tower was subscribed by people in service. Baron Anson, who sailed round the world, took his title from Soberton, and the avenue at the bottom of the church meadow, by the Meon, was believed in my day to lead to his house, now pulled down, with what truth I know not.

One of the three Soberton manors belonged to Godwin and Harold. Beaulieu Abbey also had land here. Later the manor passed to the Earls of Southampton, and then to the family of Dr. Curle, Bishop of Winchester, who retired here when he was expelled under the Commonwealth, being supported by friends and dying in the house of his sister. Afterwards it came to the Minchins. In the Lady Chapel, called both the Curle and the Minchin Chapel, is a large stone coffin dug up near by. The church possesses a seventeenth-century altar-cloth embroidered with the story of the Good Samaritan. The railway has increased this large, straggling parish.

The road to Hambledon lies among the richly wooded peaceful downs in the neighbourhood of the old racecourse. Forty years ago this attractive village, nestling under the downs in its valley, was wonderfully isolated and it was a pleasure to come upon it. Even now, though well in touch with the Portsmouth road, its picturesque old cottages and shops under the noble great church on its hill, seem to stand apart from the modern world. This boasts the remains of a pre-Conquest church, Norman and interesting later work, including a two-storeyed vestry and a fine fifteenth-century pulpit. In 1199 the manor went to the Bishops of Winchester, remaining with them, except for a break under the Commonwealth, when it was bought by George Wither, till it was taken over by the Ecclesiastical Commission.

Charles II passed a night here after a day's coursing on Old Winchester Hill, on October 13th, 1651, when, after Worcester fight, he was making for Shoreham to escape to France. His guide was Colonel Gunter and he slept at the house of his brother-in-law, which later became a gardener's cottage. The master of the house, 'who had been all day long playing the good fellow at an alehouse in the town', came in at supper and declared the king looked like 'some round-headed rogue's son', but was soon appeased. Afterwards, in the time of entertaining his guests, he did by chance let fall an oath; for which 'Mr. Jackson' (as the king was called) took occasion modestly to reprove him.

The road for the downs goes up by Park House and on to the Bat and Ball, the cricket inn, by Broadhalfpenny Down, where a large granite monument records the centenary of the Hambledon men, the real founders of modern cricket. They live in the pages of John Nyren, one of the younger of them. He was a farmer, son of the great Richard Nyren, who was the chosen General of all the matches. John was cultivated and a good musician. In London he was the friend of Leigh Hunt, Lamb, Cowden Clarke and Novello. 'No eleven in England could compare with the Hambledon, which met on the first Tuesday in May on Broadhalfpenny.' The club was founded about 1750 and refounded some 20 years later. The 20 years till 1791 were its greatest years. In that year, when Richard Nyren left it, their eleven nearly beat the Middlesex twenty-two at Lords. Thomas Lord, by the way, who gave his name to that famous ground, was a West Meon man, a further debt owed by cricket to the county. John Small, a shoemaker, was the best bat and the maker of the best cricket-balls. He, too, was a musician, the strains of whose violin, like those of Orpheus' lute, are said to have had charms to soothe the savage breast of an angry bull in a field.

The great match of the year was with All England, which Hambledon won many times. The farmers would gather on the ground ' and whenever a Hambledon man made a good hit, worth four or five runs, you heard the deep mouths of the whole multitude braying away in pure Hampshire, " Go hard! Go hard! *Tich* and run! *Tich* and run! " ' At an exciting finish Sir Horace Mann, who generally had a few hundreds on the result, would be seen walking about, cutting down the daisies with his stick, while ' the old farmers would be leaning forward on their tall old staves, and the whole multitude perfectly still '. The Bat and Ball was kept by another Nyren, who supplied the ample food and drink required for the occasion.

The big matches were always for £500 a side. For this kind of cricket Miss Mitford, who considered herself a connoisseur of the game, had no love. She saw it at Brams-hill Park, Hants *v.* All England, with Mr. Budd at the wicket, all of them in their cricketing jackets and tall hats, playing for large sums. She preferred the fine village lads.

Hambledon was a noted sporting centre in other ways. There were the races and there was the Hambledon Hunt, run by Mr. Laud of Park House. His hounds were a unique pack, which hunted the deer in summer and the fox in winter in the Forest of Bere. So well trained were they, that it needed only a few days for them to turn completely from one quarry to another. Æsop assures us that, when after a fox, they would pass the deer quite unnoticed, though they had been hunting them a week or two ago.

From the Bat and Ball you go on by Hyden Hill and through Hyden Wood, which, according to a survey of 1647, generally supplied the wood for Butser Beacon. From here you get a charming view of East Meon below. The handsome Norman tower of the church is backed by Park Down across the valley, which marks the former bishop's park, 'well stored with conies', though there were no deer. The pretty village, thatch and half-timber, runs along the tiny Meon, which rises under Childen Down. Since Henry II it has belonged to the Bishop of Winchester. In the large church is one of the Hampshire Norman fonts of black marble from Tournai, with scenes from Genesis. The villagers used to maintain that it was a present from a pope. In the south transept is the stone marked Amens Plenty, which is popularly said to mark the grave of men killed in skirmishes when East Meon was Waller's headquarters before Cheriton, since no service was said, only a number of Amens. Opposite the church stands the delightful medieval Court House, where the bishop's courts were held, changed but little since the seventeenth century.

Back at Soberton, you continue down the broadening valley of the Meon to Wickham, 'a praty townlet', as Leland calls it. Round its ample square, where tournaments were held, is a pleasing medley of houses of varying dates and sizes. The most interesting thing in the rigorously restored church is the tomb of Sir W. Uvedale (1615), which shows the transition from the Elizabethan to the

Caroline Baroque in the outbreak of skulls on the handsome canopy and even in the hand of the baby, the last of
the kneeling children. Wickham was a De Port manor, but
the Uvedales held it from the fourteenth to the eighteenth
century. Till some ten years ago the Courts Baron were still
held, and before the opening all those attending marched
in procession over the upper bridge across the Meon to a
low wall opposite the churchyard and gazed at the site of
the vanished Uvedale mansion. The timbers of the mill,
marked by shot, came from the American frigate *Chesapeke*
captured by the *Shannon* in the famous fight of 1813.

Wickham was the birthplace in 1324 of the greatest of
the bishops of Winchester, William of Wykeham, as he
called himself. Of humble origin, he was sent to school
at Winchester, probably by Sir Nicholas Uvedale, Governor
of Windsor Castle. He introduced him to Bishop Edyndon
of Winchester, who presented him to Edward III, when he
had nothing to recommend him but his knowledge of
architecture and the ' courtly attribute of a comely person '.
He was put in charge of Windsor Castle and the rebuilding
was largely the result of his advice. He soon became all
powerful with Edward III and reaped a rich crop of bene-
fices.

For Botley you go through beautiful wooded Hampshire
country, with Preshaw Down above you, by Shedfield.
While Botley was a market town, the lord of the manor,
who owned one side of the market-place, used to collect
the dues. A falling tree ruined the church and only the
chancel remains. Standing at the head of a creek, where
the Hamble River joins it from Bishops Waltham, Botley
was something of a port while the timber was of value.
To-day it is the centre of the Hampshire strawberry
industry. It is good to sit by the old wharf on the Hamble,
a little more derelict than when first I knew it, on a fine
May afternoon. The grounds where was Cobbett's home

face you : behind you are boat-houses and farm buildings. The great mill lies higher up beyond the bridge. Cobbett's house has gone, though some of the outbuildings remain. Cobbett is never quite so vigorous and fresh on Hampshire as he is on his native Surrey. Traffic may be busy on the Winchester road, Cobbett's road, ' a turnpike road of which I was the projector and indeed the maker ', for Botley is at its junction with the Fareham road. But down here it is easy to dream oneself back to the days when our prehistoric ancestors paddled up in the dug-out canoe which was found a little farther down the Hamble. Once its remains reposed in the dignified little porticoed Town Hall which sets the tone to the peaceful old square, but they are now in the Tudor House at Southampton.

The road to Bishops Waltham runs above the Hamble with pleasing views over the valley and beyond. Bishops Waltham was given the Bishop of Winchester in 904 by Edward the Elder and, except under Edward VI and Cromwell, it has belonged to the see ever since. The little red-brick, tiled and thatched town to the north of the castle is as yet little spoilt by the houses and villas that are springing up round it in all directions. Henry de Blois built the castle, but William of Wykeham gave it its final form, the ruins of which we see to-day. Its proximity to his birthplace may explain why he lavished so much wealth and labour upon it. Across the road is the Abbot's Pond, formed from head waters of the Hamble, for supplying the bishop with fish. The chief remains of the palace are the 5 handsome windows of the dining-hall facing the road. The tower beyond is older. In the second of the two courts there were towers at each angle. Here is also the kitchen, divided into two storeys, which was used as a barn after the castle was slighted. There are other ruins, as well as the great outer wall.

Here Richard I was splendidly entertained after his coro-

Bishops Waltham Palace

Beeches in the New Forest

nation at Winchester: and here, as was fitting, William of Wykeham breathed his last at the age of eighty in 1404. It was a favourite residence of the earlier bishops, who often entertained their sovereigns there. Thus Cardinal Beaufort left Margaret of Anjou ' the blue bed of gold and damask wherein the Queen used to lie when she was at the palace of Waltham '. A good fight was put up by 200 Cavaliers before they surrendered in 1644. The castle was then slighted. Though it was restored to the bishops they never rebuilt it. It stood in a park of 1,000 acres, fenced in by a mound known as the lug. Swanmore, along the built-up road to Droxford, was the bishop's swan mere or pond; and from here Stephen Leacock took his humour to mature in Canada at the age of seven. Bishop Morley disparked it. Beyond it lay Waltham Chase, really a part of Bere Forest. Hence the Waltham Blacks whose evil doings resulted in the passing of the Black Act. Deer stealing was the rage even among decent people, says Gilbert White, and ' unless he was a deer-hunter . . . no young man was allowed to be possessed of manhood or gallantry '. They were called Blacks because they blacked their faces to escape recognition. Bishop Hoadley refused to restock the Chase with deer because ' it had done mischief enough already '.

Vernon House was built by Admiral Vernon, the victor of Portobello. Sir Arthur Helps lived there later. His efforts to give the town a pottery industry and an infirmary came to nothing. During the Napoleonic Wars Bishops Waltham had a large quota of French prisoners when 20,000 are said to have been settled in the Portsmouth district. A well-known girls' school there is said to have come to grief owing to a letter from one of them to a girl in it being picked up by a servant; and that though the unfortunate girl was expelled and the servant dismissed.

I

CHAPTER X: *Odiham, Basing House and Basingstoke*

ODIHAM I have approached by various ways: from Farnham, through Crondall, where there are the remains of two Norman castles, both covered with trees. Crondall's handsome church is interesting, in spite of the restorers. The striking brick tower (1658) is copied from Battersea church. There is an excellent brass to a four-teenth-century vicar in the chancel with its finely groined roof. Or you may tackle Odiham from Alton, running up among the gently sloping fields and woods and on to the down, passing South Warnborough, a good thatched village, whose peace is threatened by the new aerodrome on the hill between it and Odiham.

About Odiham there can be no two opinions. The moment you turn into its broad high street, with its medley of houses of all periods, admirably grouped, you realize that you are in one of the most nearly perfect small towns in the county. It runs you back through the centuries, tending to linger a little in the eighteenth for the coaches. Of its many inns the George, licensed in 1540, is rich in woodwork. The best of the old houses, including the delightful alms-houses, stand to the south of the High Street, in the Bury, which is reached by a narrow drook. Here is the church with the stocks and the whipping-post in front; large and impressive with its seventeenth-century central brick tower. It has a notable thirteenth-century chalk font, where the inscription from the Vulgate is still legible, and a beautifully carved Stuart pulpit. At Odiham was born William Lily, one of the first Englishmen to learn Greek and the first to teach it in England. Colet made him the first High Master of St. Paul's School. Upon his

Brevissima Institutio all later Latin Grammars were based till comparatively recently.

Odiham belonged to the Saxon kings who seem to have had a residence here, and it was royal demesne under the Normans. About a mile away stands the shapely ruin of the octagonal keep of the castle, built by John, with its gracious coronal of firs, close to the quiet canal, a delectable contrast to the noisy Basingstoke tentacle by which I had come. From it you look across to the purple downs to the north. It stands in the marshy meadows of the Whitewater that rises at North Warnborough. It was protected by three large moats, the natural defence in marshy country, well stocked with fish. John was fond of it, visiting it 24 times. There is no escaping John in Hampshire. From it he went to Runnymede and to it he returned after signing—or rather sealing—Magna Carta. When the Barons called in the Dauphin and he besieged it, the garrison is said to have held out for a fortnight, making sallies and engaging an equal number of the foe. When they capitulated and marched out with the honours of war, the French saw to their amazement that there were only 3 knights, 3 squires and 17 men-at-arms, all unhurt. Other buildings and houses, possibly of wood, came later. Henry III granted it to his sister, the Countess of Pembroke, who had well filled stables and kennels there. She married Simon de Montfort and here he took leave of her before the fatal Battle of Evesham. David of Scotland, captured at Neville's Cross, was a prisoner at Odiham from 1346 to 1357, till his huge ransom of 100,000 marks was raised. It belonged to several queens, Anne of Bohemia and Margaret of Anjou among them. There was a large park, and in the fourteenth century the royal stud was here. It seems to have become ruinous about 1600.

For Winchfield you should follow the derelict canal as it winds round the fine woods of Dogmersfield Park. Only a canal tow-path can bring back the peace of a pre-car country lane and here, among the woods and fields, you find it to perfection. The park belonged to the Bishop of Bath and Wells. In the palace not only Henry VII but Prince Arthur first met Catherine of Aragon, to the horror of her Spanish suite, who, in Oriental style, would not have had her unveil even to her father-in-law before the wedding. However, ' there were the most goodly words uttered to each other ', though neither party understood the language of the other. Henry VIII bought it and Edward VI added it to Wriothesley's vast Hampshire estates. The Beauclerks acquired it in the eighteenth century, but sold it in 1908. The church, twelfth century, which stands away in the country, near the park, with its small chancel arch, is liberally adorned with handsome deep zigzag Norman carving. Winchfield was part of the original endowment of Chertsey Abbey. In Domesday it was held by Walter Fitzother, or De Windsor, as he was called after being made governor of Windsor Castle.

From Winchfield you can make your way through Hook along the main road. The church of Nately Scures, with the manor-house, now a farm, and the pond which you pass on your left, are interesting. The De Scures held it of the De Ports in the twelfth century. Later it went to the Uvedales and then to the Carletons, Earls of Dorchester. Many of their monuments are in this tiny late twelfth-century church of St. Swithun, one of the smallest in the county, with its apse. On the left door pillar is a mermaid. Altogether a charming group. Farther on, to the south of the road again, is Andwell, in good open country by the canal, where Priory Farm, almost islanded by the winter mud, contains a few remains of the priory built by the French Cistercians to whom Adam De Port gave the land. William of Wykeham bought it for Winchester College.

Then you turn up north by the canal to Basing, a long

Hampshire village with a good sprinkling of seventeenth-century cottages that runs out by the Loddon. Basing was the head of the De Port honour. Hugh De Port, who came from the village of Port-en-Bressin, near Bayeux, was one of the Conqueror's most trusted followers. In accordance with his system of putting the south coast and the channel ports into the keeping of his Normans, William gave him 70 manors, 55 of them in Hampshire; in addition, he held 13 others of William's half-brother Odo, Bishop of Bayeux. The De Ports were, in fact, the only large landowners in the county, where much of the land either belonged to the church or was royal demesne. 'A mighty man in this tract and of great wealth,' Camden calls Hugh. His great-grandson, Adam De Port, took the name of St. John. In 1299 we have the first Baron St. John of Basing, which passed to the Paulets by marriage in the fifteenth century.

The medieval castle on its mound with its bailey dates probably from the early twelfth century. There was a much earlier fortification on this commanding position, doubtless prehistoric. In 871 Ethelred and Alfred were probably beaten by the advancing Danes at Basing. Anyhow, this castle was rebuilt by the first Marquis of Winchester. His father was knighted at the marriage of Prince Arthur, but William Paulet, a typical Tudor man, was to go much further. Henry VIII made him Comptroller of the Household and Knight of the Garter; Edward VI President of the Council and Marquis of Winchester, while Elizabeth gave him the Great Seal. He was as loyal to Mary as to Edward VI, for, as he said, he was born of the willow, not of the oak. He had his reward, dying in 1571 at the age of eighty-seven and leaving 103 descendants. His wealth was enormous, and he turned the old castle at Basing into a magnificent mansion, covering not only the original site, but a large piece of ground beyond. It stood on a slope with 4 great towers. The ramparts were brick, lined with earth, and there was a deep, dry moat. A descendant pulled down one wing. Fuller thought it 'the greatest of any subject's house in England, yea, larger than most of the King's Palaces'. Here the Marquis entertained Elizabeth in 1560, though it was said that 'all things for so great entertainment but elbow-room and good will were wanting'; and she rewarded him with one of her compliments. 'By my troth, if my Lord Treasurer were but a young man, I could find in my heart to have him for a husband before any man in England.' Among those she knighted on her departure were Benjamin Tichborne and Colonel Norton of Alresford. The fourth Marquis so impaired his estate by entertaining her for thirteen days that his son had to live very quietly.

This 'loyal Marquis' was a conservative landlord. 'Tenants were to make hedges for the wheat field within six days of Maie Daie. No wheat was to be sown until within a fortnight of Christmas, and no fallowing done until within a fortnight of Candlemas.' He had become a Catholic and was popular with Henrietta Maria and her friends. In the Civil War Loyalty House—*Aymez Loyauté* was the motto on all the windows—was an important stronghold. It commanded the road from Kent and Sussex to Newbury and Oxford, seriously hampered the trade of London with the west, and enabled the king to levy his contributions. Roundhead Basingstoke had to pay £40 a month.

Beyond the gate, over which are the arms and the famous motto of the loyal Marquis, you soon find yourself among the brick ramparts, 36 feet high in places, the plan of which has been confused by the canal. Above rose the great circular turreted house which appears in Hollar's engraving. The site has been fully excavated. The two deep wells are there, and the brine pit where the meat was preserved in winter and the cellars. The gate-house beyond the moat to the north, with its 4 towers and its 2 courts, has been identified. Across the road is the Grange, then also walled. Beyond the old keep is the walled garden, perhaps less changed than anything, where Elizabeth walked and exchanged compliments, with its enormous dove-cot where there was room for 500 nests and the unique revolving ladder to facilitate the taking of the birds and the eggs. If the size of the place made it difficult to defend, it also made it hard to besiege. The fact that it was a Papist stronghold increased the bitterness on both sides.

At the outbreak of war the Roundheads seized the armoury for 1,500 men, leaving the Marquis but 6 muskets. Expecting an easy success, Dick Norton and Captain St. Barbe of Broadlands, Romsey, attacked it hotly with 'a ragged rabble of dragoons'. But the king sent Sir Henry Bond, whose disobedience was to lose Cheriton Fight, with 100 troopers who arrived in the nick of time and drove the enemy back to Farnham. However, Parliament was not likely to leave such a thorn in its flesh alone, and as soon as Waller was back from the west, he set about removing it. The garrison was now 500 strong and many Royalists had deposited their valuables there. Basting House, as they began to call it, as spacious as the Tower of London, writes a Roundhead, was 'built upright, so that no man can command the roof', on which some guns were mounted. Waller's artillery did little damage, and all he could accomplish was to capture the Grange and some out-houses full of provisions, from which he was later driven, even in a second desperate attempt to storm the house, when the women hurled down stones on his men, now numbering from 6,000 to 8,000. On the advance of Hopton he withdrew.

After Cheriton, Hopton's chaplain, Thomas Fuller,

remained at Basing 5 or 6 weeks. The garrison now began to lose heart, and a plot was discovered in which the brother of the Marquis, Lord Edward Paulet, was implicated. His life was spared, but he was compelled to act as executioner to his fellow conspirators. No Paulet has since been named Edward.

Once again the siege was prosecuted with vigour, guns were placed on Basing church and a tower was brought down. But the garrison hit back vigorously with a sortie into the park led by Major Cuffaud, and held trenches for a time near the Grange, thus lightening their task of going out at night to cut forage. Smallpox had broken out, desertions increased, and the Marquis was continually sending messengers disguised as Parliament men with orange tawny scarfs and ribbons to Oxford for help. Colonel Gage, a Catholic, undertook the relief and put Norton to flight with a dashing Cavalier charge on Chinham Down while the garrison made a sortie. He brought in ample supplies of provisions and powder, besides cleaning out Basingstoke for the benefit of ' brave old loyalty '. But the enemy were not completely dislodged from the park and were gathering in force round Kingsclere and Silchester, so he returned to Oxford. When things began to look threatening, Gage came on again in November, but the enemy were also in a bad way and raised the siege.

After Naseby, Parliament determined to finish with these garrisons ' which, like vipers in the bowels, infested the midland parts '. Dalbier, a Dutchman who had fought under Buckingham, was then besieging Basing. His guns were effective. Not only did a shot enter the boudoir of Lady Winchester, killing one of her maids by her, but another sent a bushel of Scotch twopenny pieces, hidden in one of the towers, flying about the ears of the prisoners. On the 21st the besiegers were encouraged by a sermon from William Beech, a Wykehamist, entitled, ' More

sulphur for Basing '. On October 8 Cromwell appeared
with his heavy guns after taking Winchester. By the 13th
the breeches were made and he decided to storm next
morning. ' The old House had stood (as it is reported)
2 or 300 years,' wrote Peters. ' A nest of idolatry, the New
House, surpassing that in beauty and stateliness, and either
of them fit to make an Emperor's Court.' The struggle
was short. The new house was taken first and then the old
house, where the besieged showed ' incredible boldness '.
' Clubs are trumps as when Basing House was taken,' runs
the Hampshire saying, for some of the guard were playing
cards when the assault began.

The Marquis was stripped of his clothes by a soldier.
That ' reverend dragoon ', Hugh Peters, began a religious
and political discussion with him, but the Marquis cut him
short by telling him that ' if the king had no more ground
in England but Basing House, he would adventure as he
did, and so maintain it to the uttermost, comforting himself in this disaster that Basing House was called Loyalty '.
Peters was much elated with this all-round victory. It was
he who took the news with the Marquis's banner to
London. The place was a nest of engravers. Wenceslas
Hollar, the Bohemian, held a commission, and was taken
with Sir Robert Peake and his pupil, William Faithorne.
So also was Inigo Jones, aged seventy-two. He had to be
carried out in a blanket, having been robbed of his clothes.
Major Robinson, an ex-comedian of Drury Lane, was shot
in cold blood by Harrison, the regicide, after he had surrendered. The women were ' coarsely, but civilly used ',
being robbed of their valuables and good clothes. Only
one was killed, the daughter of an expelled parson, when
she railed at the soldiers for their treatment of him. Of
the priests, six were killed, four hung later in London.

The booty was enormous. Rumour credited Mrs. Cromwell with receiving a liberal share of it. The soldiers took

the great stores of provisions outside and sold them to the country people. When the house caught fire owing to a neglected fire-ball, the Roundheads worked hard to retrieve everything of value. On Cromwell's advice, Basing was ordered to be slighted and any one permitted to carry off the materials. The fire had left only the bare walls standing. The roof of Basingstoke church, which had been used as a powder magazine and blown up, was repaired with 4,000 tiles from the ruins. Many men perished in the cellars, where it was impossible to rescue them, during the fire. Plentiful relics of the siege, including some skeletons, were found in the digging of the Basingstoke canal.

Basing church suffered badly, and in 1644 a brief was allowed to be read in all churches for funds for its repair. There are only two Norman arches under the striking seventeenth-century brick tower which suggests a Cambridge college, and red brick was cleverly used in the restoration. The Dukes of Bolton, the heirs of the Marquis, are buried in the Paulet chapel, but there have recently been changes there. On the bleak, bare walls are a funeral helmet and gauntlets. The Italians employed to make figures on the tombs left when the siege began without finishing the lettering. The Virgin and Child over the west door, probably dating from Sir John Paulet's restoration of 1519, escaped intact. Was it taken down and hidden during the troubles? The church has no bells, for Cromwell carried them off.

Basingstoke, at the junction of the London, Winchester and Salisbury roads, has long been important as 'a good market and a great thoroughfare'. The market was there in Domesday, and it is now a railway junction as well as the meeting-place of five main roads. It gets its name from a Saxon tribe. The Romans were here, and Winklebury Camp, close to which runs their Winchester-Silchester road, the western boundary of Basingstoke, was an important centre before them. It is on the down to the north, clearly marked, though sadly mutilated, most of the ring being fenced off for chickens. If you carry on over it to the crossroad on the top of Rooks Down, by the group of firs and the chapel, you are on the spot whence Cromwell is reputed to have surveyed Basing House, a very distant prospect, even with a perspective glass. But on a blusterous March day—visibility good—you get a gorgeous view, raised above modern vulgarities, right across the valley. You may follow the road past the mental hospital through some great fields to Sherborne and look down on the Berkshire border.

Basingstoke was a king's town. Henry III gave it its charter, the fee-farm from which was often held by the queens. It was incorporated in 1392 after a disastrous fire. The woollen trade, thanks to the sheep on the downs, flourished till the seventeenth century. Edward VI gave it with other places to Sir William Paulet for maintaining Netley Abbey. It was again burnt down while Elizabeth was at Basing House and she allowed the town to beg in London and the seven home counties, with poor results.

The modern Mote Hall with its clock-tower is on the site of the original in the market, which was very old in 1511. The old houses are mostly in the streets between the market and the late Perpendicular church, and round it, largely eighteenth century. The glass in the east window of the north aisle is from the Holy Ghost chapel. In the large garden of the handsome rectory meet two arms of the Loddon. It was the home of the Whartons, Joseph and Thomas, poet and historian of English literature, whose father was rector. The famous Walter de Merton, founder of Merton College, was also born at Basingstoke.

Inns were numerous in Tudor days. There were the Swan and the Angel, which remained the chief posting-inn to the end, when fifty coaches passed through in a day.

It stood opposite the Town Hall, on the site of the International Stores, modest externally, but with ample stabling. The sixteenth-century wall-painting, now covered up, and the beams are preserved in the buildings behind. Over the stables were the Assembly Rooms, where were held the balls that were the thrill of Jane Austen's young days. A few years ago they were used as a loft. Cromwell stayed at the Falcon in London Street, opposite the Bell, where the Marquis of Winchester was confined after his capture.

The ruins of the Holy Ghost chapel are conspicuous by the railway. During the six years' interdict under John, when cemeteries were closed, the dead were buried on this hill, the Holy Ghost liten. Later the land was consecrated. In 1525 Lord Sandys of the Vyne and Bishop Fox built the chapel, which Camden says was very beautiful, with a richly painted roof. The glass went in the Civil War. One of the two remaining battered tombs is probably that of Lord Sandys. To the chapel he attached an educational guild, suppressed under Edward VI, but revived under Mary. The boys were taught till quite recently in a building near the chapel, which suffered severely at their hands. Gilbert White, himself a pupil, was ' eye-witness, perhaps a party concerned, in the undermining of a portion of that fine old ruin '.

It is a beautiful drive to Alton through well-treed, leafy lanes and among great Hampshire farms, over the ridge. On the left is Hackwood, long the home of the Dukes of Bolton, later of Lord Curzon. It is said to have been Hawkwood, a simple hunting-lodge, much enlarged after the fall of Basing House. The present pleasing house, with its graceful portico, was built for the first Duke, the son of the Loyalty Marquis, in 1668, from plans by Inigo Jones. The view from the front looks down over the small lake, past the statue that George I gave him of himself. The park is beautifully landscaped in the eighteenth-century style, with wide vistas and the great masses of trees that are the chief charm of this part of the county. It often suggests an English garden according to Lenôtre; and the rustic theatre, rather mangled, with its temple, its avenues and terraces, with the long lake and the summer-house, are also in the French taste. The trees are magnificent, the most impressive being the aisle of huge beeches called the cathedral. Here lived the third Duke with Lavinia Fenton, the first Polly of the *Beggar's Opera*. Joseph Wharton, future Head Master of Winchester, went with him to the south of France in order to marry him to her as soon as his duchess died, but she was so long about it that he had to come home.

NORTH of Basingstoke are some interesting villages among the hills towards the Berkshire border, to which you may wander through typical unspoilt country, once you are free of the meshes of the town. First there is Sherborne St. John. The church has a good south porch with a wooden sundial and a request to pray for those who caused it to be made in 1533. The pulpit is Caroline, with tester, and on a three-sided reading-desk are the three volumes of Foxe's *Book of Martyrs*. The modern tower, with its ugly copper spire, soon becomes a landmark. In the Brocas chapel are some good brasses, notably one of a Brocas lady with veiled Edward IV head-dress.

The Brocases were lords of Beaurepaire for five centuries. Under Henry III the manor was Crockerel Hulle, later Clotely. In 1353 it was bought by Sir Bernard Brocas, to whom the owner was heavily in debt. The De Brocases were Gascons and when the French seized Gascony they came to England. Three brothers were brought up at the court of Edward II, where the Gascon, Piers Gaveston, was all powerful. Bernard, the priest, vicar of St. Nicholas, Guildford, was the lawyer and business man of the family, often employed by the king. His brother John, Master of the Horse, was one of Edward III's right-hand men. He fought at Crécy at the head of a force raised by himself, was knighted after the battle of Sluys and settled near Basingstoke. His heir, Sir Bernard, was the best of the family. He was a friend of the Black Prince and a supporter of William of Wykeham. Edward III allowed him to impark the 280 acres of Beaurepaire. He was even a suitor for/the Fair Maid of Kent after he had divorced his first wife. When she married the Black Prince, he consoled himself with a rich widow, a Des Roches of Roche Court, Fareham, who brought him great estates and the hereditary Mastership of the Royal Buckhounds, which long remained in the family. He was a no less loyal servant to Richard II, as was his son, Sir Bernard, who was beheaded at Tyburn for taking part in a last desperate rising against Henry IV.

The branches stuck together and intermarried. Under Elizabeth there was a notorious black sheep, Sir Pexsail, who was charged with forgery and riot and in 1613 did open penance at St. Paul's Cross in a white sheet, with a stick in his hand, ' for secret and notorious adulteries with divers women '. After it, says Stowe, he went ' with thirty men in scarlet that waited upon him to the Lord Mayor to demand a dinner '. In the Civil War Beaurepaire was held for the king and the heir was found dead mysteriously at Oxford, but there was also, as often, a Roundhead branch.

In 1825 that noted sportsman Nimrod, Mr. Apperley, took up farming at Beaurepaire, but the venture was so disastrous that he retired to Boulogne. ' I have known what it is to repose upon a bed of roses, and, like most of my kind, I have languished upon a bed of thorns, but to ride a good hunter over a bed of flints is a misery which was reserved for me till I came to Hampshire.' Hence he hunted there as little as possible. In his day the country was even more wooded, for he complains that the number of coverts help the foxes, as do the large hedgerows, which enable him to turn back unperceived upon the hounds.

There is no more attractive or more interesting house in Hampshire than the Vyne. Of mellow, Tudor red brick, it stands out, long and low, clearly visible from the road, in a gently undulating valley, amid its lawns and gardens and its ample park. Most people know it best from Horace Walpole, who gave his friend John Chute the eagles that still flank the entrance. There are Roman remains in the neighbourhood. At the Conquest it went to Hugh De Port, and a chantry chapel was founded there in the twelfth century. When Adam De Port inherited the St. John estates, he kept it as a hunting-lodge. It passed to the Sandys under Richard II : the first Lord Sandys rebuilt it. William Sandys was a Tudor man, who began life under Henry VII and, though he was not one of Henry VIII's favourite ' scant, well-born gentlemen ', his career was typical. In 1512 Sir William was keeper of the ordnance at Fontarabia, when Henry was allied with Spain; then Commissioner for the Field of the Cloth of Gold; later Treasurer of Caláis, distinguishing himself greatly in the French wars. In 1523 he became Baron Sandys of the Vyne and then Lord Chamberlain. He ' much amended his estate by marrying Marjorie Bray ', heiress of Sir John Bray, and cousin of·Sir Reginald Bray, another Tudor man, who was architect of Henry VII's chapel and of St. George's Chapel, Windsor.

Lord Sandys so translated and augmented the Vyne, says Leland, ' and beside builded a fair Base Court, that it became one of the principal houses in goodly building in all Hamptonshire '. The entrance was then by a bridge over the Wey brook or Sher, a tributary of ' the Loddon slow ', which was here widened, into the court. To him it owes the chapel with its handsome oak seats, its gallery and screen, and its beautiful tiles—' the most heavenly chapel in the world ' to Horace Walpole. In his dilettante way he ' carried down incense and mass books, and we had most Catholic enjoyment of the Chapel '. In the fine east window are portraits of Margaret of Scotland, Henry VII, Catherine of Aragon and Lord Sandys. This glass is said to have been hidden in the brook during the Commonwealth, when Waller occupied the Vyne to ' make it a bridle ' to Basing House.

Sandys was very unhappy about the divorce of Catherine of Aragon, but he welcomed Anne Boleyn at the Vyne in 1531, when the keeper received 13/4 as a tip from the king and the Lord Chamberlain 10/-, ' for bringing a stag to the Vine which the king had stricken before in Wolmer Forest '. Lord Sands [*sic*] appears in *Henry VIII* flirting with Anne Boleyn.

Enjoying to the last the favour of the king, he died at Calais in 1540 and was buried in his Holy Ghost chapel at Basingstoke.

The third Lord Sandys was involved in the Essex rebellion, but escaped with a short imprisonment and the huge fine of £1,000. In that year he entertained Henri IV's ambassador, who came to announce his marriage to Marie dei Medici, with a suite of 400 while Elizabeth was at Basing House. The Vyne was ' furnished with hangings and plate from the Tower and Hampton Court, and with seven score beds and furniture ' gladly lent locally at two days' notice. The fifth peer was mortally wounded at Cheriton.

In 1644 Sandys was obliged to sell it and retire to Mottisfont, where the family soon died out. It was bought by Challoner Chute, of great wit and of stately port, as Vandyke's portrait shows him, a lawyer who won universal respect for his pluck in defending his clients during the troubles. Being a moderate man, he was made Speaker of Richard Cromwell's Parliament of 1659, but died the same year. The Vyne is pretty much as he left it. He pulled down the court and built the stately portico behind, as well as the domed summer-house. In particular he replaced the mullioned windows with sashes, a novelty from Holland which gives the house a lightness and airiness one does not associate with Tudor mansions. The two long, graceful galleries, notably the upper oak gallery, are delightful. The linen panels are ornamented with the

arms of noted Tudors, such as Bishop Fox, Wolsey and
Catherine of Aragon, which show that it was finished by
1523. The beautiful panelled ceilings, white with gold
designs, are among the most attractive features of the
rooms, as in the library with its Vandykes and its striking
portrait of the Speaker's grandparents. And the contents
are admirably in keeping.

The Vyne owes its handsome staircase, as well as the
memorial to the Speaker in the tomb chamber from Vandyke's portrait, to the taste of John Chute, which saved
him from carrying out some of the wild suggestions of
Walpole, such as the two towers and the Roman theatre.
At last he gave up advising, though he admitted that
hitherto Chute 'has done nothing with his estate—but
good'. A small panelled room is called the Strawberry
Parlour, because it was kept for Walpole. The road was
such that in October ' you will find it difficult to persuade
me to accompany you there on stilts '. Chute's death was
a real blow to Walpole. A bachelor like himself, he shared
all his hobbies. Gray was also at the Vyne.

The Vyne won fame of a different kind at the end of
the century from the Vyne hunt, founded by William
Chute, a noted character and sportsman. He liked small
hounds, and put up ' *Multum in parvo* ' over his kennels.
Calvert's picture, now at Farleigh Wallop, shows a meet
with the Duke of Wellington and a number of local sports-
men. The Duke sometimes gave £400 to the Vyne. Chute
left money to support the hunt so long as it kept his name.

No one appreciated our interest in things in general that
day more than our charioteer from Basingstoke, who told
us that he had taken only two parties sightseeing in ten
years of driving.

To Silchester also I went by Bramley, Silchester, with
its furzy heath of 200 acres, over which in its September
purple Queen Elizabeth rode with some of the ' ancient

gentlemen civilly educated and who live in great amity together' when they welcomed her to their 'county pleasant of soil and full of delights for princes', as she complimented them on her way to Basing House. A brilliant pageant it must have been. Good country it is up on the Berkshire border, with the cattle over the tall hedges of the twisting lanes, the fields here and there being marled, as they were before the coming of the Romans. We took the road to the south of Calleva, where a sad massacre of noble trees was in progress, and turned up into the Roman Silchester-Winchester road, passing the woods of Rampier copse.

Experts were agreed that this was Calleva Atrebatum, the capital of the important Gallo-British tribe that spread down into the Thames valley, when the finding of a stone inscribed Calleva, the town in the wood, clinched the point. On this strong, commanding position, between Pamber Forest and the end of the Andraedswald, was a Celtic camp, the vallum of which, still 15 feet deep, is best seen in Rampier copse. Here the Atrebates had their capital till the Romans, probably in the great movement initiated by Agricola, induced them to lay it out and fortify it in the style of their conquerors. Nothing now remains except the complete circuit of some two miles of wall inside the British rampart, enclosing about 100 acres of corn land; but an impressive sight it is away in the country on this lonely height, and the impression is heightened by the shock of surprise at finding not a trace of a ruin inside. To the north the wall is at one point 17 feet high : the original height was 20 feet. The bastions at regular intervals probably carried towers. It was backed by a mound of earth.

The town was small. Only some 80 houses have been found scattered within the enclosure, though there were doubtless a number of huts for the poorer Britons. The houses were of the villa type, the rooms opening into a corridor along the front, with perhaps another behind. The larger houses might have from 12 to 20 rooms, being built with two wings round a court. The walls inside were brightly coloured. Even the poorest generally had one mosaic floor. They were all central heated.

The heart of Calleva was the roomy forum, where the roads to the four gates met, with public offices and shops, arcaded both behind and in front, on three sides, and a basilica, an arcaded Town Hall, capable of seating 4,000 people, on the other. On such a scale did Rome build. There was also an hotel, with two courtyards, a number of rooms and a bath-house. The people of Calleva went to the public baths, to which strangers were not admitted. Two small temples were under the modern church and the farm. There was also a tiny Christian church, the only one of the kind found in these islands, near the forum, a basilica not more than 42 feet long, of the fourth century. Dyeing seems to have been the chief industry, probably owing to the sheep on the downs. A dull, comfortable little town, Calleva.

Outside the walls, across the road from London to Bath, the Devil's Way, is the small amphitheatre, now covered with trees, from which the tourist is warned off. Here Calleva indulged its taste for sport, boxing, perhaps, or the baiting of a badger or a bull by British dogs, the fame of which had reached Imperial Rome; or a cock-fight, for which the weakness of the Britons was notorious. There is a good model of a cock in the Reading museum. Chariot-races, in spite of the British war-chariots, or gladiatorial shows were luxuries unknown in such a backwater.

Calleva was overwhelmed by no disaster. It simply decayed and was abandoned, becoming a quarry for the district, which was so remote that the walls escaped. The land belonged to the Duke of Wellington and the excavations were carried out under his auspices, the ground being recovered. The finds are in the Reading museum. The site must have been under the plough for centuries and it is a comfort to find it just as when Camden knew it, even to Onion's hole, through which he had difficulty in climbing, owing to the change in the level of the ground. For the Romans had become crystallized locally into the giant Onion, and the coins picked up were Onion's pennies. Is the corn on the lines of the walls below still inferior to that sown in the open spaces? It is pleasant to lunch under the walls, say by the sluice-gate on the east, in the absolute peace of the country, on a fine day in November, looking over the wooded plains and the down ridges.

The only buildings within the circle are the church and the farm, once the manor-house, which were doubtless built of material quarried from Calleva. William de Owe, who got into trouble with William Rufus, held Silchester in Domesday. The Early English church, by the farm and the pond, near which is a good piece of trench, has a fine wooden tower. Its best feature is the chancel screen, with the beautifully carved angels along the top. There is also a carved canopy over the pulpit, with its Elizabethan panels.

Monks Sherborne is reached by the quiet lane to the west. The much-restored church has a charming Edward III open wooden porch with a Norman door. Here again, as in many Hampshire churches, we are reminded of the opposition between the Puritan preacher and the ritualism of Laud in the pulpit and the altar rails, which have, unfortunately, been moved, both of them Stuart.

In Pamber, for all this wooded district was once part of Pamber forest, stands the picturesque church, with its magnificent square Norman tower, well back from the road amid the fields. It is all that remains of the priory which gave Monks Sherborne its name, though the moat can easily be traced. This was, of course, De Port land, and Hugh's son Henry under Henry I founded a Benedictine priory here, a cell of the Abbey of St. Vigor of Cérissy (Bayeux), near the home of the De Ports. Such foundations, which linked their recent conquest with the Duchy, were encouraged by the Norman kings. At the confiscation of the alien priories, Edward IV gave it to God's House, Southampton, which belonged to Queen's College, Oxford. The College turned the fine Norman choir—all that is left—of the chapel into a parish church for the scattered forest village of Pamber. There is an interesting wooden effigy of a knight, cross-legged, late twelfth century, and a very early bier.

It was Saturday. As we passed the Vyne a couple of men got into the bus with a huge trout, and then we realized that we were in the fisherman's county. The story of the struggle, during which the chief hero was nearly pulled into the water, was listened to breathlessly and commented on with expert knowledge by women as well as men, and eagerly asked for by the little knots we swept up at the stops.

Soon the manor-house of Bramley, once again a single dwelling, faced us as we came up to the crossroads, half-timbered, with delicate barge-boards under the gables of the projecting wings, and the original doors. The inside is said to be worthy of it. Yes, a delightful house, and so placed you can enjoy it to the full. De Port again and a good village as you turn into it, with a sufficient sprinkling of the right Hampshire cottages. It has just the kind of aisleless Norman church it should have, in spite of the ugly Brocas chapel with their Moor's Head crest, the crest that so intrigued Sir Roger de Coverley when he saw it on the tomb of Sir Bernard in Westminster Abbey. Nor is the Caroline tower a misfit. On the north wall, as always, is a great rough St. Christopher with mermaids gazing up to him from the water he is crossing. St. Christopher is not common in Hampshire. This north wall is Norman with Norman lights. There is also an interesting slaying of Becket. In Miss Mitford's day no road went within a mile of Bramley. When the lady of the manor visited her only neighbour, she drove right across the farmers' plough-land in her coach and four.

From Bramley the road runs down past the green of Sherfield Loddon. To the church, entirely rebuilt, Cromwell is said locally to have given all the bells from Basing that were not cracked. It was a royal manor, and from 1275 to 1603 was held by the sergeantry of marshalling the king's meretrices, now held to be washerwomen, dismembering condemned prisoners and measuring the gallons and bushels of the royal household. Truly, a strange medley of services, such as could have been devised only by an enemy.

North-east from Bramley, past Fair Oak Green, through the richly wooded, undulating Loddon country, you reach Strathfieldsay. Like Strathfield Turgis, it gets its name from the Roman road that runs from London by Silchester to Bath. This road—strata, street, paved—has taken over the job of the Loddon, which here forms the eastern boundary of the parish, running through the park. It separates Hampshire from Berkshire. Once it was Strathfield-Stoteville from the family that owned it, becoming Strathfield-Say when Sir William de Say acquired it. Under Richard II it went to the Dabridgecourts. In 1729 it was sold to Edward Pitt, son of Sir William Pitt, Comptroller of the Household. Later George Pitt became Lord Rivers of Strathfieldsay.

The estate was given to the Duke of Wellington by the

nation for the service of a tricolour flag presented to the king on June 18th, Waterloo day, which is hung in the Guard-room of Windsor Castle. There are some goodly trees in the park of 1,500 acres, including a fine elm avenue to the north. Under an oak in his own paddock is the grave of Wellington's charger Copenhagen, who was buried with military honours. The low, unimpressive house of yellow brick—'.like a great cottage '—mostly Queen Anne, is near the Loddon, which has been widened to form several lakes. In the hall are the Roman eagle, probably belonging to a legion, and two of the best mosaic pavements from Calleva, which was excavated at the Duke's expense.

The brick church (1784) in the shape of a Greek cross is most unattractive. It has some Dabridgecourt monuments from the old church, a handsome one to Sir William Pitt and his lady, and an inscription near the organ to John Howsman, rector (1626), ' who continued a paynfull Preacher by the space of 41 years '. This brings you nearer to the Carolines than all their altar-rails and pulpits.

From the park you come out by the avenue of Welling-tonias to the huge column surmounted by the Duke in Field-Marshal's uniform, which seems to have strayed from Trafalgar Square to this region of heath and woodland. To the south lies Heckfield, a De Port manor, beyond its wooded heath. Here the father of Mrs. Trollope, the mother of Anthony, who began her prolific career as a novelist when over fifty, was vicar. Here, wrote Miss Mitford to her adored Miss Barrett in Wimpole Street, on ' a common dotted with cottages and a large piece of water backed by wooded hills, with the tall trees of Strathfieldsay Park behind ', while a cricket match was in progress, she enjoyed one of those flashes of peace that come to the most harassed in surroundings contrasting completely with their everyday life. She also stood in the crowd to witness the departure of the queen from Strathfieldsay and noticed the relief of the Duke at being at last delivered from his royal guest.

I turned east from the park by Heckfield Place, lying back from the heath. Here was the home of Shaw Lefevre, Viscount Eversley, a noted Speaker. He is buried in Heckfield church, which boasts a Crusading alms-box of the thirteenth century. It was early November, a still November, the trees yet wearing their leaves of every shade of red and brown. Those on the ground were running races in the breeze or drifting helplessly, like unsubstantial ghosts. Certainly the oak is more varied in hue, but, in spite of Gilpin, I like a solid bank of yellow-brown beech in autumn uniform.

CHAPTER XII: *Aldershot, Bramshill and Eversley*

IF you enter Hampshire by the road or railway from
Woking, or even through Aldershot, there is nothing
to remind you that you have left Surrey. This barren
greensand country is common to both counties and, after
being left alone from time immemorial, it is now being
covered with desirable villa residences.

Fate willed it that my formal call upon Aldershot for the
purposes of this book should be the last trip I had to take,
when war had already broken out. We seized the chance
of another spin along the Hog's Back before the rationing
of petrol. Down the turn to the great army centre were
squads and companies of marching khaki, not, alas! on
manœuvres, as they were when I began the book, but in full
kit with steel helmets.

Hampshire, with Portsmouth and Aldershot, is the headquarters both of our army and our navy, and Aldershot has
the endless streets of small houses one associates with a
garrison town. War time though it was, there did not seem
to be more khaki about than usual.

Till 1854 Aldershot was a remote Hampshire village
with a church, a green, a couple of large houses and a few
cottages. The manor belonged to the Tichborne family
in the seventeenth and eighteenth centuries and there are
seventeenth-century Tichborne monuments in the church.
The place is healthy and the Government bought land there
for a large camp, which is crossed by the Basingstoke canal.
The huge statue of Wellington in the South Camp was
formerly over the arch at Hyde Park corner. Aldershot is
now a large and flourishing town, but it owes its interest
entirely to its military importance.

Farnborough is virtually a part of Aldershot, from which

it is separated by the Basingstoke canal, and the North Camp is in the parish. It, too, was a lonely village and the last of the great prize-fights, the one between Henan and Sayers, took place here, down by the Blackwater, which forms the boundary, so that they could slip over into Surrey, if surprised by the Hampshire police. Dick Turpin is said to have haunted the great common between it and Farnham, and the landlord of the Dick inn to have been his friend. Did the name give rise to the legend? The church is in the old village, on high ground, in the park, near the station. It has been ruthlessly restored and enlarged, but the fifteenth-century porch is good. It is interesting primarily for the twelfth-century paintings on the north wall, representing St. Eugenia and St. Agnes, the only St. Eugenia known in England. This painting of her patron saint was discovered while the Empress Eugénie lived at Farnborough Hill and interested her greatly. Outside the south door are two macabre mid-eighteenth century tombstones, one with a skull and a skeleton appearing under the raised lid of a coffin, the other with a skull and an hour glass. At Farnborough is the Benedictine church which the Empress built in 1887 over the mausoleum of Napoleon III and her son, the Prince Imperial, who was killed in the Zulu War. It is modelled on the tomb of Napoleon in Les Invalides.

Beyond the Long Valley and the Aldershot Commons you are in Fleet, prosperous and modern, the red villas scattered among the pines and the silver birches, a typical product of this district. The railway cuts its great pond in two. Then the road runs through woods or deep-treed hedges to Hartley Row, on the Reading road, with a large common and a Georgian house or two. You escape up a lane passing Hazely Heath. Bramshill dominates everything, standing high on its hill, so different from other houses of the period tucked away in the valleys. The

stately gateway ushers you up the long oak avenue and over
the pond. The house is built of beautifully mellowed rose-
pink brick with stone dressings. The south-east front with
its loggia and its balustrades and terraces is, to my mind,
the most attractive. Bramshill is, of course, a famous specimen of Jacobean architecture, but the elaborate stonework
of the main front is distinctly heavy. Here, too, a good
loggia extends from the porch and terraces, giving a
wonderful view ' looking out far and wide over the rich
lowlands '. The gardens are charmingly walled, but it is
sad to see one of them filled with the commonplace poly-
antha rose, which does not even smell. Surely a house of
that period, without a modern addition, should have roses
of Provence and the like.

Bramshill was given by Edward VI to the Marquis of
Winchester. In 1602 Lord Zouche bought it and built the
house, they say, for Henry, Prince of Wales. Hence the
great Prince of Wales' feathers, with *Ich Dien*, over the
main front. James I was here in 1620 and next year Archbishop Abbot, who had come to consecrate the chapel,
accidentally killed a careless keeper while shooting at a
deer. The decaying trunk of the oak by which he was
killed still survives. There are 1,000 acres of park and some
magnificent timber, notably the Scotch firs, the first in
England, said to have been planted by James I himself.
Bramshill has belonged to the Copes since 1700. The old
house was built round a courtyard and of this not a little
is incorporated in the new one, which also encloses a court.
The great drawing-room has a beautifully moulded ceiling
and some tapestries from designs by Rubens. It is one of
the three Hampshire claimants to the Mistletoe Bough
legend.

But a mile and a half away, through lanes, is peaceful
Mattingley with its quaint half-timbered cottage church,
where the bricks have mellowed to much the same colour

as those of Bramshill. It is fifteenth century and is credited to Bishop Waynflete. The aisles are marked off by fine timber columns. The chancel with its amusing little window is altogether original. On the west wall is an embroidered altar-piece of red velvet with gold fringes dated 1667.

Bramshill village is at the top of the park, which the road skirts, trees everywhere, the pines increasing in number. Then comes Eversley, a long village straggling down the road. The Blackwater, marking the Berkshire boundary, lies to the left, the road thither running through beautiful woods. Here is a modern suburb, suggesting Reading, but the trees along the bank show that the river has changed little since Kingsley used to throw a fly over it for an hour of an afternoon as a relaxation from his unremitting work. The Blackwater takes its name from the peat through which it flows. It joins the Loddon beyond Bramshill.

There is a pond by the turning to the church, which is virtually in Bramshill Park. The best thing near it is the roomy old Hampshire farm with its great half-timbered barn. The church, with its garish late Georgian screen, is not very attractive, either inside or out. Even the brick tower, which eighteenth-century Hampshire usually manages successfully, has failed to come off. Its redeeming feature is the finely-sculptured restful figure of Dame Mariane Cope (1852) on the tomb in the chancel. But there is the two-decker pulpit where Kingsley preached from 1842 to 1875 and where he was never known to stammer. In the churchyard is the pleasingly simple grave of himself and his wife, with the Cornish cross, near the gate to the rectory, close to which the road now passes.

The slope of the garden with its huge tree made the water and the damp most troublesome till he drained it. As the house was empty, I could wander round wondering which was the study where he worked, the swing-door of which he was never known to shut. Most of his work was thought out as he paced the little green grass plot in front of it, no matter what the weather, smoking a clay pipe. The strong, sensitive, whiskered face is not often seen now, but it belonged to one of the most attractive of the bigger Victorians, who would have sympathized with all that is best in the world to-day. An ideal companion he would make into this district, richly wooded even for bosky Hampshire. And how beautiful it can look under snow, with all around the solemn winter stillness of Milton's *Nativity Ode*. In Kingsley's day five-sixths of the parish consisted of firs and moor—' those delicious self-sown firs '. How he loved it all. ' I got home at 4 this morning after a delicious walk—a poem in itself. I never saw such a sight before as the mists on the heaths and valleys, and never knew what a real bird-chorus was ': and after seventeen years, ' It does look too blessed for a man to spend his life in.'

Eversley was a rough parish when Kingsley took it over, though not as rough as it had been, when every man there, being sprung of a long lineage of heathers and poachers, poached wood and river, and the women remembered the muffs and tippets of pheasant-feathers their husbands and lovers gave them in their young days. It was because of such weaknesses in his flock that the rector refused to carry a gun or become a magistrate. ' The clod of these parts is a thoroughly good fellow nevertheless. Civil, contented, industrious, and often very handsome; a far shrewder fellow, too—owing to his dash of wild forest blood, gipsy, highwayman and what not—than his bullet-headed and flaxen-polled cousin, the pure South Saxon of the chalk downs ', as a very little acquaintance helped him to realize. This view is echoed by W. H. Hudson.

And his parishioners soon learnt to appreciate their genuine, manly, sport-loving parson, who could swing a flail or turn his swathe with the mowers and was unremitting in his attentions when they were sick. There was not a grown-up labourer or woman in the parish who could read or write when he came. The old rector, under whom collections were made in a wooden bowl, would often send at the last moment to tell the few worshippers waiting in the church that there would be no service. When Kingsley suggested monthly communions, the churchwardens consented only on condition that the rector supplied the wine. Eversley is divided into three villages, each with its green; in the one by the cross is the cottage where Kingsley lived when curate. He was given the living by Sir John Cope after a petition from the parishioners.

Farther down the road is Yateley. The church, standing behind its jolly green, is one of the most interesting hereabouts, large and well preserved. You enter by a good Norman doorway. The tower is supported by a curious structure of beams, such as I have not seen elsewhere. In the north wall of the chancel is a blocked doorway which excavations seem to prove to have been the entrance to an anchorite's cell. The old tiles in the chancel are curious, a hound chasing a stag and the like, and fragments of similar ones were found there. But the treasure of the church is the really beautiful Yateley cup, secured in a case, at the east end of the south aisle. Crystal and silver-gilt of the end of the seventeenth century, probably Dutch, it was presented in 1675. Unfortunately it has been broken. The East window is by Morris and Burne Jones. The Dog and Partridge inn was once the church house : later it was divided between a public-house and an alms-house, surely a unique combination.

Darley Green is said, I know not with what truth, to have been named after parson Darley, who lived and preached at Eversley, but was a gentleman of the road by night and was duly hung upon the green.

CHAPTER XIII: *Basingstoke to Andover. Steventon, Laverstoke and Weyhill*

FROM Basingstoke the road runs through Church Oakley, the home of Archbishop Warham, who rebuilt the much-restored church in the pretty village a little to the south. His arms are over the west door, and there is a monument to his parents. To the north of the road, up one of the lovely lanes that take you over the ridge and then on to the high downs by Kingsclere, is Malshanger, which was bought by Warham, who came of local farmer stock. He was Keeper of the Rolls and Bishop of London under Henry VII and VIII. To-day the great octagonal tower is all that remains of his work. The present house was built by Lord Chancellor Thurlow in 1806. It belongs to the Portals.

Then comes Deane Gate and the turning by the inn, where the Janeite hesitates. The road on the right leads to Deane, the living which was bought for Jane Austen's father and in which he was succeeded by his son James. But the old rectory has gone and the church has been rebuilt, so we may safely turn left down the broad wooded valley to the railway arch beyond which lies Steventon. It is a scattered village, still small, but with few cottages that can have known the Austens. The lane was then a mere cart-track, and when the family moved, Mrs. Austen made the journey on a feather-bed placed upon some soft articles in the wagon conveying the household goods. In winter ruts would be filled up, if many friends with carriages were expected. The living was given George Austen by the Knights of Chawton in addition to Deane, which was bought for him, and here Jane was born in 1775. The rectory has gone, pulled down by brother James, but it stood in a field along the road to the church, below its more splendid successor on the hill. All that remains is the wash-house pump—one imagines Nanny Littlewart using it—with traces of a terrace. Every one knows what you want almost before you can ask. Up the field to the church ran the path ' between hedgerows, under whose shelter the earliest primroses, anemones and wild hyacinths were to be found '. And round about are some fine nut-hedges, as Jane calls them.

The road takes you up to the manor-house in its ample park and the thirteenth-century church, hardly changed, built of Isle of Wight stone. The key is a foot long. It has a pleasing pointed arch to the chancel, where are memorials to James, who was rector for half a century, and his first wife. A great-grand-niece has recently put up a brass recording Jane's connexion with the church. It is on a hill with wide prospects over to the north downs and across the well-treed valley to the west.

This is Jane's real home. Here she lived for 27 years, fainting away when she heard that her father was resigning, and here she was formed in the ' confined locality ' she loved in her books. ' Three or four families in a country village is the very thing to work on,' she wrote to a niece about her story. Here she wrote her first three novels and lived the life she brings before us in her letters with her own large family, her father and his pupils, her clever mother with the aristocratic nose and the endless visiting among relations. The Austens were cousins of the Knights, the absentee lords of the manor, and, though the house was occupied by the Digweeds, they were treated almost as their representatives. At Ashe, the turning to which you pass on the way, were the Lefroys, Tom and Jane's great friend, Mrs. Lefroy, who, to her profound grief, was killed in a riding accident. And here she joins hands with Miss Mitford, her junior by ten years, whose mother, the daughter of a former rector, left a character

L

sketch of her as a girl which scandalizes her admirers. At Deane were the Howards, and from old John Howard Fielding, who was often at Oakley Hall, may have taken hints for Squire Weston.

The Basingstoke balls were the greatest events of Jane's home life, and for these she would sometimes stay with the Bigg-Withers at Manydown Park. The Withers held the manor under Edward III, and from it William of Wykeham bought the timber for repairing the roof of Winchester Cathedral. Then there were the theatricals in the barn, where her cousin, Mme. de Feuillide, the widow of a guillotined French count, soon to become her sister-in-law, reigned supreme. This is the life she fixes for us, the life that seemed to vanish with the old Assemblies. Yet, except for Portsmouth in *Mansfield Park*, the scenes of the novels are never in Hampshire, though they were all written in the county.

Through North Waltham the road goes on to Dummer, with its interesting church. It has a fourteenth-century pulpit, good Charles II altar-rails and gallery balustrade, and above all the unique great blue wooden canopy studded with gilt bosses over the chancel arch, beneath which was the rood. It is said to be fifteenth century. George Whit-field served his first curacy at Dummer and ' mourned like a dove ' for Oxford and his friends there. The Dummers and Pophams were lords of the manor.

' I, William At-More, alias Dummer call'd, do here
    entomb'd lie,
And lordship this and of the church the patronage
    had I.
Mine ancestors me long before were owners of the
    same,
Obtain'd by match with Dummer's heirs, whereof
    they took the name.'

So runs the inscription on the tomb where William, born in 1508, Comptroller of the Chamber of London for half a century, still kneels.

The house, dating from the sixteenth century, is largely Georgian, with some Jacobean panelling. It is close to the church, a striking building. It was the home of the Austens' friends, the Terrys. Stephen, a reforming landlord of the Coke of Norfolk type, was a great figure in the hunting field in the days of Assheton Smith and William Chute. Hunting was the chief social activity of the old squires. The hounds then generally left the kennels in the dark, reaching the covers soon after daybreak. There was no regular division of the country. They were taken to any point where there might be foxes.

Assheton Smith, by the way, had his princely establishment, where he kept 50 hunters in perfect condition, at Tedworth, beyond Appleshaw, on the Wiltshire border, now a great camp region. He built Tedworth Park and transformed the rough district into good hunting country, where the farmers soon ' began to preserve foxes as if they were prize pigs '.

To the north lies Kempshott House in its great park, which the Regent had for a hunting-box. Mrs. Fitzherbert, who did the honours, is said to have superintended the laying out and arrangement of it. There were a number of good horses, but the stable was badly managed. In 1791 Kempshott was full of French émigrés, who turned out with their horns round them for a great stag-hunt given for them by the Prince. To Kempshott also the Regent brought his wife, Caroline of Brunswick, on her honeymoon.

Woodmancott, where a Roman villa has been found, lies south. You go through it to the down beyond. We drove thither on a quiet December afternoon. It is good to knit up the ravels of a summer tour in this way. This down land, the bare trees fretted against the sky above the dull browns of the fields, looks hardly more beautiful in June. Up the hill we went after a great lorry load of hay. At the top of the down the view came suddenly, a view that one does not forget, across the winter country, quiet and sober under the grey, filming sky to Winchester and the downs right across to Woolbury above Stockbridge. The distances were too vague in the late afternoon to be sure of more.

After Church Oakley comes unattractive Overton, a great place in the coaching days, the first stage out of London, when the Poyntz Hotel at the crossroads, where are now the schools, did a roaring trade. Here, too, were the kennels of the Vyne Hunt.

Beyond lies a beautifully wooded section of the road. Thanks to the Portals, Laverstoke seems to stand in a huge park. It is watered by that famous trout-stream, the Test, which began to keep us company at Overton. The Test is a stream with variations. In wet years it flows steadily from Church Oakley, but, after the way of chalk streams, it often vanishes into swallow-holes at Deane, and its regular source is near Ashe House.

Laverstoke is the home of the Portals, descended from a notable Huguenot family of Toulouse. The father was a Conseiller du Roi at Poitiers at the time of the Revocation of the Edict of Nantes, when they all fled to their château. The children were hidden in an oven for 2 nights and 2 days while the dragoons butchered the rest of the family. They tried the oven door, but luckily it stuck. Helped by some servants, the children walked to Bordeaux, disguised as peasants. Here friends hid them in barrels under a load of full wine-casks, and they successfully passed the cordon of troops, though they tapped the barrels to make sure they were full. They escaped on an English ship. At Southampton they were welcomed by their fellow Huguenots.

Henri de Portal found work in the Huguenot paper-mill at South Stoneham. He impressed Sir William Heathcote of Hursley, who readily leased him Bere Mill, near Whitchurch. So well did he do that by 1718 he had leased Laverstock Mill as well. He invented a method of watermarking the paper, and in 1727, when Sir Gilbert Heathcote, uncle of his friend, was Governor of the Bank of England, he was given the contract for making the paper for the banknotes, which the family has held ever since. Paper money was one of Cobbett's pet bugbears, and he tells us gleefully that in his day the park was known as Rag Hall.

Hyde Abbey held the manor till the Reformation. The Tudor House, pulled down by the Portals, is described in 1636 as ' seated harde by the water, but so high from it that it is not nor can be in any whit annoyed by it ', in country excellent for hawking and hunting. The Test is but small, ' but a cleare streame such as should seem to have good trout '. The Portals have owned it since 1759, and the church in the park is their mortuary chapel. The old church at Freefolk, built in 1265, still sometimes used, stands down by the Test, flowing clear and pure with its grebes and dabchicks among the water-meadows, on the other side of the bridge, beyond the rectory garden. I could only peep through the windows, but this tiny chapel gives a good idea of what many a village church that was pulled down to make room for a larger one must have been like.

If you are going on by bus towards Andover about closing time, you will find yourself in the stream of girls from the mills, all knitting, all hatless, some as dark as Italians.

Whitchurch, a mile farther on, was busy in coaching days, as our Salisbury road here meets the road from Winchester to Newbury and Oxford, which runs through the gap in the downs. Charles I stayed there before the second battle of Newbury in 1644. The Great Western also has a tryst with the Southern at Andover. The White Hart, dating from Queen Anne, is the inn, and here Kingsley once came to fish with Froude, but was let down by his brother-in-law. Whitchurch, the Witbury of *Two Years Ago*, is still a charming little town, which formerly sent two members to Westminster. The one thing to be set off against the merciless restoration of the church is the discovery of the tombstone of the Saxon lady Frithburga (Pledge of Peace) with its Latin inscription in Saxon lettering and the quaint bust of Christ above. Doubtless it came from the church known to have been here in 800. The impressive tower, with its familiar great spire, is old and contains an original staircasing. The Portway crosses the Newbury road in this parish at Chapgate, clearly the old gathering-place of the merchants with their pack-horses.

Just outside Whitchurch are the north gates of Hurstbourne Park, a noble park of 1,000 acres, running right down to Hurstbourne Priors in the Bourne valley. In a moment of enthusiasm Kingsley called it the finest park in the south of England. The manor belonged first to Hyde Abbey, whence the name of the village, then to the Bishops of Winchester, who held it till the Reformation. The Duke of Somerset had it till his attainder. In 1638 it was sold to Henry Wallop of Farleigh Wallop (of which John Wallop died, seized in 1486): his regicide son Robert died in the Tower. His grandson, after fighting at Oudenarde, visited Hanover on the grand tour, where the future George I took a fancy to him. Hence he became Earl of Portsmouth in 1743. His son married Newton's great-niece, thus coming into possession of the Newton manuscripts and his portrait by Kneller. These, with the collection of books on Hampshire, are now at Farleigh Wallop, the original home of the family, since Hurstbourne Park has been sold. So also is the noted flock of black, four-horned sheep, such as were kept in noblemen's parks in Spain, which are said to be descended from some wrecked in the Armada. The modern house—the old one was burnt down—stands high, with a glorious view out towards Bury Hill and Winchester.

A mile along the Winchester road from Whitchurch is Tufton, a tiny hamlet with an ideal village church standing away in the fields close to the Test. The small chancel arch is Saxon and in size all but one of the chancel lancets might be too. Facing the south door, as usual, are the remains of a painting of St. Christopher, never more needed than now, seeing that a prayer to him guarantees you against accidents for the day. Even the brick floor is in keeping. Tufton belonged to Wherwell, and Abbess Euphemia took it under her reforming wing, building the manor-house here.

In the fading light we went up on to the down, where the moon had just risen over the fields. Then the woods closed in and we enjoyed the evening peace of the unspoilt country to the Hurstbourne Tarrant corner.

To Andover you can go by well-named Longparish, when you will pass through Harewood Forest, where trees are now rare; or along the main road, when you will skirt it and enter Andover by the Ladies' Walk, which is off the road near the iron bridge. It is a good road, often wooded, with fine views here and there over the fields to the south from the downs, but the cars have driven the ladies, when not in them, to more secluded haunts.

Andover is an important road-junction and agricultural centre at the crossing of the Anton, and the view up and down it from the bridge with the ducks by the chapel is perhaps the best this flourishing market-town has to offer. Still, there are some charming peeps into old Andover down yards in High Street, where all the fronts are modern. The Town Hall, like others in the south, is early nineteenth

century. Doubtless with the hill camps round, Andover
was well known to our Bronze Age forbears. There is no
proof that it was a Roman settlement, though it is just
south of the crossing of the roads to Salisbury and Winchester, but the sites of no less than 16 Roman buildings
and villas have been found within a radius of 6 miles of
it. With their large farms they continued to flourish long
after the decay of the towns, to the very end of the Roman
period. The old church was pulled down, except for the
Norman arch, now the entrance to the churchyard, where
there is a fragment of the wall of the small Benedictine
priory. Founded when the Conqueror gave the church to
the Abbey of St. Florent, Saumur, it was suppressed in 1441
and given to Winchester College, which still holds it.

Andover was often visited by the Saxon kings. It is
closely associated with Edgar's life as a lover, notably with
the story of his third wife, the fair Elfrida, daughter of the
Earl of Devon. Hearing of her beauty Edgar sent Ethelwold, Earl of Hampshire, to woo her for him. So overwhelmed was he by her charms, that he wooed and won
her himself, telling the king that she was not much to look
at. When Edgar came to visit him, Ethelwold bade her
disguise her beauty. Instead, she laid herself out to captivate him and was completely successful. Soon afterwards,
while hunting in Harewood Forest, Edgar stabbed the earl
in the back and married his widow. A monument marks
the traditional spot, Dead Man's Plack, and records the
legend, for it is nothing more. But the story of the many
loves of Edgar the Peaceful is not forgotten in Hampshire.
Wherwell is said to have been founded by Elfrida in expiation for her murder of his son by his first marriage, Edward,
to make way for her own Ethelred. But again her guilt is
doubtful. However, Winchester was the capital of his
flourishing kingdom and Andover his favourite hunting
seat. He it was who made Ethelwold, the great reformer

and refounder of English monasteries, Bishop of Winchester. Like Edgar, Ethelred held a witenagemot at Andover. Here he met Olaf of Norway, who had seized the Southampton coast with Sweyn of Denmark. Ethelred gave him rich presents and he was baptized by the Bishop of Winchester, who had escorted him. He kept his promise never to attack England again. Near Andover, too, Edmund Ironside fought a drawn battle with Cnut, the Dane.

The borough was royal demesne and often held by queens, as by Eleanor of Provence, who kept it even when a nun at Amesbury. Later it went to Catherine of Aragon, who stayed at the Angel inn, still there near the church, when she came to England. In the fourteenth century Andover had an iron market and important tanneries. Elizabeth gave it its charter. James II was here when he ordered a retreat on hearing of the landing of William of Orange. Here he was deserted by his son-in-law, Prince George. ' Is " *Est-il possible?* " gone too? After all, a good trooper would have been a greater loss.' And by the Duke of Ormond, who had also supped with him.

South of Andover in a beautifully wooded valley lies the delectable village of Upper Clatford. The view up and down the troutful tributary of the Test from the bridge, with the not uninteresting, though much restored church beyond, and a couple of men gathering water-cresses near by, compels you to linger. The church was given to the convent of Lire in Normandy by the Conqueror and here Roger, Earl of Arundel and Shrewsbury, gave Adeline the singer, of whom he was enamoured, a virgate of land. The manor ultimately went to Roger, Earl of March, and then to Edward IV. Henry VIII gave it to Lord Berners, the translator of Froissart, and his daughter.

At the top end of the village take the real untarred lane to the left up to the high down. On your right lies Bury

Hill, a well preserved round camp of a dozen acres, with a strong double rampart and deep ditches, at the end of a long chalk spur. It is among the easiest of these camps to visit and, though in places the firs are thick, the inner ditch is generally clear. Strengthened with palisades, it must have been a formidable defensive position. It commands wide views south to Danebury and beyond and to Quarley and the downs north.

The road goes on among the broad fields of a great Hampshire farm to Redrice. General Webb, the hero of Wynendael, planted the trees and avenues so as to represent the arrangement of Marlborough's men at Malplaquet.

We followed the fine avenue past St. John's Cross, then down into the valley, with the sun coming out just after a shower, by the farm, to Abbotts Ann, standing attractively down by the Pillhill brook. In the red-brick church built by Governor Pitt, ancestor of the great Pitts, who was lord of the manor, you will find the ' virgin crants ' of Ophelia. For here the custom lingers of carrying paper garlands at the funerals of young women—and also bachelors—of the parish ' reputed to have died virgins ', as Gilbert White cautiously puts it. Quite a number still hang high up in the church. The last case was in 1921. In White's day it had died out at Selborne, but he recollected ' to have seen the clerk's wife cutting in white paper the resemblances of gloves and ribbons to be twisted into knots and roses, to decorate these memorials of chastity '. The glove shape symbolized a challenge to any who might doubt the purity of the deceased.

From Abbotts Ann it is easy to make one's way through good country to Weyhill—more pleasant than to follow the main road from Andover. It stands at the top of a hill with wide views into the valleys and over to the glorious downs in every direction. If Weyhill is nothing but the fair—all that there is to see are the buildings and outhouses for the animals—it has none the less been from time immemorial at the centre of English life. No fewer than 8 roads or prehistoric tracks converge upon it, and here the Harroway meets the Portway. In the Roman villa at Appleshaw was unearthed that unique find of pewter vessels, one of them, marked with the Christian PAX symbol, being almost certainly a communion chalice.

Weyhill was one of the greatest of English fairs. We know nothing certain of its origin. Latterly it was primarily a sheep fair, and its importance when these downs were covered with flocks can be imagined. 'At Wy and Winchester I went to the fair,' says Piers Plowman. The village, on the Wiltshire border, is Penton Grafton and belonged to the wife of Edward the Confessor. On her death William gave it to the Abbey of Greistain, in Normandy, of which Grafton is said to be a corruption. In 1442 the Earl of Suffolk bestowed it on his foundation of Ewelme Hospital, God's House, at Oxford. At the Dissolution Edward VI granted it to his sister Elizabeth and with it seemingly the fair, for she complains, thus early, to Cecil of the attempt, among other evil doings of the paymaster 'of myne almeshouse, of Ewelme', to transfer the fair to Andover, to the great damage of her tenants at Weyhill.

It is still held on October 10th. It is difficult to realize the importance of these fairs right up to the coming of the railway, when there were no shops in the villages and stores had to be laid in when opportunity offered. Henry White, vicar of Fyfield, Gilbert's brother, bought his cheese at Andover in May and at Weyhill in October. Hence his concern to stop the holes in his ceiling through which the mice came after it. Once 'ye shelves behind ye kitchen fell with 21 cheeses . . . weight sufficient to have broken ye ablest head'; and we can believe him when brother Thomas sent him a 60-lb. Cheshire from London.

The sheep came first. In the early years of last century 150,000 would change hands in a day. After the sheep came the horses and lastly the hops. A special place was reserved for the ' Farnham row ', the best hops in England. The competition among the wagoners to get in first with their hops was like a race of the old tea-clippers. They would drive all night. Ribbons were given to the horses with the first load and the honour was much coveted. The day after the sales came the hiring fair for farm-hands all over the county.

Horning was the regular initiation ceremony for the newcomer; and horns, fastened to a cap fitting on the head, were kept at the two inns. This is the horning song, which the greenhorn had to sing:

' So fleet run the hare, so cunning run the fox,
Why should not this young calf grow up to be an ox,
For to get his living through briars and through thorns,
And die like his daddy with his long pair of horns.
    Horns, boys, horns!
    Horns, boys, horns!
And drink like his daddy with the long pair of horns.'

Then he stood the company a quart of ale. Along one of the roads to Weyhill from Dorset came the future Mayor of Casterbridge, when he sold his wife to the sailor, in Hardy's novel.

CHAPTER XIV: *The Cleres and the Camps*

THE country between the main road and the downs from Basingstoke to Andover is all of a piece. For Hurstbourne Tarrant you go out of Andover, through Knights Enham, over the hill, through Dole's Wood, then down to the village folded in the valley by the stream. The bourne is a typical chalk stream, varying greatly in its level according to the season, the lavants, as they are called, appearing much higher up in winter. Here it is dry in summer. Hurstbourne Tarrant was part of the royal demesne of the Cleres till Henry III gave it to Tarrant nunnery in Dorset, to which his queen was a good friend. Hence the name. At one time it belonged to Ludlow, the regicide. It is pronounced Ussebourne locally, the first syllable being the same as Ouse: Cobbett calls it Up-Husband—it was also called Up-Hurstbourne—just as Hurstbourne Priors was called Down-Husband. Cobbett was very fond of Up-Husband, where he stayed with his Roman Catholic farmer friend at the Rookery, whither chance also took W. H. Hudson. 'The homesteads in the sheltered bottoms with fine lofty trees about the houses and yards form a beautiful contrast with the large open fields. The little villages running straggling along the dells (always with lofty trees and rookeries) are very interesting objects, even in winter. You feel a sort of satisfaction, when you are out upon the bleak hills yourself, at the thought of the shelter which is experienced in the valleys.' And its unspoilt character makes it doubly attractive to-day.

From Up-Husband a lesser road continues up the ridge to Ashmansworth, where some old wall-paintings have been discovered in the tiny church. Then a deep wood-fringed lane takes you to the Three-Legged Cross inn. Opposite this is a cart track that passes the gate to Highclere Park and continues between a field on the left and a wood on the right to Sidown, one of the great camps along the ridge of the down. The hill is thickly wooded, but the view extends into Berkshire, with Pilot Hill on the left, to the north; and to Danebury and the Winchester downs in the other direction. Sidown is in the magnificent domain of Highclere Park, which belongs to the Earl of Carnarvon. Within its thirteen miles of circumference is some of the finest and most varied scenery in the county. It contains several large lakes. 'According to my fancy the prettiest park I have seen,' says Cobbett. The trees and shrubs, many American, are of all kinds. From this side you go down by a great box hedge. Near the house, which is modern, are some finely layered cedars and many kinds of firs and pines, as well as a wealth of rhododendrons and azaleas. The house occupies the site of the palace of the Bishops of Winchester, to whom it belonged. As you approach it, you catch sight of Pilot Hill and Wadbury to the left. Wadbury I omitted, since only half of it belongs to Hampshire; but it is the largest camp hereabouts, containing 80 acres. You come out into Highclere village, set deep in woods. It has the appearance of having been annexed by Newbury.

You may, however, carry on through the woods to Burghclere, where again Cobbett often stayed in the country he loved—'high chalk bottom, open downs or large fields, with here and there a farm-house in a dell, sheltered by trees'. The second of the Cleres, it belonged from 794 to Winchester, like Highclere, from which it was in early times undistinguished. It was acquired by Edward VI and passed for a time by marriage to the Lucys of Chalcote. They sold it to Sir Robert Sawyer, Attorney General to Charles II and James II and defender of the seven bishops. Through his daughter, who married the Earl of

Pembroke, Lord High Admiral, it came to the Carnarvons. Burghclere, on the Berkshire border, commands the gap between the two great camps on Beacon Hill and Ladle, through which runs the road, and now the railway, from Portsmouth and Winchester to Newbury and Oxford, a great road all through the Middle Ages and a salt road in the days when stock was killed off and salted down in winter, because there was keep for so few. 'The flock hath eaten nothing but straw this six weeks,' writes Cary Stewkeley from Preshaw in despair in February 1658; and hay was £4 a ton. It was a road familiar to many a clerk of Oxenforde from the south and west. It can never have been busier than at the time of the great fairs at Winchester and Weyhill. The Romans do not seem to have used it through this wild country, but the men of the prehistoric camps understood its value.

The great bare chalk bluff of Beacon Hill, 858 feet, 14 feet less than Sidown, is a well-known landmark, a twin of Butser, from which it can be seen on a fine day. You are now on the great ridge of chalk that runs in from Wiltshire and lies between the valleys of the Thames and the Test and other Hampshire streams, continuing right through Surrey and Kent. Beacon Hill is one of the most important hill-top fortresses of this district, which is so rich in them. These camps are nearly all on treeless ground and were constructed when the lower country was covered with forest. The entrenchment naturally follows the shape of the hill, and the entrances, always on the flat of it, were cleverly and often most intricately defended. Thus on Beacon Hill the entrance is protected by two detached guard-houses. Within the camp are the remains of a prehistoric village. In his admirable book Dr. Williams-Freeman holds that they were not originally camps of refuge, but regular settlements, as the variety of objects found in them proves, into which the cattle could be driven when necessary. They were probably continued in the Bronze Age and were often inhabited much later. The Romans sometimes camped in them. As to the water-supply, the climate was then much more moist and the water-level much higher—there is evidence that it has fallen 50 or 60 feet—and the value of dew-ponds and the making of them was probably already understood.

You can approach the camp from Burghclere by the turning to the golf-course or by the path from Sidown. All these hills rise very little above the main level of the ridge, but the Beacon's great groined buttresses on the north are very steep and can only be approached comfortably by the path from this side. Time has, as usual, so completely subdued the line of the trenches to their surroundings that they seem to form a natural whole. This is, to my mind, the best of the camps and my favourite peak of the Hampshire downs. The narrow top gives you a unique view both ways. South you look down the Test valley, of which this ridge is the head, to Danebury and Quarley, with Salisbury Plain and the downs by the Candovers and Winchester. On the other side is the wooded Kennet valley with the Berkshire downs, and the Goring gap. This I have not seen myself, nor the Chilterns beyond the Thames, nor the possible Hindhead to the south-west.

Looking down from the north side, as Dr. Williams-Freeman points out, you have before you a strip of the primeval forest. 'Winding along, following the shape of the hill, exactly where the richer valley land abuts upon the chalk, they may be mistaken at first glance for hedges; but they consist of the natural undergrowth of the country such as springs up self-sown in every ancient hedge.' To the south are the Seven Barrows, once a well-known landmark, close to the railway. They are in Litchfield, the wrong derivation of which from the Anglo-Saxon word for a corpse gave rise to the belief that they mark the site

Beacon Hill, Highclere

of a great battle in Saxon times. They have been opened and belong to the Bronze Age.

Ladle, broad and round, lies on the other side of the Newbury road and can be reached up a lane by Ladle House, a good, old-fashioned lane. The ditches are little impaired. It is now given over to sheep, which seemed astonished at my intrusion and so little perturbed by it that it is clear their solitary reign is not often invaded—an impression one gets on most of these camps. There is a clearly marked track connecting all of them, following the ridge from Walbury by Beacon and Ladle and Kingsclere right on to Winklebury. It was a regular drove road till quite recently, where the drovers could escape the tolls on the turnpikes. But there are now often so many obstacles, hedges and the like, on these old tracks, that I refrained from following it through. The road runs under the downs. It is so high itself that the camps do not rise much above it and even less above the main ridge. A beautiful walk it is under the pale blue of the autumn sky, chequered by ragged clouds which every now and then shut out the sun with a shower : on the right was the long green line of Waterlip Down, with the fields and the spinneys and the woods on the other side. Yet even here, even on Beacon Hill, you realize what Hudson means when he says that Hampshire lacks sublimity. The downs do not impress like the south downs in Sussex.

From the top of the hill above Kingsclere you look down into Berkshire and out towards the Thames valley. On the downs to the right are the famous Kingsclere stables. Over the perfect turf have galloped many of the greatest of English race-horses, such as Ormond, Common and Flying Fox, in training under John Porter. The stables are now owned by a company. Below, in the hollow, nestles Kingsclere, at the head of a valley with a stream that runs north to the Enborne, which is here the county boundary.

M

Kingsclere belonged to the king, as the other Cleres belonged to the Bishop of Winchester. Alfred left it to his second daughter, who was Abbess of Shaftesbury, and it was royal demesne till Henry I gave it to the canons of St. Mary, Rouen. Canon Heath Down recalls them. Later it went to the Paulets.

All this was long a wild, wooded hunting district: indeed, this border region is still known as Woodlands. Freemantle, a little south of Kingsclere, was a royal park, where fair Rosamund is credited with a bower. This is a region of royal forests, as at Odiham, or on the Weald at Woolmer. Restless John is recorded to have hunted here 37 times. In 1212 5s. was given to the groom of Master Ernald de Auckland when the dogs caught a wolf in the park, a fact which goes to prove the wildness of this district. John, indeed, is said to have had a castle on the hill that bears his name, the last of the peaks, also known as Cottington Hill, from which there is a magnificent panorama. Once, says legend, there were witches enough in the neighbourhood to draw a ton load up, so the castle may have been built by magic. One thing is certain, there was never one there built by the hand of man.

The striking great church of Kingsclere, ruthlessly restored, with its solid central tower, has been claimed as ' the finest in the county of non-conventual origin '. The handsome top to the font and the beautifully carved pulpit are Jacobean. Is any county richer than Hampshire in Stuart woodwork? This charming, remote downland village has a number of old cottages. The Falcon inn here belonged to Archbishop Warham and was given by him to Winchester College.

The chalk ridge flops by Basingstoke and on past Odiham. You may return to Basingstoke by Hannington through some delightful lanes. Sydmonton, which lies north of the road we followed to Kingsclere, was part of the original endowment of Romsey Abbey. Later the Kingsmills owned it. William Kingsmill's account of his troubles during the Civil War, in a petition to the Parliament to be allowed to return to his estate, reminds one of the Buckinghamshire Verneys. Though for the Parliament, he had been compelled by the king to go to Reading and to be sheriff there. He had then been plundered by the king's command and had been no better treated by Waller. Moreover, since his house lay between the two armies, he had been compelled to entertain the forces of both sides freely.

For Quarley you go from Andover by Grateley, where a Council was held in Saxon days. Some of the beautiful glass from Salisbury Cathedral, which was removed in the eighteenth century, is preserved in the church. You turn into the green road of the Portway, the Roman road from Silchester to Salisbury. It is irresistibly attractive as it runs straight up over the hill into Wiltshire, straight as a die, seeming to embody Schiller's line about all roads leading to the end of the world. Till well into the eighteenth century it was the main road to Exeter. You must fight your way up through a thick growth of juniper, which is more natural to the chalk even than the yew; and an admirable defensive hedge it would make. Quarley hill, 200 feet high, rises isolated from the plain. The oval camp is most interesting, the banks and ditches being in excellent condition. The centre is planted with beeches and firs. It is the only hill-camp in the county with 4 entrances, and the proximity of the villa at Thruxton, the Portway and other signs of Roman life in the neighbourhood have led to the suggestion that the Romans adapted it for the use of their legions. The panorama is magnificent, right over Salisbury Plain with the cathedral spire, the high ground above Alton, and the chain of the north downs behind.

Quarley is the centre of the great string of camps, Beacon Hill, Ladle, Bury Hill, Danebury and Woolbury, the navel of these strange, prehistoric settlements that stretched right over Salisbury Plain, where Stonehenge was the heart of the religion of their people, who possessed this country with a completeness that no one since has rivalled. Agriculture they practised, but at first, one imagines, like the Britons of Cæsar's day, they lived largely on the flesh and milk of their flocks and herds. It is a world that has vanished too completely for any one but the specialist to be able to grasp it, high though the civilization was that it attained towards the end. First came the Neolithic people of the long barrows, miners and potters and herdsmen, a small, long-headed, dark race. They were followed by the round-headed men of the Bronze Age, who burnt their dead and buried them in the round barrows scattered all over Hampshire. Then, apparently about 400 B.C., came the Goidels and the Brythons, who were acquainted with iron, the builders of the strongest hill-forts. The Brythons settled in Hampshire. The Celtic tribes from Gaul did not emigrate to our shores long before the invasion of Julius Cæsar. All this remote world is slowly coming to light, thanks to the spade of the archæologist.

As we made our way down the other side of Quarley, we realized that this is the easiest way of approach, though hardly the most interesting. We came out from the fields to the charming thatch of the village. Quarley belonged to Harold and then to the Conqueror, who gave it to the Norman abbey of Bec. Later, it fell to the Regent Bedford, brother of Henry V, and on his death it went back to the Crown. Then Duke Humphrey of Gloucester had it. In 1442 it was granted to the hospital of St. Katherine by the Tower of London, which sold it after 550 years of ownership to the Marquis of Winchester. Formerly the parson had to keep a bear and a bull for the parish, and when he failed to do so in 1597 the parishioners refused him his tithe of milk.

We went on with Quarley Hill—the pines and beeches on the top alone visible—and the sun behind us, a big storm-cloud flanked by puffs of white in front, between hazel hedges and two great fields which were being ploughed, to Thruxton. It is a long, typically Hampshire village. A very fine Roman tessellated pavement was found here and given to the British Museum. As the Museum has no room to display such treasures, it seems a pity that some of them are not transferred to local museums, which are now quite competent to look after them. The church stands within the ramparts of the manor-house, now an orchard. It has some notable monuments. The yews outside are good specimens of the topiary art, in which Hampshire attains considerable success.

Barely a mile away is Fyfield, five fields, the ideal manor. Here the brother of Gilbert White was vicar. He also was a naturalist and a scholar. He did not live in the small rectory—he had 10 children—which he used for the school he ran, but in the large house next it. He it was who ' tried all the owls that are in his near neighbourhood with a pitch-pipe set at concert pitch, and finds they all hoot in B flat '. Next year, Gilbert tells us, he was to examine the nightingales, but there is no record of the result. He was a good musician who could quill his own harpsichord and a welcome visitor in houses round where people were fond of making music.

To the south lies Amport or Anne de Port, on the Ann (which, by the way, means a spring), a De Port manor, belonging to a junior branch, as it did later of the Paulets, till its lord succeeded the last Duke of Bolton as Marquis of Winchester. It is now the chief seat of the family. The peaceful thatched village stands charmingly back from the green with its big pond and the thick woods behind, beyond the bridge over the Ann, by the park gates. This corner of the county has lost little of its rural character. In the east window of the church is some curiously twisted flamboyant tracery, and there is an interesting portable altar found in a cottage in a near-by village. We returned to Andover along a section of the Portway, passing the Monxton aerodrome. The Air Force is getting its claws into all this region as firmly as the men of the Bronze Age. The noise of the planes is incessant.

CHAPTER XV: *The Valley of the Test*

FROM Andover the road goes up on to the down with Goodworth Clatford church and a fine version of the familiar view over the great valley to Danebury and the hills to the south on the right before turning off to Wherwell. As you wind down its zigzags you catch glimpses of the thatched cottages from varying angles. To my mind this is another almost perfect Hampshire village, its beautiful main street meandering along a bosky combe, on a tributary of the Test. Outside the White Lion hangs one of Cromwell's cannon balls, said to have been dropped down the chimney; was it dropped to clean it?

The chief interest of Wherwell—or Horrell, as it is said to be pronounced by your true son of the county—lies in its Benedictine nunnery. It was founded in 986 by Edgar's widow Elfrida after her share in the tragedies with which legend associates her name. Here she withdrew, and here she died abbess in 1002. It was fashionable in Saxon days, when the kings were often in the Andover district. Edith, the wife of Edward the Confessor—the Lady of England, or the Young Lady, as she was called—was sent here by her husband. The convent was burnt down in the wars under Stephen. From 1226 to 1257 it was ruled by that remarkable woman, the blessed Euphemia. 'Realizing that the Lord had called her to the rule of the abbey of Wherwell, not that she might live there at ease, but that she might, with care and dispatch, uproot, destroy and dissipate all that was most noxious and erect that which would be useful', she rebuilt the insanitary buildings in the court of the abbey manor and 'under her pharmacy she made a water channel through which a stream of sufficient force swept all refuse that might corrupt the air'. Indeed,

' she seemed to have the spirit of a man rather than of a woman '. Under her rule, exemplary in every way, the numbers rosé from 40 to 80, and great was her fame. On the whole, the nunnery continued to have a good record. In the neighbourhood it owned Goodworth Clatford, Little Ann, Longparish and Bullington, as well as 31 messuages in Winchester. At the Dissolution Lord De La Warr wrote to Cromwell, ' I would gladly have the said abbey, because it stands wholesomely in the country where I was born, and my wife has no house to dwell in if I should die before her, and it is but a reasonable house as I hear say.' And to him it was assigned in exchange for 5 Sussex manors, though it had been destined for John Kingsmill, the brother of the obliging last abbess. There are a few remains of the nunnery in Priory House which replaced it, and the stream, now troutful, still runs under it, as Euphemia ordained. The church is modern, standing beautifully by a bridge over the stream.

From here we made our way to the Test, dividing its stream where it lists to make islands, as it wanders through this rich, lush valley, with its grey-green willows, its poplars and alders, its sedges and reeds and the streaming hair of its water-grass. If Hampshire is ' the home of the most finished school of fishing in the world ', the Test is its Mecca, but only a rich man's Mecca, in the honours of which its tributaries share. Like other chalk rivers, it is fed by powerful springs, as at Mottisfont, or by streams, clear and swift and pure from the chalk downs. Such are the Anton, which gives Andover its name, and the Pillhill that comes in by Upper Clatford. ' Most pure and piercing the aire of this shire,' says Fuller : ' and none in England hath more plenty of clear and fresh rivulets of troutful water.' All this area is a network of streams haunted by water-fowl.

Just by Wherwell the Test is joined by the Bullington

or Dever, rising near Micheldever. Soon after its rise it fringes the large meadow in which stands the delectable little church of Stoke Charity. You may reach the village by Sutton Scotney, a busy, high-lying road junction, with two old inns facing each other. The Dever flows through it and by Bransbury common with its snipe. It is good to escape from it down to thatched Wonston, of which Sutton Scotney is a highway off-shoot. Then up on to the hill by two great open fields looking towards Itchen Down and Worthy Down, and below lies beautiful Stoke Charity. The manor-house stood in Pretty Meadow, north-west of the church. Edward the Elder gave it to Hyde Abbey. By the thirteenth century it belonged to Henry de la Charité, whence its name. In the fourteenth the Hamptons bought it; then it came to the Wallers by marriage. Charity Waller was the second wife of Sir John Ogle, who held Winchester for the king, in whose cause her son was killed. Cromwell permitted her to leave the besieged castle, but she died worn out when she had barely got outside Winchester.

The church is by the manor farm. The tiny arch in the north aisle was the chancel arch of the original Saxon church. The present chancel and its arch are fine Norman work. The Saxon chancel was enlarged into a Hampton chapel in the fourteenth century. Here is the tomb of Thomas Hampton (1483) with his wife and 8 children, and the brass, with the pleasing head-dresses and the expressive faces of the 6 daughters. There are other interesting Hampton and Waller monuments. On the wall is a curious piece of sculpture, found walled up, obviously to preserve it from vandalism, in 1849, depicting our Lord's miraculous appearance to Gregory the Great while celebrating mass. There are full printed descriptions over each monument, but one cannot help wishing for a little account of the church left on sale.

If the Test valley is a paradise for the fisherman, it is hardly less so for the walker. Across the river, now flowing rapidly, you go on to Chilbolton, another charming village. The houses in these villages may increase a little, but time has mellowed them as completely to their surroundings as their grey churches, giving them ' an air of immemorial quiet and a human life that is part of nature's, unstrenuous, slow and sweet '. Would W. H. Hudson still find them so? The car has brought many changes. But on the whole the description is true to-day. Chilbolton is said to have been given to St. Swithun's by Athelstan after the defeat of the Danish giant by Guy of Warwick. Through the village now and out on to the ' carmon ', as we were directed, where are some valuable, little-spoilt remains of a prehistoric village; then across the long bridge by the very beautiful tryst of the Test with a Wherwell arm, a great expanse of marsh and water-meadow with a little wood flanking it and a picturesque inn in front. The road follows the valley to the broad opening where the Anton comes in on the right, peaceful and tree-shaded. Crossing to the other bank, under the tree-fringed hill, with the railway between you and the river, I saw what looked like an Italian village cemetery as I entered Leckford, a colour-washed daub wall, common here, with its broad, red-tiled coping, and a row of cypress-like firs behind. In the Edward I church is a good Jacobean pulpit with tester.

Across the river again is Longstock, and right in the centre of the village is Charity Farm, now a private house, to which I had long wanted to make a pilgrimage. Down behind it, by a large arm of the Test, are the clearly marked remains of a dock, some 130 yards long and 30 broad, running by the river, from which it is separated by a great bank formed of the earth that was excavated. This effective screen is also continued along the channel that connects it with the river. Dr. Williams-Freeman gives the work unquestionably to the Danes, who were at Romsey. It is well suited to their flat-bottomed boats. Close as it is to the point where the important British road connecting the camps fords the Test, it may have been a dock for the fleet of Cnut himself. It is difficult not to feel something like a thrill at thus finding oneself in contact with the great rovers and pirates, Sweyn, Cnut and the like, men whom a few pages of the sagas bring before us in all their vigour and brutality as nothing else can.

For Danebury you turn up by the church and follow the old farm track that dates from prehistoric times up on to the downs, which soon bring back to you the glorious sense of space that they alone can give. Over the old Stockbridge race-course you go, now a training-ground for the Danebury stables. Here the Days, father and son, once ruled supreme, and here the Cannons rose to fame. There were bluebells and cowslips on the gallops as we made our way to the hill that is crowned by the strongest of the great hill-camps in the county. The centre is thickly covered with beeches and a few firs. You look back on the sun-drenched Test valley and over to the line of the north downs and the other camps in the neighbourhood. The name comes from the Celtic dun, a fort, and it was formerly often written Dunbury. The two mounds that guard the western entrance stood out clearly. The inner vallum is on an average 25 feet above the bottom of the ditch and 12 above the level of the dozen acres it encloses. The second rises 9 feet above the ground, and there is a third beyond. The defences of the only entrance to the east are very complicated. Dr. Williams-Freeman considers that this great fortress, Neolithic in origin, was occupied continuously right down to the Iron Age, when it was strengthened as we see it to-day, and even through the

Roman period. Like much of the country inhabited by our prehistoric ancestors, this downland camp region has never been possessed to the same extent by later generations, which settled where their forbears could not penetrate. It has remained remote and little altered except by the plough, and has therefore been preserved for us as a precious relic. Nothing of the kind that I have seen in Hampshire impresses more than Danebury.

From Danebury, by the racing-stables, it is but a step to Nether Wallop, an attractive village, where the gardens are above the Hampshire average. The Wallop estates were royal demesne, held by Gytha, Earl Godwin's wife, before the Conquest. Hugh De Port's holdings were in Over Wallop. Henry II gave Nether Wallop to the nuns of Amesbury, who held it till the Dissolution, when it went to Wriothesley. Nether Wallop Buckland is named after the Buckland family, from which it passed to the Tiptofts, including the noted first Earl of Worcester, who was executed as a Yorkist in 1470. Later the Paulets acquired it with the rest of Nether Wallop. The church has a good eighteenth-century tower and some interesting fourteenth-century wall-paintings, recently discovered, including an excellent mounted St. George slaying the dragon and a St. James; also a good brass to a prioress, Mary Gore (1436). The nuns are said to have had a rest-house here.

Cromwell wrote a letter from Wallop 2 days after taking Basing House. The Wallops lie in the wooded valley of the Wallop brook, which is almost hidden in water-cress beds and masses of other water-plants. It rises in the hill by Over Wallop and joins the Test at Bossington. A flock of 25 bustards was seen on the Wallop downs early in the nineteenth century. Beyond Over Wallop, held of Earl Godwin by the famous Lady Godiva, wife of Leofric, Earl of Mercia, the road rises towards the downs and Grateley. You can return to Andover by the Salisbury road, which passes between Quarley and Danebury and through Abbotts Ann.

The characteristic, attractive, long, broad street that makes Stockbridge may still be described as 'a noted thoroughfare, with some good inns'. It owed its rise to the weekly market in the Street, as the place was called, granted by Richard I to William Briwere. In the fifteenth century it was almost deserted owing to the plague. Elizabeth gave it two members and later the elections became notorious. The electors were known as 'sixty-pounders', this being a fishing village. Steele was a member, but was warned not to stand again, as he had not sent his promised 'apple stuck full of guineas' to the bailiff's wife. There is a delightful view up and down the Test from the bridge that has replaced the old one where you were besought to 'say of your cheryte a pater noster and an ave for the sowllys' of its founders and makers. In the Middle Ages a legacy for a bridge was a wise and approved form of charity. Two small arms also flow under the town. If you follow the path by one of these to the south, you come out among the water-meadows criss-crossed with irrigation ditches. You can see what the Test can do in the way of trout in the Grosvenor hotel, the angler's centre, with its porch bearing up the bulging room above, next door to the red-brick market-house. The houses are as pleasantly varied as in other old Hampshire market-towns, but there are few half-timbered.

At Stockbridge Stephen's men caught up with the Empress Matilda after her flight from Winchester in 1141. She escaped through the devotion of her half-brother, Count Robert of Gloucester. After the fight he took refuge in the church, only the chancel of which remains, at the east end of the town, and then surrendered. Interesting relics of the old church are embodied in the new. James II dined at the Swan here in the fateful November of 1688.

For Woolbury Ring you turn off to the left out of
Stockbridge along the London road. At the top of the hill
a grass lane takes you up among the junipers to the long
down. Doubtless it was part of the prehistoric track crossing the valley to Danebury. On the highest point is the
camp, a large one, of 20 acres, with plentiful firs on the
top. At the south-west end the bank is still 16 feet above
the bottom of the ditch. The view carries over the New
Forest and to the Isle of Wight, with Danebury and
Quarley and Salisbury Plain on the other side, and to the
high north downs. The ridge continues to St. Catherine's
Hill, over Beacon Hill and Old Winchester Hill, to Butser
and then by the downs above Harting into Sussex.

The road on the east of the Test next passes John of
Gaunt's Hunting Park of 400 acres. Just outside Horse-
bridge, towards King's Somborne, can be seen part of the
great bank that once formed its boundary, and the dams
of the fish-ponds are also easy to trace. Eastwards lies
King's Somborne, with a branch of the Test running
down its main street. Here John of Gaunt had his palace,
which has disappeared. The stables are said to have been
at Place Farm, where there are some ruins and a good deal
of old work. A king's manor in Domesday, Somborne
was granted in 1190 to William Briwere. He was a man
of note and a friend of King John, whom he supported
against the barons. John often stayed with him here to
hunt in the western Forest of Bere, which stretched away
to the Itchen valley. The manor came to ' time-honoured
Lancaster ' by marriage and was, till recently, part of the
Duchy.

The road to Ashley, a charming little wooded village,
runs through delightful country up on to the down, where
the small aisleless church stands in a commanding position. The chancel arch, only 4 feet across, and the 3
characteristic lights in the chancel, are late Saxon. The

large squints on each side of the arch, very necessary additions, are later. The curious wooden pillar-shaped alms-box is dated 1595. Close by, covered with trees, is the mound of a castle with its bank and deep ditch. The ring of the bailey, enclosing the church, can also be traced. This was very probably the castle of William Briwere.

Less than a mile farther along the road, which runs under the wood, on a jutting spur of the down, to the left, is a Roman camp. The remains, including especially three of the entrances, are well marked, though they have been much spoilt. Beside the path that leads up to the main gate runs a bank. Genuine Roman earthworks are not common in England and it is quite possible that this was the permanent camp of a legion. Numerous coins, pottery and other remains have been found here.

Just below it runs the Roman road from Winchester to Old Sarum, and a delightful walk it is back to Winchester over Farley Down by Farley Mount with its obelisk. The mount is a burial mound, and to the east of it is a camp with a clear ditch. Under the obelisk is buried a horse which, while hunting with its master on its back in 1733, jumped into a chalk-pit 25 feet deep and, next October, won the Hunters' Plate on Worthy Down at the Winchester Races, being entered under the name of Beware-Chalk-Pit. At Bossington Farm, by the way, where this road crosses the Test, was found in the eighteenth century the famous pig of lead of Nero's day (A.D. 60), from the Mendips, which is in the British Museum.

Michelmersh, on a hill to the east, is said to have been given by Queen Emma, mother of Edward the Confessor, to St. Swithun's, in gratitude for having successfully walked bare-foot over the nine red-hot ploughshares in the nave of Winchester Cathedral to clear herself of the charge of unseemly conduct with Bishop Alwin. Stanbridge, back of the road, is the reputed home of Ethelwulf, father of Alfred the Great.

The Test here disports itself freely in a much-widened valley in a number of branches which actually enisland Romsey besides flowing through it. One of them, running under Church Street, divides it into Romsey Infra and Romsey Extra. It now ceases to be a trout stream. Salmon leap here in the season. Romsey has an attractive little market-place, which seems hardly big enough for whiskered and frock-coated Palmerston on his pedestal. The houses in the older part of the town are not striking, but they are well enough shuffled for there not to be too many of a suit together. The roads from Winchester, Stockbridge and Salisbury meet here.

Romsey owes its rise to the abbey and an admirable situation it had in Romsey Infra on the Test, where Edward the Elder founded it in 907. Two of his daughters were here, and one of them, Ethelflaeda, was probably abbess. A second Ethelflaeda, a notable saint who is joint patron of the abbey with the Virgin, was also a nun here in the reign of Edgar. Her miracles are duly recorded. The nunnery was burnt down by the Danes in 994, but the abbess, warned in a vision, fled to Winchester. She was succeeded as abbess by St. Ethelflaeda, and the nunnery flourished, especially while the Saxon kings frequented this part of Hampshire.

To Romsey, after Domesday, came the daughters of Queen Margaret of Scotland, to be educated under their aunt, the redoubtable abbess Christine, sister of Edward the Aethling, who seems to have done her forcible best to induce Maud to take the veil. According to the well-known, if not well-authenticated story, William Rufus came over to call while hunting in the New Forest. The abbess bade Maud, much against her will—she vividly remembered the blows and the language with which her

Wherwell

The Bolder Wood, New Forest

aunt reinforced her orders—put on nun's dress and go into vespers. Then she let in the king and invited him to come and see her roses, giving him to understand that Edith (Maud) had taken the veil. The girl had a better fate before her. Henry I sought her hand and seems really to have loved her. There was everything to be said for the match, since it would unite the Norman and the Saxon royal lines. But there was the question of the taking of the veil. It was brought before an assembly of bishops and nobles, and, Edith, having declared that she had never taken vows, was blessed by the Archbishop and became the good Queen Maud. Her attainments speak well for the teaching of Romsey. They would do credit to some of our most up-to-date institutions to-day.

More unhappy is the story of another of the Romsey nuns, Mary of Blois, Stephen's daughter, and great-niece of Queen Maud. She was abbess. When her brother, the Count of Boulogne, died, she became his heiress, and Henry II encouraged a son of the Earl of Flanders to marry her. She yielded to the pressure put upon her and was heartily welcomed by her subjects; but her husband later repented and allowed her to retire to a French convent. The Pope legitimized her daughters, one of whom made no less than 4 husbands Counts of Flanders.

Romsey continued to flourish, though hardly on so aristocratic a scale, till the Black Death, after which the numbers and the morals fell off sadly. Towards the end it went rapidly downhill. Among other things, two abbesses were blamed for ' immoderate habits of intemperance ', nuns were forbidden to frequent taverns in the town, and there were other scandals. At the Dissolution it was valued at £528. The north aisle of the church had long been reserved for the inhabitants of the town. It was shut off by a carved screen, the remains of which were unearthed by an energetic rector and now form part of the chancel

N

screen. At the Dissolution the people of Romsey saved their magnificent abbey by buying it from the king for £100.

This glorious, lofty church, with its Norman strength and dignity, commands reverence. It is a veritable epitome of the development of our ecclesiastical architecture. The interior is, as a whole, early twelfth-century Norman, as pure and perfect as can be found; but the last three bays of the nave, like the East window, are hardly less beautiful Early English. It would be difficult to exaggerate the wonderful richness and variety of the mouldings of the columns and arches, especially round the choir.

Foundations of the pre-Conquest church were uncovered in 1900, a portion of an apsidal east end, under the pavement in the centre. At the end of the choir aisle is the famous Saxon rood, found built face inwards into the wall, obviously to preserve it from desecration. It is small, but has an unusual number of figures. Outside, near the door of the south aisle by which the nuns entered, is the other rood with the hand of God above it appearing from a cloud. This also is Saxon. It owes its preservation to a store-house having been built round it. In the abbey is kept the beautifully illuminated Romsey Psalter (1440), with its list of abbesses, which was discovered at Quarritch's. Among other relics is the hair believed to be that of a Roman lady. There is no proof that Romsey was a Roman station, but this was found in a lead coffin under the abbey, the position of which showed that it was not Christian.

In the choir is the monument to Sir William Petty, the son of a humble Romsey clothier, whose granddaughter was a wealthy ancestress of the Lansdownes. At Oxford, when assistant Professor of Anatomy, he won both fame and money by reviving Ann Green, who had been hung, and exhibiting her. In Ireland he did good work as a surveyor and acquired considerable property round Kil-

larney, then a very remote district, where he founded
Kenmare. He developed the fishing and opened up the
mines with his usual energy. At the Restoration he found
little difficulty in winning the favour of Charles and James.
He was one of the founders of the Royal Society. Evelyn,
who gives a long account of him, had the greatest admira-
tion for him, saying he had never known such a genius.
He is now best remembered as a pioneer economist.

The abbey suffered at the hands of the Roundheads, who
were encouraged in their godly work of destruction by
a zealous brother of the ministry, dwelling not far off, for
the space of two hours, from the pulpit.

Next to the abbey the most interesting building in
Romsey is King John's recently discovered hunting-box.
It was then separated from it only by the river, now by
Church Street. Henry II bought the land, but it was restless John, with his passion for hunting, who built the lodge.
Converted into cottages, it had been completely lost sight
of. It was the appearance of the handsome west window,
facing the abbey, with the dog-tooth moulding on both
sides, proof of a royal residence, from behind the lath and
plaster while it was being repaired that led to the discovery. One of the earliest private dwellings to be built
with two storeys, it also had glazed windows. In such
luxurious style did John build. The entrance door in the
east wall is all that remains of the chapel. John's daughter,
Johanna, afterwards queen of Scotland, was sent here to
be educated in privacy—not to the convent, be it observed
—her governess being paid 2d. a day.

Henry III gave the hunting-box to the abbey for a guest-
house, and so it remained till the Dissolution. In February,
1306, when Edward I visited the abbey, his barons were
put up here, and they or their squires, like cockney tourists,
covered the walls with a most interesting series of scratched
armorial shields, mottoes and drawings. Among them is

a life-sized sketch of the king with his crown.

John Foster was granted the guest-house at the Dissolution, and hither he brought his bride, a nun of the abbey, enlarging it by building the Tudor cottage beyond.

White-porticoed Broadlands, down by the Test, built from plans by Capability Brown, who also laid out the grounds, made a fitting home for the great Whig statesman. It belonged to the St. Barbes, who sold it to the first Viscount Palmerston in 1736.

West of Romsey lies East Wellow, not a regular village. King Alfred left it to his daughter Ethelfleda, Lady of the Mercians. It belonged to Netley Abbey from the thirteenth century to the Dissolution. Embley Park, covering 100 acres, with beautiful gardens looking over the Wiltshire hills, was bought by the father of Florence Nightingale for a winter residence. As a girl, she dreamt of turning it into a hospital. The chief interest of the church on a hill by the river lies in the extensive remains of crude thirteenth-century paintings, including a murder of Becket on the south wall of the chancel. Florence Nightingale lies in the family grave, her initials on one side of the column, while another records her sister Parthenope Verney, to whom we owe the Verney letters : Parthenope because she was born at Naples. We may be thankful that her greater sister was born at Florence, seeing that to her we owe its popularity as a Christian name. In the church are the typical Victorian text that hung over her bed and her cross made of Crimean bullets.

Farther down the Test, about half-way to Redbridge, is Nursling. In the monastery here, probably destroyed by the Danes, Winfrid, St. Boniface, the Apostle of the Germans, spent 20 years in the eighth century. Elizabeth once used Tudor Grove Place, with its fine linden avenue, as a hunting-box.

CHAPTER XVI: *Lyndhurst and Burley*

LYNDHURST, at the junction of the roads from Romsey to Lymington and from Redbridge to Bournemouth, is the capital of the New Forest. This thoroughly modern tourist centre is 2 miles from its station and they make an excellent introduction to the Forest. On the right are regular fir plantations, while on the left is a stretch of the natural forest such as it was before the Conquest. This is how Manwood describes it in his *Forest Laws*, ' A certen territorie of wooddy grounds and fruitfull pastures, privileged for wild beastts and foules of Forest Chase and Warren to rest and abide in, in the safe protection of the King for his princely delight and pleasure.' Though the deer went in 1851, it is good to remember this great tract of English woodland, much of it still in its primitive state, where the birds and beasts can dwell undisturbed, as symbolized by the confidence of the Forest ponies. They have been thinned down owing to the fall in their value, but they are no less aware of their rights and able to maintain them.

As to the plantations, the idea is to enclose and plant certain tracts, and throw them open to the public when the timber is sufficiently mature. Since the Forest was surrendered with other Crown property by Queen Victoria, it has become a source of pleasure and delight to an ever-growing number of His Majesty's subjects whom the car is bringing to it and, above all, through it in numbers that are threatening its most vital characteristic as a reserve of rare species. The one hope is that the recommendations of the recent Commission will be put into force and that building and road development will be strictly controlled.

It was William the Conqueror who, in 1079, with his

passion for the chase, turned the great tract of land lying roughly between the Avon, Southampton Water and the borders of Wiltshire into a forest by placing it under Forest Law and made it a worse offence to poach a deer than to kill a man. For long it was universally believed that he had laid waste a flourishing country-side and destroyed a number of villages with their churches. But he found much of his New Forest a forest already, known as Ytene, a wild, furzy tract. So poor is the land that it could never have been fertile or supported a large population. Otherwise, it would long have been under the plough. Domesday, indeed, shows that some 30 manors in the heart of it, which can never have been very profitable, went out of cultivation. But other villages remained. Brockenhurst and Milford, the only churches in Domesday, still exist, nor are there any ruins of a single one of the churches that he is said to have destroyed. Moreover, Boldre church, standing high on its hill like a beacon to guide the traveller through one of the wildest tracks, was finished soon after the enclosure.

Such charges are due not a little to the severity of the Conqueror's forest laws. Even he seems to have hesitated at the unpopularity he might incur by substituting them for the mild Saxon regulations. So a Charta Canuti, embodying his own ruthless system almost to the letter, was duly forged and opportunely discovered at Winchester. The death of Rufus and of his nephew in the Forest were regarded as divine retribution on the family for the Conqueror's cruelty and the lesson was duly rammed home by the Church, with which Rufus had quarrelled.

The Forest Laws were long a grievance. From Henry III was wrung the Forest Charter, which modified the cruelty of the old laws. But things remained much as they had been under John's oppressing hand till the barons forced Edward I, in whose reign the Forest was at its greatest, to order a second perambulation in accordance with Henry's charter, with the result that it was brought more or less within its present limits. Charles I, who is said to have released a number of wild boars, which were promptly killed by the natives, was reduced to mortgaging the Forest. Parliament kept it, but made sadly free with the oaks and the deer. As the officers were not paid, they naturally recouped themselves out of its products. Charles II tried in vain to improve matters, but they were as bad as ever till the first enclosure act under William III. The oaks were needed for the navy. The Great Storm of 1703 did immense damage. There was little real progress. The officers were dishonest and incompetent. The Forest was haunted by sturdy vagabonds and squatters, poachers and heathers. Gilpin remembered all the materials for a cottage being brought together, the cottage built, roofed and a fire lit in the course of a single moonlight night. Once up, it was either winked at or the offence was punished with a small fine. The deer and the timber continued to disappear wholesale till 1848, when a beginning was made with sound administration.

Lyndhurst, then, was the capital, and, with the wardenship, a royal manor. In early days it was often granted to the queen. Thus Henry III gave it to Eleanor of Castile, wife of the future Edward I. It was also held by Margaret of France, by Isabella, queen of Edward II, and, on her imprisonment, by Philippa of Hainault. The kings often hunted here from their lodge at Lyndhurst. The present King's House dates from about 1640. Happening to be a court kept for the Foresters, wrote Baskeville in 1679, ' were much good company gathered together, and they had a good feast at a small inn near the King's House '. The Lord Warden is there when he comes to hunt and hawk, and, according to Celia Fiennes, ' he is served in plaite, those that hunt with him all day comes and dines

or supps with him '. And she describes the tameness of
the Browne deer, as she calls them, when the keepers call
them and feed them by each lodge at certain times a day.
Afterwards they are as wild as ever in the Forest.

George III stayed a week at the Lodge on his way to
Weymouth in 1789, but he was generally a guest of George
Rose, Pitt's friend, at Cuffnells. It is now the residence
of the Deputy Surveyor. The Forest Courts are held in
the Verderers' Hall with its solid timber dock and oak
seats. Six of the 7 verderers are elected by the commoners.
The Forest is divided into Walks for administrative purposes, and the commoners' rights are under four heads :
Common of Mast (the turning out of pigs); of Pasture; of
Torbary (turf-cutting); of Estovers (firewood). The commoners are smallholders. Large sections of the Forest are,
of course, privately owned, and thus outside the manor.

In the hall is the stirrup. If it is not the stirrup of Rufus,
as it used to be called, since it is not earlier than the sixteenth century, at least it is a Forest antiquity, the stirrup
through which all dogs must pass if they were to escape
lawing. This meant the cutting of three claws on the fore-
paw so that the dog could not hunt. The dogs of the
Abbess of Romsey and the Abbot of Beaulieu were among
the few exempt.

The railway made this pretty village popular in Victorian
days, when it was quite small. Leighton and Millais and
other artists and writers frequented it, and for the characteristic church, which superseded an ugly Georgian structure,
Leighton painted the altar-piece of the Wise and Foolish
Virgins. The spire is a familiar landmark. Of recent
years Lyndhurst has grown and in summer it is a little
too crowded for some of us. Indeed, this applies to the
whole of the Forest, which to my mind is far more attractive in autumn.

Certainly it is easy to get from Lyndhurst into some of

the best of the true Forest scenery : out past Swan Green, for instance, by some beautiful patches of it, to Emery Down, a charming old village, with amusing alms-houses and an inn, which has much increased of late. Then on by the farm into the gate of Minstead Manor House, finely wooded, with a wealth of rhododendrons along the path, out to the road. This leads to the stream, Bartley Water, very picturesque by the splash, with a farm beyond. Here was a sow with a goodly progeny that sent one back to the Aeneid, an independent lady, obviously used to fend for herself, very different from her sisters on farms. I remembered that it was a pannage month (September 25 to November 22) when, in old days, the hogs of the commoners were taken out by the village swineherd to feed on the acorns and beechmast. Bolderwood Walk, where are the magnificent beeches of Mark Ash, was a favourite pasture. The hogs of to-day, completely domesticated, may run in the Forest all the year round. Hampshire hogs and Hampshire bacon were considered the best in the land when most of Hampshire was covered with woods. Pork and pudding were the food of farm-hands, except for the Sunday joint. In the eighteenth century, when there was a great felling of timber, the bacon lost its special flavour. Does that of the New Forest differ from other bacon in the land, or has its flavour also faded into the light of common day and the true Hampshire hog become merely as other hogs?

Minstead village stands high in the north-eastern corner of the large Forest parish, with a number of characteristic outlying cottages. Under Edward the Confessor Geodric Malf owned three and a half hides here, but in Domesday only half a hide : a hide, by the way, was about 120 acres. This is an interesting instance of the effect of the Conqueror's enclosures. It has been suggested that Malf gave his name to Castle Malwood. You pass the Trusty

Servant, an inn with the well-known Wykehamist sign, and there, right above the green, stands the church, a curious and interesting mixture. It has a seventeenth-century three-decker intact with two original private pews entered from the porch for Castle Malwood and Minstead Lodge, the home of the Comptons, one with a fire-place. Such relics are rarer to-day than the curiously carved square bowl of the Norman font, dug up in the parsonage garden. The red and blue brick tower is 1774 and pleases. There are two Compton hatchments in the gallery and one of the Earl of Errol in the chancel arch. He is said to have died so deeply in debt that his creditors seized his body, but Squire Compton intervened and had it buried from his own house in his family tomb. Back up the hill the road has a prospect stretching from the Winchester to the Wiltshire downs. To the left is Castle Malwood and Malwood Lodge with its earthwork, the much loved home of Sir William Harcourt, on the right. From the top a path to the left through Forest woodland will deliver you from the cars along the main Cadnam-Ringwood road, till it brings you close to the Rufus Stone, which stands by it at Stoney Cross, in Canterton Glen. There is little peace here, but it stands in one of the finest and best-treed stretches of the Forest into which it is a delight to escape. Deer, one feels, should bound off down these quiet glades, as they did in Norman days, rising up from the thick bracken. There are still a few left, which are hunted by the New Forest deerhounds. The view over the tops of the acres of trees, mostly beech, just touched by the deadening hand of autumn, was something to remember; for here and in Castle Malwood Walk is much of the best timber of the Forest. The Walk has probably changed less than most others in appearance.

And this is as it should be, seeing that it was the scene of the culminating tragedy of the Conqueror's family, which is still the great tragedy of the New Forest. One of the Conqueror's sons, Richard, had already been accidentally killed here, and in May 1100, another Richard, a natural son of Robert, had met a like fate. No wonder people talked of a judgment from Heaven. Now, on August 1st, ' King William was shot by an arrow while hunting by one of his men and afterwards brought to Winchester and buried in the bishopric '. That is all that the contemporary Anglo-Saxon chronicle says, but round it tradition and later monkish writers have spun an elaborate story, which has naturally caught the imagination. The king came to Malwood Castle, where he was troubled by a dream, which so frightened him that his attendants stayed the night with him. He drank heavily at dinner, recovered his courage, and determined to hunt, in spite of another dream by a monk, information of which was sent him by the Norman Abbot of Gloucester. But he sent the monk 100 shillings, exclaiming, ' He is a monk and dreams for money, like a monk.' His huntsman brought him 6 new arrows, two of which he gave to Sir Walter Tyrrell, Lord of Poix and Pontoise, who was just back from Normandy, with the remark, ' The best arrows to the best shot.' Towards evening Tyrrell was left alone with the king. As they stood near Stoney Cross a stag bounded by. The king wounded it and watched it spring off with his hand over his eyes. Then he bade Tyrrell shoot. He did so, and the arrow glanced off a tree and pierced the king's breast. He dropped dead. Tyrrell at once took horse and escaped to France. The red king's body was found by a charcoal-burner named Purkess, who took it on a cart to Winchester, the blood dripping along the road. The direct line of Purkess died out in 1821, but the name still exists in Minstead. The king was buried in the cathedral next day without any ceremony.

Meanwhile Henry I, in a different part of the Forest,

chanced to break his bow-string and went to a forester's hut, where he was greeted as king by an old woman. Hurrying to Winchester, he seized the treasure, though De Breteuil, who was of the party, spoke up loyally for the rights of his elder brother Robert, who was overseas.

The Church had no reason to love Rufus, who had banished Anselm, denied the authority of the Pope and refused to pay Peter's pence. Clearly he was treacherously killed, but Tyrrell was almost certainly not the murderer. He repeatedly declared that he had not seen the king that day. A friend of Anselm, he doubtless knew of the plot and hurried off to tell the good news. The foreknowledge of the event shown by some priests is also in favour of a clerical conspiracy. Doubtless the priests also spread it about that Rufus was killed on the site of a church destroyed by the Conqueror. Leland saw a chantry there, built for masses for his soul. The memorial stone marks the place where the oak stood from which the arrow is supposed to have glanced. Charles II had it railed off, but it has long since disappeared. There are some splendid oaks in the neighbourhood.

If it is oaks that you want, you should leave Lyndhurst by the Bournemouth road—a road intolerable to a walker with a shred of self-respect, except at an off hour, say early in the morning or during lunch on Sundays. Fortunately, it is easy to slip off into the forest and possibly to avoid it altogether, if you are sufficiently familiar with the paths. The woods were turning in the October mist, the bracken reddening and the leaves beginning to fall. The ponies were more numerous than usual, especially round Allum Green. In older days they often died in great numbers. Some 300 perished of hunger in Bolderwood Walk alone in the hard winter of 1787. The lawns running back into the forest are especially beautiful here. The whole picture suggested the English garden of the continent in its naturalness, sending one back to Fontainebleau or Corinne and Oswald. The road crosses what looks like a Highland stream and then on your right comes the Knightwood enclosure. It is a pity they do not put up the names of the enclosures instead of the eternal Forest By-laws and directions about fire. However, at this famous one there is generally an impecunious gentleman ready to put his services at the disposal of the bewildered novice, at least on Sundays and holidays.

A truly magnificent glade of oaks escorts you up to their chief. There it stands, the Knightwood Oak, the living embodiment of the Conqueror, Norman with the strength of the Normans and of the greatest of their cathedrals, its branches rising straight up, instead of spreading. You must come to the New Forest to understand what an oak is. And those round it might be his barons, Adam De Port and the rest. As one gazes, one realizes that the New Forest belonged to the Conqueror, as of right. Its oaks seem to embody all that he and the best of his descendants gave to England, and the darker side of the gift, his cruelty —did not he punish the slaying of a deer with mutilation and his son with death?—was the obverse of their strength.

From the Knightwood Oak it is not far to Mark Ash, where the beeches, fine as they are, fail to impress like the oaks. All the way thither are large regular plantations of firs; and all the way one is beset by the car, which is filching the very New Forest from the walker and pursuing him into its remotest recesses, with small benefit to its rarer fauna and flora.

Instead of crawling back in the gutter of the Bournemouth road, the wise man escapes into the comparative peace of the Burley road, which has recently lost much of its primitive Forest character, or the new Lyndhurst road, as they call it in Burley. The hill leads down to the Blackwater, with Vinney Ridge enclosure and its heronry on the left and Burley Lodge and its pond on the right; a noble forest road, giving you a better idea of the true Forest in its peace and beauty than any other I know. At the elbow in the road a path runs off from the lodge gate, near which is a very fine beech, into the grounds of Burley Lodge for about half a mile to a meadow, where are the battered stumps of the Apostles, only 9 of them now. Doubtless they were famous because they were 12. My companion, Naaman-like, asked whether we had not passed dozens of oaks infinitely finer and why we had troubled to come and see these stumps in such weather, for it was raining hard. True, but the others were not the Apostles, and they are certainly about the oldest group of oaks in the Forest.

Back behind them, in Oakley enclosure, is the Old House, where Auberon Herbert, a typical wealthy Victorian aristocrat and individualist, who had led an adventurous life, been an M.P., declared himself a Republican and written a good deal, spent his last years. He is a legend in Burley, with the annual teas he gave to Burley, to Ringwood and to the Forest gipsies, and the strawberry feast to the children. They tell you how, every morning, he used to go up to the top of his tower to enjoy the view from a revolving barber's chair, and how he was buried in an enormous coffin filled with earth and his precious prehistoric flints.

Beyond the lodge this newly made road passes through a beautiful stretch of country, a broad glade on each side, covered in spring with yellow gorse. To the right is Oakley enclosure, nearly all of oaks, fenced in by some fine conifers; across the road the new Oakley enclosure. At the end comes Burley, a pretty village, the parish formed out of Ringwood and embracing Burley Walk and Holmesley Walk. Lyndhurst has become too busy a centre for me, and, if the scheme of the Commission goes through, is destined to become even more busy. Burley is growing too, the houses tucked away in every possible corner among the trees; but it is quiet still, a real village, large though it is, from which it is easy to escape into the best the Forest has to offer, whether of heath or wood, and, to my mind, far preferable for a stay. The church is modern, but attractive, and up on the heath is the cricket-ground, which has been in use for over a century.

The road goes through the pretty heart of the village, by the green, and from it, on the right, a path leads up to Burley Beacon. A group of noble oaks stands sentinel at the edge of the wood, and others, hardly inferior, with some great hollies, keep you company all the way. From the edge of the Beacon comes the view right over Holmesley Walk to the sea, with the Avon valley and St. Catherine's Hill on the right. Though Burley has forest proper of the best, it is essentially the centre for the moorland, which is as true a part of the New Forest, rolling purple, with a touch of green here and there, apparently down to the sea. It is curious how the yellow of the gorse is lost almost at once.

Higher up is Burley Castle, or Castle Hill, now crowned with villas. But the vallum of the prehistoric camp or castle is clearly marked, and a good defensive position it must have been. On the other side is Burley Street, a hamlet with an old house or two, among them Stocks Farm, so called because the stocks used to be there. At the Rest and Be Thankful stone, just as you get out on to the moor, they tell you that loaves used to be distributed to the poor on a certain day in accordance with a charitable bequest. The distribution now takes place at the baker's.

From here the road runs over the moor, which reminded Scott of the Highlands. To me it suggested the more-recently visited Camargue. There were periwinkles in plenty amid the gorse and the heather and, in late autumn, the red bracken. By the inn at Picket Post is a glorious panorama, with the downs about Breamore on the Wiltshire border to the north, Cadnam to the right, and the hills of the Isle of Wight in the other direction. Unfortunately, the crowded road from Cadnam to Ringwood gives it a touch of Hampstead Heath.

On the other side of Burley, beyond Holmesley Heath, towards the south-east, is the Naked Man, standing quite alone on the moorland, a lightning-blasted oak-shell that is always pointed out. They tell you it got its name because a naked man was once found by it. Beyond it the road winds through beautiful wooded country to Brockenhurst. To the south-west of Holmesley, towards Boldre, is the village of Sway with its curious tower, 200 feet high, which catches the eye all over these parts. It was built in the 1860s by one Peterson, with unskilled labour, of concrete quite without reinforcing, to show what concrete could do, and is something of an historic monument as one of the first erections in which concrete was used.

It is good Forest most of the way from Lyndhurst to Brockenhurst, with wide patches of heath. Brockenhurst church, up a deep wooded lane, stands on its hill embowered in Forest trees apart from the hustle of road and rail, as becomes a church that was already there in its first form before Domesday, when the great yew in the churchyard may have been alive. There is also the ruin of an oak which is locally said to date from the Conquest. The font and the chancel arch, like the south door with its good dog-tooth moulding, are Norman : the chancel Early English of Edward I. The church also has a shady relation in the shape of an eighteenth-century brick tower, but it would take more even than the brick north aisle to vulgarize a church with such a heritage and in such a position.

In 1212 the manor was held by sergeantry of finding litter for the king's bed and forage for his horse when he came here to hunt, and later by serving the king for 11 days when at war in England. A survey of New Park, still Crown land, of 1615, records that oaks and beeches to the number of 270 had been thus early marked out for the navy. Here Charles II kept a herd of French deer. Beyond the church is Brockenhurst Park, held by the Morants since the eighteenth century, which runs down to the Lymington or Boldre River. Brockenhurst, though car and rail have done it no good, and it is also to be opened up further by the Commission, is a good centre for some very beautiful Forest country. In old days, Wise tells us, the deer would gallop through the village at night chased by the dogs, who would often pull one down.

CHAPTER XVII: *Lymington and Beaulieu*

THERE is a delightful Forest road along the Lymington river from Brockenhurst which, by the way, means Badger Wood; or you can take the Lymington road from Lyndhurst and turn off to the left by a wooded road to Boldre, the picturesque village of heavily thatched cottages down by the river, hidden away with its farm-lands in the Forest. It seems only natural that the Conqueror should have thrown the manor into his chase. Formerly it was a huge parish, embracing Lymington and Brockenhurst as chapelries of Christchurch. At the end of the sixteenth century the churchwardens and inhabitants of Lymington still went to Boldre on Midsummer's Day and offered 3s. and a wax candle to the churchwardens there in consideration of a dinner for two priests, clerks and choristers. Over the bridge and to the left, between the forest—good forest, running right up the hill—and the sown, goes the path to the church. Though it stands high, it is so embowered in trees that one does not notice it. A church was built here soon after the Conquest and there are Norman and Early English features, as well as a curiously placed tower. The fine old glass in the *fleur-de-lys* window in the north chapel was taken away in the 1860s. On the top of the west wall is a gooseberry bush, which bears fruit regularly.

The church has its associations. William Gilpin of *Forest Scenery* fame was vicar (1771-1804), having been given the living by Mitford, the historian, his pupil at Cheam. The well-known inscription over his grave under the Field Maple, suggested by himself, begins, ' In a quiet mansion beneath this stone, secure from the afflictions and still more dangerous enjoyments of life . . .' Both as headmaster, when he abolished corporal punishment, and

210

as vicar, he was in advance of his time. He refused other livings because he disapproved of pluralism and he devoted the profits of his many books to parish purposes. His parishioners, with the Forest offering every kind of temptation for poaching and smuggling, were little better than a herd of banditti, and he was no more disposed to leave them as they were than Kingsley. Nor would he let them tread the primrose path in ease. A rich farmer, a notorious evilliver, and his fair companion in sin were made to do public penance in white sheets, on pain of excommunication, before a large crowd. Richard Warner, the historian of Hampshire, was his curate in later years.

There is no ground for the tradition that Monmouth was buried in the churchyard after his execution, but Southey married Caroline Bowles, the poetess, in his old age in the church.

It is best to turn off down the beautiful valley along the water-meadows and cross the river by the footbridge. As you look back you see the goodly estate of Vicar's Hill which was Gilpin's home, across the valley, crowning the wooded slope. A noble, broad, peaceful, well-treed valley it is, the river, now tidal, running in a single stream. It is filling up with good-sized houses, but, luckily, in very open order. It takes courage to lay out a garden with Gilpin's ghost to watch you from his hill. His views on the placing of trees were decided and forcibly expressed. He might even condemn your labours as disgusting.

The road joins the main Lymington road opposite a large, half-timbered house. Here was Buckland Cottage, the home of Caroline Bowles. A path immediately beyond the railway bridge leads up to Buckland Rings with its deep autumn carpet of beech leaves. It is a strange combination, the railway running by this big, well-placed prehistoric camp with its triple row of strong, deep trenches. The inner bank rises 7 feet. It stands close by the river, flanked by small valleys. Between the Rings and the river, by Ampress Farm, is Ampress Hole, a river camp with a dock dug at right-angles to the river, probably of Danish origin.

A stretch of tree-lined road takes you to the extensive modern suburbs of Lymington, a charming old town, some 2 miles from the river mouth. It climbs up the hill from the mud and marsh by the estuary. The broad High Street has the bright, pleasing look of these Hampshire towns, the low houses of all sizes and shapes, brick or stucco, the best of Georgian red brick. They carry you down to the harbour for the Isle of Wight and round it and beyond to the west. You can go right back through Dickens and Thackeray to Fielding, and here and there the tile or half-timber brings you up to Stuart or Tudor times. It is a place where it is a pleasure to sit in the window of a solid Georgian house flush on the pavement, once a business house or a bank, when a passer-by was an event and the clerks knew every one by sight. On a quiet afternoon you almost expect to see a French *émigré* officer mincing along with a keen eye for a pretty girl, or a couple of Germans, already well on, quarrelling violently on their way back to barracks. In 1756 Hessians were quartered here and a house near Church Lane is called Quadrille Court because the officers played quadrille there. During the Revolution Lymington was an important centre for French refugees. Here was formed a regiment, some 300 strong, which was wiped out at Quiberon Bay. They were followed by a rough, mixed crew called Germans, who had barracks along the quays till the Peace of Amiens. Their colonel lived in the Masonic Hall and the tithe barn was the hospital. In 1803 all wagons in the town were registered to take the people into the Forest if Napoleon landed. Stories of these days and the duels fought lingered long. Some of these foreigners settled in Lymington.

The cupola-towered church stands at the top of the High Street and here, blocking the middle of the road, was the Town Hall, pulled down in 1820, with a row of booths below it. The butchers long slaughtered in the street. The noble lime-walks in the roomy churchyard doubtless date from the seventeenth century. Samuel Baldwyn, we learn from the registers, sojourner in the parish, who died in 1836, was immersed without the Needles in Scratchell's Bay, *sans cérémonie*, in order to spite his wife, who had declared that she would dance on his grave.

Lymington has an interesting history. In Domesday it had gone to the Earls of Shrewsbury after William had sliced off something for his Forest. On their rebelling, Henry I gave it to Richard de Redvers. The widow of Baldwin de Redvers, Isabella de Fortibus, whose confirmation of the charter is the first that Lymington possesses, took refuge in Breamore during the Barons' Wars. But the prior proved to be a supporter of Simon de Montfort and compelled her to sign a deed giving him the manor of Lymington before he would release her. The manor was duly restored to her. Later, it was granted to the Courtenays. In early days Lymington was an important port which supplied twice as many ships as Portsmouth for the navy in 1345 to Edward III for his invasion of France. The French are said to have burnt it 3 times in early days. From the first 'the wines of the continent were wafted into this port' and it had a good share in the New Forest timber trade till the special privileges of Southampton sapped its prosperity. It was Royalist in the Civil War, but had to mend its manners under the Commonwealth. A burgess lost his rights on his third offence for drunkenness, vain swearing and profanation of the Lord's Day. Lymington seems to have gone all out for Monmouth. The mayor raised 100 men for his support and proclaimed him king. A handsome red-brick house opposite the church is known as Monmouth House, since there is an absurd tradition that he took refuge in it. Lymington returned 2 members to Parliament till the Reform Bill. Latterly it was a pocket borough of the Burrards. Gibbon sat for it. For a time it had some name as a watering-place. But its chief sources of wealth were the salterns, which can still be traced in the neighbourhood. They produced 5,000 tons of salt in 1804. Celia Fiennes gives a detailed description of their working. When they were abandoned, Lymington was in a very bad way. Later it revived as a Solent yachting centre. Coventry Patmore spent his last years here, and William Lyte, author of ' Abide With Me ', was a curate.

For Beaulieu the road crosses the river by the bridge above the harbour where the Isle of Wight boats lie and passes Wolhampton House, the home of the Burrards. A Burrard was mayor of Lymington in 1574. George III visited Sir H. Burrard Neale there. The mother of Caroline Bowles was a Burrard. Beyond its ample grounds is the wide expanse of Beaulieu Heath with the ugly cottages along the road. The valley of the river lies off to the left. W. H. Hudson finds in Beaulieu a distinction above all Hampshire villages : ' it is unlike all others in its austere beauty and atmosphere of old-world seclusion and quietude '. But it is the village of the Lords Montagu of Beaulieu rather than of the monastery, in spite of the mill on the tidal Beaulieu River, a model village where the thatch and the half-timber are in as good order as the newest cottages : a village, however, which it is a pleasure to see.

It would be hard to find a more ideal spot for a Cistercian abbey. The object of the Cistercians was to return to the stricter rule from which the Benedictines had lapsed. Their founder decreed that they must build by a stream remote from the conversations of men. Here the Exe joins the Beaulieu River at the head of the long creek, forming a large pond by the modern mill and another above the village. You cross it by a bridge to the ruins of the abbey. Wild indeed this district must have been in the early thirteenth century, and the monks had every opportunity for opening up new country, which was probably the most important of their civilizing influences in any district where they settled. Unfortunately, their admirable business methods and strict accountancy, which lay land-owners were glad to imitate, generally ended by throwing the spiritual aspect of their life, with the inevitable wearing off of the first enthusiasm, somewhat into the background. They became hard and grasping taskmasters and led the luxurious lives that brought them hatred and contempt in this country.

Legend says that John, who did not love these austere White Monks, had threatened to have all their abbots trampled to death. Then in a dream he saw them assembled beside a judge who, having heard their statements, bade them scourge the royal persecutor. So thoroughly did they do their work that he said he could feel the effects when he awoke. His chaplain recommended him to spare the abbots. In expiation he founded Beaulieu for the Order and always treated it with special favour. He is said to have wished to be buried there. The lands of the Cistercians alone were not confiscated during the interdict.

The name is said to be Beo-lea in Anglo-Saxon, becoming Beaulieu, the Bellus Locus Regis of the charters. Beaulieu was a favourite name among the Cistercians; one might almost call it a tribute to their taste in choosing their localities. The abbey, founded in 1204, was endowed by the king with lands in the New Forest and in Hertfordshire. Like so much else in Hampshire, it was built of Binstead stone from the Isle of Wight. It was completed in 1246, when it was dedicated in a splendid ceremony, which was attended by Henry III and his queen and Richard, Earl of Cornwall. So pleased was the king, who was also a benefactor, with the feast that he remitted a heavy fine which the abbot had incurred for poaching in the New Forest. The nearness of the Forest was a sore temptation to an abbot with sporting tastes and a weakness for game. In 1278 Abbot Dennis was fined 40 marks for making 3 breeches in Beaulieu Close, placing therein stakes and engines for taking the deer and driving the deer on to them, as well as for hunting a stag and taking a buck in the Forest. The young prince was taken ill during the festivities and nursed in the abbey by the queen for 3 weeks, in spite of the trouble made about admitting a woman. Richard, Earl of Cornwall, King of the Romans, brother of Henry III, who was granted Dibden when it fell to the Crown with other St. Valery property, wished to be buried at Beaulieu. The rare heart coffin found in front of the High Altar may well be his, since it is close to the grave of his first wife. It was not uncommon to have your heart buried away from your body, as your soul thus had the advantage of prayers in two churches.

The abbey had many privileges, among them the exemption of the abbot from the expensive duty of attending Parliament. Edward III granted it a tun of wine annually for mass which the Corporation of Southampton had to deliver. People of distinction sought sanctuary here. On Easter Eve, 1471, the eve of the Battle of Barnet, where her husband was killed, Anne, Countess of Warwick, took refuge here, having just landed at Southampton. Queen Margaret of Anjou had also just landed at Weymouth with reinforcements. She went first to Cerne Abbey, then to Beaulieu, whence she joined the Lancastrian army for Tewkesbury, only to be beaten and captured. To Beaulieu also came Perkin Warbeck on the advance of Henry VII, shamelessly leaving his men in the lurch. The abbey was surrounded and at last he surrendered on promise of his life. But he was hung at Tyburn.

A wall a mile and a quarter in extent surrounded the abbey grounds. Inside it were also the fish-ponds, which can still be traced. The destruction of this noble foundation, built just when the Early English was breaking into the Decorated, was thorough, for the stone was needed for Calshot and Hurst Castles. The church has completely gone, though the plan has been recovered and bricked out. Three fine arches of the cloisters, now a green meadow, are standing. They formed the entrance to the chapter-house, but now look out into the open country. The north wall is fairly complete. Opposite these, in good preservation, thanks to having been used for residential purposes, are the refectory and dormitory of the lay brothers, with the stairs that led into the chapel. The interesting museum is in their dorter. The model there shows that the abbey was built on the regular Cistercian plan.

On the south side are the remains of the monks' lavatory, a remarkably fine building for the trifling operation that washing then was in such establishments. Here, too, is the Refectory (Frater), which has long been the parish church, though it runs north and south : and a fine church it makes, which is obviously appreciated by those in charge. Its most beautiful feature is the arcade in the wall leading to the pulpit where the Lector read to the brethren at meals. The heads decorating the bosses in the roof are interesting. Among them are those of King John, Richard of Cornwall and Innocent III, who placed John under the interdict.

In the churchyard was buried a famous witch, Mary Dore, who died about 1750. The Duke of Montagu, who respected her gifts, 'surrounded her grave with a neat railing', and put on it an inscription recording them.

These have now disappeared. Was a witch ever so honoured before?

The ruins about a hundred yards north of the church are said to be those of the wine-press and brew-house, and some ground near by, with a good south slope, was called the vineyard. The Duke of Montagu's steward told Warner that he had in the cellar a little brandy made from grapes there about 1720.

Beaulieu, famous for its hospitality, increased in luxury as it grew in wealth. At the Dissolution Wriothesley bought it for £1,350. The property was estimated to yield £326 a year. The Earl of Southampton was loyal to Charles I, who was often here. Yet in 1635 he claimed the property, and a Forest Court deprived Southampton of land worth £2,000 a year, which Charles later gave back to him. Beaulieu passed by marriage to the Duke of Montagu in the eighteenth century and then to the Duke of Buccleuch, who left it to his second son. He was made Baron Montagu of Beaulieu. Palace House, the residence of Lord Montagu, was the gate-house of the abbey. Wriothesley chose it for his house, and it has since suffered many changes and additions, though portions of the old building remain. The outer wall, with its 4 towers and its moat, was built by the Duke of Montagu in 1704 to protect it from possible French privateers advancing up the Beaulieu River.

Monks were not, like Warner, romantics, though we may agree with him that in general they displayed an elegant taste in the choice of their situation. Possibly the stream afforded the recluse an emblem of human life ' and at the same time that it soothed his mind by a gentle murmuring, led it to serious thoughts by its constant and irrevocable lapse '. But they were also great shepherds and farmers, and in this lovely, unspoilt country, where there are so many traces of their busy life, however it may have degenerated later, we are brought into closer touch with them than anywhere else in the south that I know. They had several granges. St. Leonards lies some 3 miles to the south along a delightfully wooded road. Here are the ruins of the great storage barn—there can hardly have been a larger in the country—226 feet long. The huge east gable gives an idea of its size, and the length of the lower part of the north wall helps us to judge of its proportions. As there were monks in these granges as well as lay brothers and workmen, a chapel was needed. The picturesque ruins of that of St. Leonard are in the gardens of the manor-house near by. In Cobbett's day they had long served the ignoble purpose of a goose-house and a pigsty. Bargery, the sheep farm, has disappeared.

Beaulieu Abbey, cradled in hills and woods, is a spot you leave reluctantly as you go back to the village and turn down the path over the fields by the estuary. It runs straight as a die through the woods, once you have crossed the road, a perfect walk for a hot summer's day, to Buckler's Hard. As it breaks out, it gives a fine view of the estuary and the meadows by it where the cows are feeding. The place is almost as remote to-day as when the monks left it, and the country can have changed hardly at all.

It is difficult to realize that where there is now little more than a row of cottages and a landing-stage was once a busy shipyard, turning out a number of three-deckers and other ships for the navy. Three of them fought at Trafalgar, the *Euryalus*, the *Swiftsure* and the *Agamemnon*, which Nelson long commanded and where he lost his eye. The Duke of Montagu owned the island of St. Vincent and hoped to make Montagu Town, as he called it, a profitable port for its products. When this scheme failed, he turned to shipbuilding. He had plenty of oaks and rights of free harbour inherited from the monks. The slips can still be traced, and near the landing-stage is the Duke's mud bath. The broad, eighteenth-century street of roomy cottages leads down to the jetty. The largest of these, the last on the left, now an hotel, belonged to Adams, the famous master, whose ruin involved the ruin of the yard and the village. The ideal way to visit Buckler's Hard is up the estuary by boat. It is difficult to imagine a ship like the *Agamemnon* being towed down to Lepe between its muddy banks. Naturally, it was a great place for smugglers. In almost the last run made a keg slipped from a horse in Boldre and broke, and an old man remembered the smugglers taking off their shoes and drinking the spirit from them.

Lepe was a Roman as well as a medieval port, though it is now silted up; and there was a Roman road thither, clearly traceable from Dibden, connecting it thus with Clausentum. Long tradition maintains that in Roman days tin was taken by cart from Lepe to the Isle of Wight, and there is no good reason to doubt this, any more than that well within historic times it was possible to cross to the Island on land at low tide. It is probably not long since the sea severed the connexion between these two parts of Hampshire.

At Buckler's Hard were found some fragments of the rare Southampton glass, specimens of which are in the Alton Museum. It has been suggested that the kilns were between it and Beaulieu.

From here it is good to run south through the brilliant green of the spring fields, broken by an occasional patch of wood, with the hills of the Island to the left. Then the Needles swim into your ken, and at last, through a gap in the hedge, there is a glimpse of Sowley, a pond of 90 acres, once called Freshwater, the largest pond in the New Forest. It was made by the monks for their fish. Later the water was used to work the hammer of the Sowley ironworks, which supplied iron for the ships at Buckler's Hard and also for Southampton. To-day it is again a preserve, well stocked with fish and a great haunt of water-fowl. Not far away is Park Farm, another Beaulieu grange, the ruined chapel of which was still standing early in the nineteenth century.

CHAPTER XVIII: *Christchurch and the Avon*

TO the west of Lymington stretches the low-lying coast which continues to Bournemouth and Poole Harbour and the borders of the county. It can never have been beautiful, except where covered with pines, but such beauty as it has, the low sand cliffs and the open fields and country that remain, contrast sadly with the works of man in red brick or stucco that are rapidly devouring them. But for an occasional oasis most of this coastal district might be a second-rate suburb of Greater London in process of development. At these we need do no more than glance and pass on along the new road to Christchurch.

Milford-on-Sea bids one pause. It lies down towards the sea, and its church shares with that of Brockenhurst the honour of representing the New Forest in Domesday. There is some Norman work in the nave, but most of the rest, including the low tower with its early, lead-cased spire, is Early English. Like the village, it stands back from the coast, from which a long, shingle bank runs out a good 3 miles towards the Isle of Wight. This curious, solid spit is ' a submarine cliff of shingle 200 feet high, the depth of the channel close to the castle being 33 fathoms ', and the tide often rushes through it with extraordinary rapidity. From it there is a view of the cliffs of the Island running out to the Needles. On the end of this spit Henry VIII built Hurst Castle, one of the series protecting the coast, of which Calshot Castle and Netley Castle are others. Hurst Castle, little more than a strong tower, has the interest of having been the prison of Charles I for 18 days in 1648 when he was taken by order of the army from Carisbrooke to Windsor.

Christchurch is the nucleus of all this region, the mother of modern Bournemouth with its pines and its chines, its smart modern shops and shoddy suburbs, and its huge Victorian houses, its memories of Stevenson, who was long ill there, and of Keble, who died there. Situated above the confluence of the Avon and the Stour, with a good harbour, Christchurch has long been a genuine town. The antiquity of the site is proved by St. Catherine's Hill, which is a couple of miles to the north and is now washed by a dreary suburb. It lies between the two rivers and its 160 feet give a wide, if not an attractive view, out to the sea and to the woods behind. On it are several barrows and the remains of a small camp, as well as the foundations of a chapel dedicated, of course, to St. Catherine, the saint of heights. Legend says that the monks wished to build on the hill, but their work was destroyed every night and the beams always proved too short till they began to build at Christchurch, when all went well. Does this legend symbolize the over-throwing of the heathen god of the height?

The stone bridge over the Avon, which was probably Norman, takes you into this 'little unfortified fisher-town', as Clarendon calls it. Clarendon, by the way, owned land in the neighbourhood and had a great scheme for making the river navigable as far as Salisbury, which came to nothing. Before you is the keep of the castle by the ruins of the Norman house. Twyneham Castle—Christchurch was originally Tweoxneham or Twyneham, the town by the two rivers—standing on its artificial mound, is one of the few mound and bailey castles in Hampshire, and a good deal of the shell of the keep remains. It was probably built by Richard de Redvers, a cousin to whom Henry I gave this royal manor as a reward for supporting him against his brother Robert after the death of the Red King. The Norman house, on a branch of the Avon, which, after serving as a moat, turned a mill belonging to the priory, was probably built for the governor. It is a good example of twelfth-century work of the kind and a most interesting specimen of domestic architecture of the time of Henry II. The castle played a part in the Civil War, being captured from the Royalists by Waller. In 1645 Colonel Goring with his rascally dragoons advanced from Romsey, where they left not a sheep or a hog, plundering through the Forest. They drove the Christchurch garrison into the church and the castle, where they resisted vigorously. A fire at Poole, taken to be a beacon signalling relief, though it was nothing of the kind, threw them into a panic and they fled. In any case, relief was on the way from the Isle of Wight. The Roundheads slighted the castle and sent the guns to Poole.

The priory overshadowed all else so effectively that the old name soon gave way to that of Christchurch. Under Edward the Confessor 24 canons held property here. They belonged to no Order, but they recognized an elder. Flambard, the evil minister of William II, got them and the minster into his hands, because its wealth in relics and fame for miracle-working made it rich. And it is to him that we owe the priory, for he induced the canons to cede him their property in return for a small pension, suppressed their rights when they died and used the money to build his magnificent church. When Richard de Redvers was granted the manor, he restored their rights to the canons and placed a dean over them. His son, Baldwin de Redvers, Earl of Devon, treated them even more generously. At times, however, the De Redvers seem to have abused their position and occupied the priory almost like an hotel. On the high altar is an inscription to Baldwin (1216). The De Redvers' chapel is at the west end of the north aisle. The monks were, it is true, excluded from the salmon fishing at the confluence of the Avon and the Stour, but they were entitled to the first salmon of the season.

The Test near Stockbridge

Ringwood

The priory was called Christchurch in 1142, when it became an establishment of Austin canons. By 1234 the choir and the nave were finished. The monks were notoriously generous to the poor. So wealthy were they in 1302 that they supplied a ship to the king's navy. The visitations shed the usual interesting light on their lives. In 1402 there were sad doings. Some of them, animated by a devilish spirit, swore upon the sacrament to eject the prior and others and then fled. They were punished with exemplary severity. At another visitation it was ordained that only the prior might keep hounds. In 1492 there was only one complaint by that true Englishman, Canon Thomas Selby: the beer was not strong enough. At the Dissolution Christchurch was valued at £519. It was rich in jewels and plate, ' whereof some be meet for the King's Majesty's use ', notably a ' litell chalys of golde '. Leland found but one book in the library, a treatise on the English laws. Henry VIII's commissioners spoke most favourably of the state of the priory, but, of course, to no purpose. The chantry of the last prior, John Draper, who was well rewarded for being so ' conformeable ', is at the end of the south aisle of the choir. At least he spoke up eloquently concerning the importance of the church for this great Forest region, and, though the commissioners put it down among superfluous buildings, it was handed over to the town in 1540. The nave had long been screened off and used as the parish church.

I am not going to attempt to describe in detail this beautiful priory, the architecture of which ranges from Norman to Perpendicular. The approach is by the avenue of elms across the ample churchyard to the north door through the long, beautiful thirteenth-century porch. Among its most striking features is the great stone reredos, recalling that of Winchester, of the Tree of Jesse, who sleeps below, flanked by David and Solomon. In the centre

P

are the Magi. It suffered a good deal at the Reformation.
The carvings of the choir stalls are quaint and amusing,
recalling the local name for the monks, ' priory lubbers '.
A cowled ape lolls on a pillow, and a fox, also disguised
as a monk, preaches to a flock of geese. The roomy Lady
Chapel is noteworthy. Above it is St. Michael's Loft,
which was used as the grammar school from 1660 to 1870.

To the north of the altar is the Salisbury chapel, built by
the Countess Margaret, daughter of the Duke of Clarence.
The last of the Plantagenets, she was the mother of
Cardinal Pole, to whom Henry VIII gave the manor. She
was beheaded at the age of seventy. This, reported the
visitors in 1539, ' we have causyd to be defacyd and all
the arms and badges clearly to be delete '. Under the tower
is the curious monument erected to Shelley by his son, who
lived at Boscombe, where he had his private theatre. It is
well executed, but, as Murray put it, ' painfully suggestive of
a designed caricature of an Italian *pietà* '. His naked body
lies on the lap of his wife. The restoration of the priory,
which has been long in progress, has by no means given
general satisfaction.

Wriothesley had the priory, which was, as usual, to the
south of the nave. The doors from the nave into the
cloister are still there, as also a piece of wall. Near by is
Priory House, where Louis Philippe stayed, an exile, in
1807.

The manor belonged to Isabella de Fortibus, who left it
on her death-bed to Edward I. The document may well
have been forged. He gave it to his second wife and then
to the queen of the future Edward II. Like other property
round here, it came to George, Duke of Clarence, through
his marriage with the daughter of Warwick the Kingmaker. Henry VII gave it to his mother.

Beyond the castle and the priory there is a pleasing
glimpse of the river, here full of pleasure craft of every

kind, sail still being plentiful. It is as well to remember the méringues of Christchurch, since there is nothing old to take the eye, though the town has too long a history not to possess a character of its own, and the centre is not uninteresting, before setting out further, or becoming engulfed in the endless suburbs that lead to Bournemouth.

At Mudeford, by the mouth of the harbour, dwelt the Rose family, who long controlled the borough. They also owned Cuffnells at Lyndhurst. More than one of them sat for Christchurch, among them John Stuart Rose, translator of Aristotle—Rogers said he ought to have printed the original beside it to make it intelligible—and a poet of some note in his day. He called his house by the characteristically romantic name of Gundimore. It is built in the shape of a Turkish tent with his gilt Arabic inscription on a red ground still in position to remind him of his Oriental travels. Round it is a circular passage, which connects with the wings where he housed his guests and his servant, Dan Hinves, who was well known to his friends and had acquired a useful knowledge of exotic cooking while with him on his travels. It looks straight out over the rough beach to the sea. The long sand and shingle bank fronting it has been broken by a recent gale. Here Rose was visited by Coleridge and Scott, who dedicated to him the first canto of *Marmion*, some of which he wrote here. The great Italian poet, Ugo Foscolo, freshly exiled, was also his guest. He was enchanted with the seashore and enjoyed watching the pretty girls and children returning from their bathes, for Mudeford had some name as a sea-side resort. On the other side of the harbour, where the Stour, which separates Christchurch from its mushroom daughter, Bournemouth, joins the Avon, is the long, low line of Hengistbury Head. Here Hengist is said to have landed and here was found a hoard of Saxon coins. The rare Christchurch salmon are caught hereabouts. This

p*

coast also had its smugglers. Warner once saw 20 or 30 carts loaded with kegs, guarded by 200 or 300 men, each carrying 2 or 3 tubs, coming over Hengistbury Heath in broad daylight towards Christchurch, making for the Forest.

Highcliff Castle, in its beautiful park, is about a mile away. The Adam brothers built a house here for Lord Bute which was destroyed by falls of the cliff. The existing house is built in the style of the French fifteenth century and is not unsuccessful. The Kaiser hired it for a cure in 1907.

It does not take long to shake off the suburbs of Christchurch, once you start north, and to find yourself among the peaceful meadows of the broad valley over which the shy Avon, generally divided into several streams, wanders at will. It is remarkably successful in hiding itself from the gaze of such as follow the road. At Burton, just beyond the railway, Southey had a cottage for some time, and Lamb spent a fortnight with him there. Somewhere in this neighbourhood was the home of Mr. Hastings.

'In the year 1638 lived Mr. Hastings, by his quality son, brother, and uncle of the Earls of Huntingdon. . . . His clothes, always of green cloth, and never all worth when new £5.

'His house was perfectly of the old fashion, in the midst of a large park, well stocked with deer, and near the house rabbits to serve his kitchen, many fish ponds, great store of wood and timber, a bowling-green in it, long, but narrow, full of high ridges; it being never levelled since it was ploughed, they used round sand-bowls; and it had a large banqueting-house like a stand, built in a tree.' This kind of raised banqueting-house was not uncommon in Elizabethan days. 'He kept all manner of sport, hounds that ran buck, fox, hare, otter, and badger; and hawks long and short winged. . . . He had a walk in the New Forest and the manor of Christchurch—those last supplied

him with red deer, sea and river fish; and indeed all his
neighbours' lands and royalties were free to him, who
bestowed all his time on these sports, but what he borrowed
to caress his neighbours' wives and daughters. This made
him very popular, always speaking very kindly to the
husband, brothers, or father, who was besides always a
welcome guest to his house. There he would find beef,
pudding, and small beer in great plenty; a house not so
neatly kept as to shame him or his dirty boots; the great
hall strewed with marrow bones, and full of hawks' perches,
hounds, spaniels, and terriers; the upper side of the hall
hung with the fox-skins of this and the last year's killing,
with here and there a pole-cat intermixed.

' The parlour was a large room, curiously furnished.
. . . The windows, which were very large, served for
places to lay his arrows, cross-bows, stone-bows. . . . An
oyster table stood at the lower end, of constant use twice
a day, all the year round, for he never failed to eat oysters
before dinner and supper through all seasons; with these
the neighbouring town of Poole supplied him.

' The upper part of the room had two small tables and a
desk, on the one side of which was a church Bible, and
on the other the Book of Martyrs. On the table were
hounds' loops, bells, and such like ', and some old green
hats in the thrust-in crowns of which were 10 or 12
pheasants' eggs. Tables, dice, cards and boxes were not
wanting. The beer and wine came in in single glasses,
since he never exceeded himself, nor allowed others to do
so. He was good-natured, but soon angry, calling his
servants by coarse names. He lived to be a hundred and
never lost his eyesight. Yes, Mr. Hastings certainly de-
served this record from the first Lord Shaftesbury.

Bidding farewell to the haunts of that fine old sporting
squire, I followed the road to Sopley, a large, picturesque
village. The church stands on a bluff, with a view over

the valley towards St. Catherine's Hill, and here you run down the Avon, flowing strongly. Hard by is the mill which, like the church, belonged to the monks of Christchurch, having been granted them in 1140, and here, a wise choice, they are said to have had their infirmary. The interesting church was Early English, but there are many Perpendicular alterations and restorations. The rather battered male and female figures now standing on each side of the door are said to be the effigies of the founders. In the east window is some old armorial glass, including the beacon of the Berkeleys, who owned the manor for a short time under Elizabeth. The Wool-Sack—this valley must have been well stocked with sheep—is an inn such as Sopley ought to have, the long, beamed parlour, hung with amusing prints and the like, if not with ballads, one to which Izaak Walton would have taken Viator, if he had brought him to fish in the Avon.

The road continues up the lovely valley. Clad in all the splendour of spring, it suggests Tuscany in the softness of its outlines, in spite of the paleness of the English sky. About 2 miles on is Tyrrell's ford, some way from the road, ' beyond the gate where the cows go ', near some pleasing cottages. The Avon is split into many streams again, flowing round osier-clad islands. It is the ford through which, according to tradition, Walter Tyrrell rode after he had slain the Red King on his way to take ship for France. A little higher up in the village of Avon Tyrrell is the forge that is the lineal descendant of the one where the blacksmith shod his horse backwards and which long paid a yearly fine to the Crown in expiation. The murder of Rufus seems to dwarf every other event in the Forest.

Ringwood is another of those bright, busy, prosperous little towns which are among the joys of Hampshire, recalling the time when a town was an oasis in the wild, such as Ringwood must have been almost to within living memory, though hardly white and clean, as Morris liked to picture such places. In fact, it is a real market-town which has sprung up gradually to supply a local need and to which it is a pleasure to escape after the builders' residential erections along the coast. The low houses are of all periods, many Georgian, some with bow windows on the street; and the newer shops testify to its continuing prosperity. Collars and cuffs are still made there, and, of course, Ringwoods, the white woollen gloves that were once very fashionable with young men.

Earl Tostig, Godwin's son, held it before the Conquest, but by Domesday it had virtually gone into the New Forest. Later, it belonged to Nevill, Earl of Salisbury, who was beheaded after the battle of Wakefield, and then to his son, Warwick the Kingmaker, through whose daughter it passed to the Duke of Clarence. It returned to the Crown when his son, the Earl of Warwick, was executed after Perkin Warbeck's rebellion. Later, it was granted to the Duke of Somerset, and, on his attainder, to Sir John Gates, a favourite of Edward VI, who lost it with his head for his support of Lady Jane Grey. Altogether, a tragic manor. And it was at Ringwood that Monmouth, after Sedgemoor, wrote the three abject letters begging that his life might be spared. Nor must it be forgotten that at Bisterne, which is part of Ringwood, Sir Maurice Berkeley, son of Sir John Berkeley and Elizabeth de Bettesthorne, slew in Dragon Fields a devouring dragon that did much mischief upon men and cattle, ' making his denne neere unto a Beacon '—that is Burley Beacon. Hence the Berkeley Beacon.

For quiet and beauty, follow the lovely wooded road on the left of the river, which takes you by Ashley Heath and the firs and moors of the ample grounds of Somerley Park, a true bit of the undeveloped Forest which has been largely planted with conifers. It keeps in unspoilt country to Fordingbridge, but you will not get a glimpse of the Avon all the way. And at Fordingbridge, should you desire to escape from the haunts of men, you can slip through the woods over the border by Damerham into the downland of Dorset and Wiltshire.

But it is our duty to follow the east bank, where men congregate, and where it is possible to keep an occasional eye on the Avon, flowing at its own sweet will among the water-meadows. Hampshire has little better to show than this beautiful, broad valley. The low hills stand out clear in the bright sunshine, often flecked with blue firs.

Ellingham church, with a large farm, stands off to the left among trees down by the Avon. This small, Early English church has been sternly restored, but it is interesting, among other things, for the Black Letter Commandments, Creed and Lord's Prayer over the chancel screen, the elaborate seventeenth-century parclose of the Moyles Court pew, a Jacobean pulpit and a good Flemish picture of the Last Judgment by Golzius. This was carried off from a church at the sack of Cadiz by Admiral Lord Windsor of Moyles Court in 1702 and was long the altar-piece. It now hangs at the west end.

Outside, by the south wall, is the tomb for which every one looks. Here Alice Lisle is buried with her daughter: ' Alicia Lisle dyed the second of Sept., 1685.' The heiress of Sir William Beckenshaw of Moyles Court, she brought the manor to her husband, John Lisle, the regicide, created Viscount Lisle by Cromwell. He was assassinated in Switzerland, whither he fled at the Restoration. Moyles Court stands back a mile on the other side of the road, lonely and peaceful in lovely country. On the way to Picket Post the road crosses a water-splash close to it, still staked. The house was in a ruinous condition when taken by the present owner, who has done his best to restore it to its original state, clearing the moats and ponds and laying out beautiful gardens. Beyond are the woods. Originally much larger—parts of it go back to Henry VII—it straggles comfortably over a wide extent of ground with its many picturesque outbuildings. There is a beautiful old walled garden and a good half-timbered barn. Lady Lisle was here when two fugitives from Sedgemoor, Hickes, a preacher, and Nelthorpe, sought shelter. Hickes is said to have been hidden in the malt-house, still there. Their presence was betrayed. Dame Alice was arrested and taken to Winchester, riding pillion behind a trooper. At Gorley the horse lost a shoe. When she bade the people round not to weep, as she would soon be back, the trooper, according to the story handed down there, grumbled, ' Yes, you will, but with your head off.' Moyles Court was sold by the Lisles to Lord Normanton in 1810.

The fine avenue that fringed the road from the boundary of Ibsley to the church has been cut down, like others of its kind, because the elms were not safe. The road continues up the spreading Avon valley, beautiful as ever, with the low hills to the west and the Forest to the east. Fordingbridge is an important road-centre and, like Ringwood, one of the eastern gates of the New Forest. It is also the centre for the Avon fishing, the pike being more notable than the trout. The river, which continues to indulge to the full its licence as a river of the plain, here pulls itself pretty well together and there is a beautiful view from the bridge down it by the island. This bridge, indeed, made the place. In 1252 there was a grant of pontage for a year owing to the traffic over it. Until 1848 the lord of Fordingbridge had to guard it for one month, the ' fence month ', in summer, and arrest any one caught poaching deer in the New Forest. It was also frequently used by the smuggling fraternity. From the fifteenth century till 1878 Fordingbridge was governed by a constable chosen at the Court Leet of Nether Burgate manor.

The church, standing high above the Avon, is interesting. The north chapel, with the arcade separating it from the nave, is strikingly handsome. The open roof— Richard II, Early Perpendicular—is beautifully carved, and among the bosses is a fine head. There is also an amusing brass to William Bulkeley, his wife and 8 children (1565). Canvas and sail cloth are among the local industries. In the distress after the Napoleonic wars there was trouble. Mills were destroyed in the riots of the thirties. The rioters then marched on Ringwood, where the men were gathered to defend their property, and they had to withdraw. The car has brought back some of the prosperity that went with the railway, and the attractive old core of the town is now set in a ring of modern buildings.

It is to the north-east of Fordingbridge, in Ashley Walk, at Ashley Rails, Sloden and other sites, that have been found the extensive remains of the potteries which flourished here in the later days of Roman rule. Apparently the potters lived in rough huts, built their own kilns and changed their quarters as soon as they had exhausted the fuel round them. Mr. Sumner thinks they hawked their wares about on donkeys in the neighbourhood, using the primitive tracks round, and possibly sending them by boat down the Avon from Horse-port, three miles away, now a part of Fordingbridge. The ware, thoroughly Romanized, is found all over south England, and, according to Professor Collingwood, these nomad potters ' show a spontaneity in their design and a taste in their decoration which make their work far more pleasing than the stereotyped patterns of Castor ware '.

Three miles higher up the valley is Breamore. The stocks are in the garden of a house on the left, just as you enter. It is an attractive village with a great green which entirely offsets the effects of the inevitable modern buildings. A communicative native assured us that it was founded by a Scot from Braemar; also that everybody may feed 3 geese upon the common except the miller and the vicar, who is compensated with a picturesque vicarage and the tithe-barn near by. The history of the manor is interesting. Breamore-Courtenay, some of which went into the New Forest, was royal demesne. Henry I seems to have given it to the Earls of Devonshire, lords of the Isle of Wight, who held it for half a knight's fee. They forfeited it in 1461. Henry VIII gave it to Catherine Howard and Catherine Parr. On the execution of her fourth husband, Lord Seymour, it came back to the Crown. When Baldwin and Hugh de Redvers founded their Austin priory here in 1129, they settled on it lands known later as Breamore-Bulborn. These Henry VIII gave to Anne of Cleves and his 2 Catherines and then to the Princess Elizabeth. She granted both Breamore manors to Sir Christopher Hatton, who sold them. The priory was visited by Richard II in 1384. Near the station are a few remains, and some good fourteenth-century tiles have been found.

Interest in Breamore centres round the 'most valuable and unusually complete specimen of a pre-Conquest church' which stands to the north of the green, in the grounds of the park. The walls are built of whole flints set in herring-bone fashion, from which the plaster has gone, and are late tenth or early eleventh century. Over the south arch of the tower is the famous Anglo-Saxon inscription in letters 6 inches long, 'Here the Covenant becomes manifest to thee.' Probably there were others over the other arches. There are also remains of painting in the room over the porch as well as good Saxon long and short work outside.

From the church the path goes up through the park, where the fine cedars were ruined by the winter's snow.

An old lady took the noise of the cracking branches for the rifle-fire of men returning from manœuvres. It passes the modern house, a good imitation of the old one which was burnt down, to the top of the hill, and then follows a long avenue of yews, a pleasing reminder that you are once more on the chalk. It is Hampshire of the chalk, north Hampshire, that will always be Hampshire for me. The path curves round the down, past the dew-pond, and there in a copse before you is the miz-maze, walled in completely by its carefully clipped hedge. It seems curiously prehistoric and uncanny right away here on the downs. It should be the work of the camp-building Celts, who made the downs their home, safe above the damp, impenetrable forest. There is a long barrow on the next hill and a path down to Grim's Ditch, which may have been a tribal boundary. It is a round maze and the path to salvation is easier to thread than at Winchester. Doubtless this maze, too, was cut right up here on the down for May games. It is the most interesting maze I know. At least it should have been cut with a religious import by the monks of the priory while tending their sheep on the hill.

Down to the right, on the border, is Rockbourne. Near the church, which is at the end of the long village street, are the remains of the manor-house, the home of Sir John Cooper, father of the first Earl of Shaftesbury. The Ashley Coopers have owned the manor since 1608. The mansion was Elizabethan and there was a thirteenth-century building, probably a chapel, and a huge barn, probably fifteenth century. It has become a farm and the chapel a barn. Sir Eyre Coote bought West Park House, where a column has been erected in the park to his memory as the conqueror of Pondicherry.

From the hill by the miz-maze there are glorious views over the great rolling Wiltshire downs, but they could not tempt me on this occasion. When I am busy with one county, I have an almost superstitious feeling against crossing the boundary into another. We followed the path back round the wood, with Clearbury Ring and its camp warning us off, past a farm folded in the skirts of the Wiltshire downs, with its great stretches of sown, by a track that led down once more to the clear, deep-flowing Avon, cooler and fresher than ever from its home in the chalk.

PRINCIPAL BOOKS CONSULTED

Aesop. *Sporting Reminiscences in Hampshire.* 1864.

Baigent, F. J., and Millard, J. E. *History of Basingstoke.* 1889.

Benham, W. *Winchester.* 1884.

Burrows, M. *Family of Brocas.* 1886.

Capes, W. W. *Scenes of Rural Life in Hampshire among the Manors of Bramshott.* 1901.

Chute, C. W. *A History of the Vyne in Hampshire.* 1888.

Clarke, F. *A School History of Hampshire.* Oxford, 1909.

Clutterbuck, R. H. *Notes on the Parishes of Fyfield, Kimpton, Penton Mewsey, Weyhill and Wherwell.* Salisbury, 1898.

Cobbett, W. *Rural Rides.* Everyman's Library.

Collingwood, R. G., and Myers, F. W. L. *Roman Britain and the English Settlements.* Oxford, 1936.

Crawford, O. G. S. *The Andover District.* Oxford, 1922.

Crawford, O. G. S., and Keiller, A. *Wessex from the Air.* 1928.

Curtis, N. *A Short History of Alton.* 1896.

Davies, J. S. *A History of Southampton.* Southampton, 1883.

Duthy, J. *Sketches of Hampshire.* Winchester, 1839.

Englefield, H. C. *A Walk through Southampton.* 1835.

Fiennes, Celia. *Through England on a Side-saddle in the time of William and Mary.* 1888.

Fowler, J. K. *A History of Beaulieu Abbey.* 1911.

Gasquet, F. A. *The Hampshire Recusants in the Reign of Queen Elizabeth.* 1895.

Godwin, G. N. *The Civil War in Hampshire.* Southampton, 1904.

Hampshire Field Club Papers and Proceedings.

Hampshire Notes and Queries. 9 vols. Winchester, 1883-98.

Harper, C. G. *The Portsmouth Road.* 1923.

Hudson, W. H. *Afoot in England.* 1909.

Hudson, W. H. *Hampshire Days.* 1903.

Hutchinson, H. G. *The New Forest.* 1904.

King, E. *Old Times Revisited in Lymington.* 1879.

Kitchin, G. W. *Winchester.* 1890.

Liveing, H. *Records of Romsey Abbey.* Winchester, 1906.

Lucas, E. V. *The Hambledon Men.* 1907.

Massingham, H. J. *Downland England.* 1936.

Milner, J. *Antiquities of Winchester.* 2 vols. 1809.

Montagu of Beaulieu, Lord. *Buckler's Hard and its Ships.* 1909.

Read, D. H. M. *Highways and Byways in Hampshire.* 1908.

Robertson, A. J. *A History of Alresford.* Winchester, 1938.

Shore, G. W. *History of Hampshire.* 1892.

Slight, H. J. *The Chronicles of Portsmouth.* 1828.

Sparks, H., and J. *The Story of Portsmouth.* Portsmouth, 1921.

Stirling, A. W. *The Diaries of Dummer.* 1934.

Sumner, H. *Excavations in New Forest Pottery Sites.* Southampton, 1927.

Varley, T. *Hampshire.* (Cambridge County Geographies.) Cambridge, 1922.

Vaughan, J. *The Wild Flowers of Selborne.* 1906.

Victoria County History. Hampshire. 5 vols. 1900-12.

Warner, R. *Collections for the History of Hampshire.* 1795.

White, Gilbert. *The Natural History and Antiquities of Selborne.* 1837.

Williams-Freeman, J. P. *An Introduction to Field Archaeology as illustrated by Hampshire.* 1915.

Wise, J. R. *The New Forest: Its History and Scenery.* 1867.

Yonge, Charlotte. *John Keble and His Parishes.* 1898.

INDEX

Printed in Great Britain by Butler & Tanner Ltd., Frome and London